THE LIFE AND TIMES OF CLEOPATRA, QUEEN OF EGYPT

This comprehensive treatment of Cleopatra and the political and social world in which she lived will be an indispensable resource for anyone interested in Cleopatra or in ancient Egypt. Laying bare the "injustice, the adverse partiality, of the attitude assumed by classical authors," the author offers the reader a new, more balanced look at the life of one of history's most important women. The book is divided into sections on Cleopatra and Caesar and Cleopatra and Antony and is supplemented by a number of maps and illustrations.

www.keganpaul.com

THE KEGAN PAUL LIBRARY
OF ANCIENT EGYPT

CLEOPATRA.

THE LIFE AND TIMES OF CLEOPATRA, QUEEN OF EGYPT

A Study in the Origin of the Roman Empire

ARTHUR E. P. BROME WEIGALL

KEGAN PAUL
London • New York • Bahrain

First published in 2004 by
Kegan Paul Limited
UK: P.O. Box 256, London WC1B 3SW, England
Tel: 020 7580 5511 Fax: 020 7436 0899
E-Mail: books@keganpaul.com
Internet: http://www.keganpaul.com
USA: 61 West 62nd Street, New York, NY 10023
Tel: (212) 459 0600 Fax: (212) 459 3678
Internet: http://www.columbia.edu/cu/cup
BAHRAIN: bahrain@keganpaul.com

Distributed by:
Extenza-Turpin
Stratton Business Park
Pegasus Drive
Biggleswade, Bedfordshire SG18 8QB
United Kingdom
Tel: (01462) 672555 Fax: (01462) 480947
Email: books@extenza-turpin.com

Columbia University Press
61 West 62nd Street, New York, NY 10023
Tel: (212) 459 0600 Fax: (212) 459 3678
Internet: http://www.columbia.edu/cu/cup

ISBN: 0-7103-1001-3

British Library Cataloguing in Publication Data
A catalogue record for this book is available from the British Library.

Library of Congress Cataloging-in-Publication Data
Applied for.

I DEDICATE THIS BOOK

TO MY FRIEND OF MANY YEARS,

RONALD STORRS,

ORIENTAL SECRETARY TO THE BRITISH AGENCY IN EGYPT,

SCHOLAR, POET, AND MUSICIAN.

PREFACE.

I HAVE to thank most heartily the Honourable Mrs Julian Byng, Mrs Gerald Lascelles, Mr Ronald Storrs, and my wife, for reading the proofs of this volume, and for giving me the benefit of their invaluable advice.

CONTENTS.

ILLUSTRATIONS.

MAPS AND PLAN.

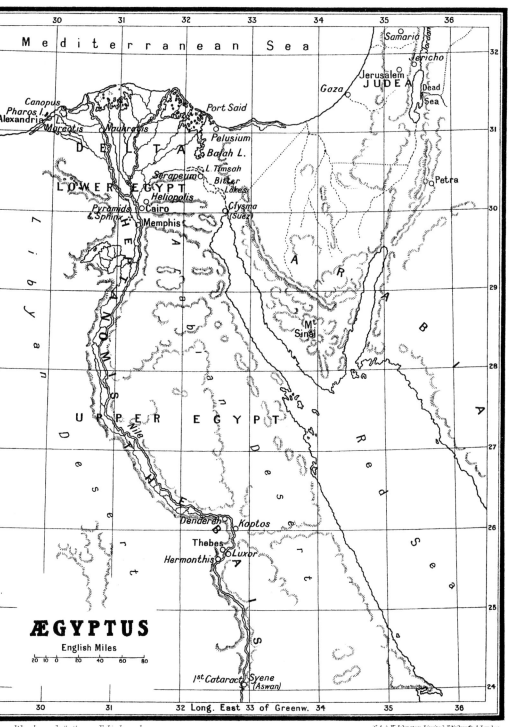

Mediterranean Sea

30 31 32 33 34 35 36

32

Samaria
Jericho
Jerusalem
Gaza JUDEA Dead
Sea

Canopus
Pharos I.
Alexandria L. Mareotis Naukratis
DELTA
Port Said
Pelusium
Balah L.
LOWER EGYPT
Serapeum L. Timsah
Bitter Lakes
Heliopolis
Pyramids Cairo Clysma
& Sphinx (Suez)
Memphis

Petra

31

30

Mt
Sinai

A R A B I A

L i b y a n

UPPER EGYPT

Nile

Arabian

Desert

D e s e r t

Red Sea

Denderah Koptos
Thebes
Hermonthis Luxor

ÆGYPTUS

English Miles
20 10 0   20   40   60   80

1st Cataract Syene
(Aswan)

29

28

27

26

25

24

30 31 32 Long. East 33 of Greenw. 34 35 36

un Blackwood & Sons, Edinburgh   & A.K.Johnston, Limited, Edinburgh & London

INTRODUCTION.

In the following pages it will be observed that, in order not to distract the reader, I have refrained from adding large numbers of notes, references, and discussions, such as are customary in works of this kind. I am aware that by telling a straightforward story in this manner I lay myself open to the suspicions of my fellow-workers, for there is always some tendency to take not absolutely seriously a book which neither prints chapter and verse for its every statement, nor often interrupts the text with erudite arguments. In the case of the subject which is here treated, however, it has seemed to me unnecessary to encumber the pages in this manner, since the sources of my information are all so well known; and I have thus been able to present the book to the reader in a style consonant with a principle of archæological and historical study to which I have always endeavoured to adhere—namely, the avoidance of as many of those attestations of learning as may be discarded without real loss. A friend of mine, an eminent scholar, in discussing with me the scheme of this volume, earnestly exhorted me on the present occasion not to abide by this principle. Remarking

that the trouble with my interpretation of history was
that I attempted to make the characters live, he urged
me at least to justify the manner of their resuscitation
in the eyes of the doctors of science by cramming my
pages with extracts from my working notes, relevant or
otherwise, and by smattering my text with Latin and
Greek quotations. I trust, however, that he was speaking in behalf of a very small company, for the sooner
this kind of jargon of scholarship is swept into the
world's dust-bin, the better will it be for public education. To my mind a knowledge of the past is so
necessary to a happy mental poise that it seems absolutely essential for historical studies to be placed before
the general reader in a manner sympathetic to him.
"History," said Emerson, "no longer shall be a dull
book. It shall walk incarnate in every just and wise
man. You shall not tell me by languages and titles a
catalogue of the volumes you have read. You shall
make me feel what periods you have lived."

Such has been my attempt in the following pages;
and, though I am so conscious of my literary limitations
that I doubt my ability to place the reader in touch with
past events, I must confess to a sense of gladness that
I, at any rate, with almost my whole mind, have lived
for a time in the company of the men and women of long
ago of whom these pages tell.

Any of my readers who think that my interpretation
of the known incidents here recorded is faulty may easily
check my statements by reference to the classical authors.
The sources of information are available at any big
library. They consist of Plutarch, Cicero, Suetonius,
Dion Cassius, Appian, 'De Bello Alexandrino,' Strabo,
Diodorus Siculus, Livy, Velleius Paterculus, Seneca,

Lucan, Josephus, Pliny, Dion Chrysostom, Tacitus, Florus, Lucian, Athenæus, Porphyry, and Orosius. Of modern writers reference should be made to Ferrero's 'Greatness and Decline of Rome,' Bouché-Leclercq's 'Histoire des Lagides,' Mahaffy's 'Empire of the Ptolemies,' Mommsen's 'History of Rome,' Strack's 'Dynastie der Ptolemäer,' and Sergeant's 'Cleopatra of Egypt.' There are also, of course, a very large number of works on special branches of the subject, which the reader will, without much difficulty, discover for himself.

I do not think that my statements of fact will be found to be in error; but the general interpretation of the events will be seen to be almost entirely new throughout the story, and therefore plainly open to discussion. I would only plead for my views that a residence in Egypt of many years, a close association with Alexandria, Cleopatra's capital, and a daily familiarity with Greek and Egyptian antiquities, have caused me almost unconsciously to form opinions which may not be at once acceptable to the scholar at home.

To some extent it is the business of the biographer to make the best of the characters with which he deals, but the accusation of having made use of this prerogative in the following pages will not be able to be substantiated. There is no high purpose served by the historian who sets down this man or that woman as an unmitigated blackguard, unless it be palpably impossible to discover any good motive for his or her actions. And even then it is a pleasant thing to avert, where possible, the indignation of posterity. An undefined sense of anger is left upon the mind of many of those who have read pages of condemnatory history of this kind, written by scholars who themselves are seated comfortably in the artificial atmosphere of modern righteousness. The story of the Plantagenet kings of England, for example, as recorded by Charles Dickens in his 'Child's History of England,' causes the reader to direct his anger more often to Dickens than to those weary, battle-stained, old monarchs whose blood many Englishmen are still proud to acknowledge. An historian who deals with a black period must not be fastidious. Nor must he detach his characters from their natural surroundings, and judge them according to a code of morals of which they themselves knew nothing. The modern, and not infrequently degenerate, humanitarian may utter his indignant complaint against the Norman barons who extracted the teeth of the Jewish financiers to induce them to deliver up their gold; but has he set himself to feel that pressing need of money which the barons felt, and has he endeavoured to experience their exasperation at the obstinacy of these foreigners? Let him do this and his attitude will be more tolerant: one might even live to see him hastening to the City with a pair of pincers in his pocket. Of course it is not the historian's affair to condone, or become a party to, a crime; but it certainly is his business to consider carefully the meaning of the term "crime," and to question its significance, as Pilate did that of truth.

In studying the characters of persons who lived in past ages, the biographer must tell us frankly whether he considers his subjects good or bad, liberal or mean, pious or impious; but at this late hour he should not often be wholly condemnatory, nor, indeed, need he be expected to have so firm a belief in man's capacity for consistent action as to admit that any person was so invariably villainous as he may be said to have been. A natural and inherent love of right-doing will sometimes lead the historian to err somewhat on the side of magnanimity; and I dare say he will serve the purpose of history best when he can honestly find a devil not so black as he is painted. Being acquainted with the morals of 1509, I would almost prefer to think of Henry the Eighth as "bluff King Hal," than as "the most detestable villain that ever drew breath."[1] I believe that an historian, in sympathy with his period, can at one and the same moment absolve Mary Queen of Scots from the charge of treachery, and defend Elizabeth's actions against her on that charge.

In the case of Cleopatra the biographer may approach his subject from one of several directions. He may, for example, regard the Queen of Egypt as a thoroughly bad woman, or as an irresponsible sinner, or as a moderately good woman in a difficult situation. In this book it is my object to point out the difficulty of the situation, and to realise the adverse circumstances against which the Queen had to contend; and by so doing a fairer complexion will be given to certain actions which otherwise must inevitably be regarded as darkly sinful. The biographer need not, for the sake of his principles, turn his back on the sinner and refuse to consider the possibility of extenuating circumstances. He need not, as we so often must in regard to our contemporaries, make a clear distinction between good and bad, shunning the sinner that our intimates may not be contaminated. The past, to some extent, is gone beyond the eventuality of Hell; and Time, the great Redeemer, has taken from the world the sharpness of its sin. The historian thus

[1] Dickens.

may put himself in touch with distant crime, and may attempt to apologise for it, without the charge being brought against him that in so doing he deviates from the stern path of moral rectitude. Intolerance is the simple expedient of contemporaneous society: the historian must show his distaste for wrong-doing by other means. We dare not excuse the sins of our fellows; but the wreck of times past, the need of reconstruction and rebuilding, gives the writer of history and biography a certain option in the selection of the materials which he uses in the resuscitation of his characters. He holds a warrant from the Lord of the Ages to give them the benefit of the doubt; and if it be his whim to ignore this licence and to condemn wholesale a character or a family, he sometimes loses, by a sort of perversion, the prerogative of his calling. The historian must examine from all sides the events which he is studying; and in regard to the subject with which this volume deals he must be particularly careful not to direct his gaze upon it only from the point of view of the Imperial Court of Rome, which regarded Cleopatra as the ancestral enemy of the dynasty. In dealing with history, says Emerson, "we, as we read, must become Greeks, Romans, Turks, priest and king, martyr and executioner." Even so, as we study the life of Cleopatra, we must set behind us that view of the case that was held by one section of humanity. In like manner we must rid ourselves of the influence of the thought of any one period, and must ignore that aspect of morality which has been developed in us by contact with the age in which we have the fortune to live. Good and evil are relative qualities, defined very largely by public opinion; and it must always be remembered that certain things which are considered to be correct to-day may have the denunciation of yesterday and to-morrow. We, as we read of the deeds of the Queen of Egypt, must doff our modern conception of right and wrong together with our top-hats and frock-coats; and, as we pace the courts of the Ptolemies, and breathe the atmosphere of the first century before Christ, we must not commit the anachronism of criticising our surroundings from the standard of twenty centuries after Christ. It is, of course, apparent that to a great extent we must be influenced by the thought of to-day; but the true student of history will make the effort to cast from him the shackles of his contemporaneous opinions, and to parade the bygone ages in the boundless freedom of a citizen of all time and a dweller in every land.

PART I.

CLEOPATRA AND CÆSAR

CHAPTER I.

AN INTRODUCTORY STUDY OF THE CHARACTER OF CLEOPATRA.

To those who make a close inquiry into the life of Cleopatra it will speedily become apparent that the generally accepted estimate of her character was placed before the public by those who sided against her in regard to the quarrel between Antony and Octavian. During the last years of her life the great Queen of Egypt became the mortal enemy of the first of the Roman Emperors, and the memory of her historic hostility was perpetuated by the supporters of every Cæsar of that dynasty. Thus the beliefs now current as to Cleopatra's nefarious influence upon Julius Cæsar and Marc Antony are, in essence, the simple abuse of her opponents; nor has History preserved to us any record of her life set down by one who was her partisan in the great struggle in which she so bravely engaged herself. It is a noteworthy fact, however, that the writer who is most fair to her memory, namely, the inimitable Plutarch, appears to have obtained much of his information from the diary kept by Cleopatra's doctor, Olympus. I do not presume in this volume to offer any kind of apology for the much-maligned Queen, but it will be my object to describe the events of her troubled life in such a manner that her aims, as I understand them, may be fairly placed before the reader; and there can be little doubt that, if I succeed in giving plausibility to the speculations here advanced, the actions of Cleopatra will, without any particular advocacy, assume a character which, at any rate, is no uglier than that of every other actor in this strange drama.

The injustice, the adverse partiality, of the attitude assumed by classical authors will speedily become apparent to all unbiassed students; and a single instance of this obliquity of judgment is all that need be mentioned here to illustrate my contention. I refer to the original intimacy between Cleopatra and Julius Cæsar. According to the accepted view of historians, both ancient and modern, the great Dictator is supposed to have been led astray by the voluptuous Egyptian, and to have been detained in Alexandria, against his better judgment, by the wiles of this Siren of the East. At this time, however, as will be seen in due course, Cleopatra, "the stranger for whom the Roman half-brick was never wanting,"[1] was actually an unmarried girl of some twenty-one years of age, against whose moral character not one shred of trustworthy evidence can be advanced; while, on the other hand, Cæsar was an elderly man who had ruined the wives and daughters of an astounding number of his friends, and whose reputation for such seductions was of a character almost past belief. How anybody, therefore, who has the known facts before him, can attribute the blame to Cleopatra in this instance, must become altogether incomprehensible to any student of the events of that time. I do not intend to represent the Queen of Egypt as a particularly

[1] Sergeant.

exalted type of her sex, but an attempt will be made to deal justly with her, and by giving her on occasion, as in a court of law, the benefit of the doubt, I feel assured that the reader will be able to see in her a very good average type of womanhood. Nor need I, in so doing, be accused of using on her behalf the privilege of the biographer, which is to make excuses. I will not simply set forth the case for Cleopatra as it were in her defence : I will tell the whole story of her life as it appears to me, admitting always the possible correctness of the estimate of her character held by other historians, but, at the same time, offering to public consideration a view of her deeds and devices which, if accepted, will clear her memory of much of that unpleasant stigma so long attached to it, and will place her reputation upon a level with those of the many famous persons of her time, not one of whom can be called either thoroughly bad or wholly good.

So little is known with any certainty as to Cleopatra's appearance, that the biographer must feel considerable reluctance in presenting her to his readers in definite guise; yet the duties of an historian do not permit him to deal with ghosts and shadows, or to invoke from the past only the misty semblance of those who once were puissant realities. For him the dead must rise not as phantoms hovering uncertainly at the mouth of their tombs, but as substantial entities observable in every detail to the mental eye; and he must endeavour to convey to others the impression, however faulty, which he himself has received. In the case of Cleopatra the materials necessary for her resuscitation are meagre, and one is forced to call in the partial assistance of the imagination in the effort to rebuild once more that body which has been so long dissolved into Egyptian dust.

A few coins upon which the Queen's profile is stamped, and a bust of poor workmanship in the British Museum, are the sole[1] sources of information as to her features. The colour of her eyes and of her hair is not known; nor can it be said whether her skin was white as alabaster, like that of many of her Macedonian fellow-countrywomen, or whether it had that olive tone so often observed amongst the Greeks. Even her beauty, or rather the degree of her beauty, is not clearly defined. It must be remembered that, so far as we know, not one drop of Oriental blood flowed in Cleopatra's veins, and that therefore her type must be considered as Macedonian Greek. The slightly brown skin of the Egyptian, the heavy dark eyes of the East, full, as it were, of sleep, the black hair of silken texture, are not features which are to be assigned to her. On the contrary, many Macedonian women are fair-haired and blue-eyed, and that colouring is frequently to be seen amongst the various peoples of the Eastern Mediterranean. Nevertheless, it seems most probable, all things considered, that she was a brunette; but in describing her as such it must be borne in mind that there is nothing more than a calculated likelihood to guide us.

The features of her face seem to have been strongly moulded, although the general effect given is that of smallness and delicacy. Her nose was aquiline and prominent, the nostrils being sensitive and having an

---

[1] The Egyptian reliefs upon the walls of Denderah temple and elsewhere show conventional representations of the Queen which are not to be regarded as real portraits. The so-called head of the Queen in the Alexandria Museum probably does not represent her at all, as most archæologists will readily admit.

appearance of good breeding. Her mouth was beautifully formed, the lips appearing to be finely chiselled. Her eyes were large and well placed, her eyebrows delicately pencilled. The contour of her cheek and chin was charmingly rounded, softening, thus, the lines of her clear-cut features. "Her beauty," says Plutarch, "was not in itself altogether incomparable, nor such as to strike those who saw her"; and he adds that Octavia, afterwards Antony's wife, was the more beautiful of the two women. But he admits, and no other man denies, that her personal charm and magnetism were very great. "She was splendid to hear and to see," says Dion Cassius, "and was capable of conquering the hearts which had resisted most obstinately the influence of love and those which had been frozen by age."

It is probable that she was very small in build. In order to obtain admittance to her palace upon an occasion of which we shall presently read, it is related that she was rolled up in some bedding and carried over the shoulders of an attendant, a fact which indicates that her weight was not considerable. The British Museum bust seems to portray the head of a small woman; and, moreover, Plutarch refers to her in terms which suggest that her charm lay to some extent in her daintiness. One imagines her thus to have been in appearance a small, graceful woman; prettily rounded rather than slight; white-skinned; dark-haired and dark-eyed; beautiful, and yet by no means a perfect type of beauty.

Her voice is said to have been her most powerful weapon, for by the perfection of its modulations it was at all times wonderfully persuasive and seductive.

> "The Devil hath not, in all his quiver's choice,
> An arrow for the heart like a sweet voice,"

says Byron; and in the case of Cleopatra this poignant gift of Nature must have served her well throughout her life. "Familiarity with her," writes Plutarch, "had an irresistible charm; and her form, combined with her persuasive speech, and with the peculiar character which in a manner was diffused about her behaviour, produced a certain piquancy. There was a sweetness in the sound of her voice when she spoke. "Her charm of speech," Dion Cassius tells us, "was such that she won all who listened."

Her grace of manner was as irresistible as her voice; for, as Plutarch remarks, there seems to have been this peculiar, undefined charm in her behaviour. It may have been largely due to a kind of elusiveness and subtilty; but it would seem also to have been accentuated by a somewhat naïve and childish manner, a waywardnesss, an audacity, a capriciousness, which enchanted those around her. Though often wild and inclined to romp, she possessed considerable dignity and at times was haughty and proud. Pliny speaks of her as being disdainful and vain, and indeed so Cicero found her when he met her in Rome; but this was an attitude perhaps assumed by the Queen as a defence against the light criticisms of those Roman nobles of the Pompeian faction who may have found her position not so honourable as she herself believed it to be. There is, indeed, little to indicate that her manner was by nature overbearing; and one is inclined to picture her as a natural, impulsive woman who passed readily from haughtiness to simplicity. Her actions were spontaneous, and one may suppose her to have been in her

early years as often artless as cunning. Her character
was always youthful, her temperament vivacious, and
her manner frequently what may be called harum-scarum.
She enjoyed life, and with candour took from it whatever
pleasures it held out to her. Her untutored heart leapt
from mirth to sorrow, from comedy to tragedy, with
unexpected ease; and with her small hands she tossed
about her the fabric of her complex circumstances like a
mantle of light and darkness.

She was a gifted woman, endowed by nature with ready
words and a happy wit. "She could easily turn her
tongue," says Plutarch, "like a many-stringed instrument, to any language that she pleased. She had very
seldom need of an interpreter for her communication
with foreigners, but she answered most men by herself,
namely Ethiopians, Troglodytes, Hebrews, Arabs, Syrians,
Medes, and Parthians. She is said to have learned the
language of many other peoples, though the kings, her
predecessors, had not even taken the pains to learn the
Egyptian tongue, and some of them had not so much as
given up the Macedonian dialect." Statecraft made a
strong appeal to her, and as Queen of Egypt she served
the cause of her dynasty's independence and aggrandisement with passionate energy. Dion Cassius tells us that
she was intensely ambitious, and most careful that due
honour should be paid to her throne. Her actions go to
confirm this estimate, and one may see her consumed at
times with a legitimate desire for world-power. Though
clever and bold she was not highly skilled, so far as one
can see, in the diplomatic art; but she seems to have
plotted and schemed in the manner common to her
house, not so much with great acuteness or profound
depth as with sustained intensity and a sort of conviction.

Tenacity of purpose is seen to have been her prevailing characteristic; and her unwavering struggle for her rights and those of her son Cæsarion will surely be followed by the interested reader through the long story before him with real admiration.

It is unanimously supposed that Cleopatra was, as Josephus words it, a slave to her lusts. The vicious sensuality of the East, the voluptuous degeneracy of an Oriental court, are thought to have found their most apparent expression in the person of this unfortunate Queen. Yet what was there, beyond the ignorant and prejudiced talk of her Roman enemies, to give a foundation to such an estimate of her character? She lived practically as Cæsar's *wife* for some years, it being said, I believe with absolute truth, that he intended to make her Empress of Rome and his legal consort. After his assassination she married Antony, and cohabited with him until the last days of her life. At an age when the legal rights of marriage were violated on every side, when all Rome and all Alexandria were deeply involved in domestic intrigues, Cleopatra, so far as I can see, confined her attentions to the two men who in sequence each acted towards her in the manner of a legitimate husband, each being recognised in Egypt as her divinely-sanctioned consort. The words of Dion Cassius, which tell us that "no wealth could satisfy her, and her passions were insatiable," do not suggest a more significant foundation than that her life was lived on extravagant and prodigal lines. There is no doubt that she was open to the accusations of her enemies, who described her habits as dissipated and intemperate; but there seems to be little to indicate that she was in any way a Delilah or a Jezebel. For all we know, she may have been a very moral woman : certainly she was the fond mother of four children, a fact which, even at that day, may be said to indicate, to a certain extent, a voluntary assumption of the duties of motherhood. After due consideration of all the evidence, I am of opinion that though her nature may have been somewhat voluptuous, and though her passions were not always under control, the best instincts of her sex were by no means absent; and indeed, in her maternal aspect, she may be described as a really good woman.

The state of society at the time must be remembered. In Rome, as well as in Alexandria, love intrigues were continuously in progress. Mommsen, in writing of the moral corruption of the age, speaks of the extraordinary degeneracy of the dancing girl of the period, whose record "pollutes even the pages of history." "But," he adds, "their, as it were, licensed trade was materially injured by the free act of the ladies of aristocratic circles. Liaisons in the first houses had become so frequent that only a scandal altogether exceptional could make them the subject of special talk, and judicial interference seemed now almost ridiculous." Against such a background Cleopatra's domestic life with Cæsar, and afterwards with Antony, assumes, by contrast, a fair character which is not without its refreshing aspect. We see her intense and lifelong devotion to her eldest son Cæsarion, we picture her busy nursery in the royal palace, which at one time resounded to the cries of a pair of lusty twins, and the vision of the Oriental voluptuary fades from our eyes. Can this dainty little woman, we ask, who soothes at her breast the cries of her fat baby, while three sturdy youngsters play around her, be the sensuous Queen of the East? Can this tender, ingenuous, smiling mother of Cæsar's beloved son be the Siren of Egypt? There is not a particle of trustworthy evidence to show that Cleopatra carried on a single love affair in her life other than the two recorded so dramatically by history, nor is there any evidence to show that in those two affairs she conducted herself in a licentious manner.

Cleopatra was in many ways a refined and cultured woman. Her linguistic powers indicate a certain studiousness; and at the same time she seems to have been a patron of the arts. It is recorded that she made Antony present to the city of Alexandria the library which once belonged to Pergamum, consisting of 200,000 volumes; and Cicero seems to record the fact that she interested herself in obtaining certain books for him from Alexandria. She inherited from her family a temperament naturally artistic; and there is no reason to suppose that she failed to carry on the high tradition of her house in this regard. She was a patron also of the sciences, and Photinus, the mathematician, who wrote both on arithmetic and geometry, published a book actually under her name, called the 'Canon of Cleopatra.' The famous physician Dioscorides was, it would seem, the friend and attendant of the Queen; and the books which he wrote at her court have been read throughout the ages. Sosigenes, the astronomer, was also, perhaps, a friend of Cleopatra, and it may have been through her good offices that he was introduced to Cæsar, with whom he collaborated in the reformation of the calendar. The evidence is very inconsiderable in regard to the Queen's personal attitude towards the arts and sciences, but sufficient may be gleaned to give some support to the suggestion that she did not fall below the standard set by her forefathers.   One feels that her interest in such matters is assured by the fact that she held for so long the devotion of such a man of letters as Julius Cæsar.   There is little doubt that she was capable of showing great seriousness of mind when occasion demanded, and that her demeanour, so frequently tumultuous, was often thoughtful and quiet.

At the same time, however, one must suppose that she viewed her life with a light heart, having, save towards the end, a greater familiarity with laughter than with tears.   She was at all times ready to make merry or jest, and a humorous adventure seems to have made a special appeal to her.   With Antony, as we shall see, she was wont to wander around the city at night-time, knocking at people's doors in the darkness and running away when they were opened.   It is related how once when Antony was fishing in the sea, she made a diver descend into the water to attach to his line a salted fish, which he drew to the surface amidst the greatest merriment. One gathers from the early writers that her conversation was usually sparkling and gay; and it would seem that there was often an infectious frivolity in her manner which made her society most exhilarating.

She was eminently a woman whom men might love, for she was active, high-spirited, plucky, and dashing. To use a popular phrase, she was always "game" for an adventure.   Her courageous return to Egypt after she had been driven into exile by her brother, is an indication of her brave spirit; and the daring manner in which she first obtained her introduction to Cæsar, causing herself to be carried into the palace on a man's back, is a convincing instance of that audacious courage which makes so strong an appeal on her behalf to the imagination. Florus, who was no friend of the Queen's, speaks of her as being " free from all womanly fear."

We now come to the question as to whether she was cruel by nature. It must be admitted that she caused the assassination of her sister Arsinoe, and ordered the execution of others who were, at that time, plotting against her. But it must be remembered that political murders of this kind were a custom—nay, a habit—of the period; and, moreover, the fact that the Queen of Egypt used her rough soldiers for the purpose does not differentiate the act from that of Good Queen Bess who employed a Lord Chief Justice and an axe. The early demise of Ptolemy XV., her brother, is attributable as much to Cæsar as to Cleopatra, if, indeed, he did not die a natural death. The execution of King Artavasdes of Armenia was a political act of no great significance. And the single remaining charge of cruelty which may be brought against the Queen, namely, that she tested the efficacy of various poisons on the persons of condemned criminals, need not be regarded as indicating callousness on her part; for it mattered little to the condemned prisoner what manner of sudden death he should die, but, on the other hand, the discovery of a pleasant solution to the quandary of her own life was a point of capital importance to herself. When we recall the painful record of callous murders which were perpetrated during the reigns of her predecessors, we cannot attribute to Cleopatra any extraordinary degree of heartlessness, nor can we say that she showed herself to be as cruel as were other members of her family. She lived in a ruthless age; and, on the whole, her behaviour was tolerant and good-natured.

In religious matters she was not, like so many persons
of that period, a disbeliever in the power of the gods.
She had a strong pagan belief in the close association
of divinity and royalty, and she seems to have accepted
without question the hereditary assurance of her own
celestial affiliation. She was wont to dress herself on
gala occasions in the robes of Isis or Aphrodite, and to
act the part of a goddess incarnate upon earth, assuming
not divine powers but divine rights. She regarded herself as being closely in communion with the virile gods
of Egypt and Greece; and when signs and wonders were
pointed out to her by her astrologers, or when she noted
good or ill omens in the occurrences around her, she
was particularly prone to giving them full recognition
as being communications from her heavenly kin. Her
behaviour at the battle of Actium is often said to have
been due to her consciousness of the warnings which
she had received by means of such portents; and on
other occasions in her life her actions were ordered by
these means. It is related by Josephus that she violated
the temples of Egypt in order to obtain money to carry
on the war against Rome, and that no place was so holy
or so infamous that she would not attempt to strip it
of its treasures when she was pressed for gold. If this
be true, it may be argued in the Queen's defence that
the possessions of the gods were considered by her to
be, as it were, her own property, as the representative
of heaven upon earth, and in this case they were the
more especially at her disposal since they were to be
converted into money for the glory of Egypt. As a
matter of fact, it is probable that in the last emergencies
of her reign, the Queen's agents obtained supplies wherever they found them, and, if Cleopatra was consulted

at all, she was far too distracted to give the matter very serious thought.

It is not necessary here to inquire further into the character of the Queen. Her personality, as I see it, will become apparent in the following record of her tragic life.   It is essential to remember that, though her faults were many, she was not what is usually called *bad*. She was a brilliant, charming, and beautiful woman; perhaps not over-scrupulous and yet not altogether unprincipled; ready, no doubt, to make use of her charms, but not an immoral character.   As the historian pictures her figure moving lightly through the mazes of her life, now surrounded by her armies in the thick of battle; now sailing up the moonlit Nile in her royal barge with Cæsar beside her; now tenderly playing in the nursery with her babies; now presiding brilliantly at the gorgeous feasts in the Alexandrian palace; now racing in disguise down the side-streets of her capital, choking with suppressed laughter; now speeding across the Mediterranean to her doom; and now, all haggard and forlorn, holding the deadly asp to her body,—he cannot fail to fall himself under the spell of that enchantment by which the face of the world was changed. He finds that he is dealing not with a daughter of Satan, who, from her lair in the East, stretches out her hand to entrap Rome's heroes, but with mighty Cæsar's wife and widow, fighting for Cæsar's child; with Antony's faithful consort, striving, as will be shown, to unite Egypt and Rome in one vast empire. He sees her not as the crowned courtesan of the Orient, but as the excellent royal lady, who by her wits and graces held captive the two greatest men of her time in the bonds of a union which in Egypt was equivalent to a legal marriage. He sees before him once more the small, graceful figure, whose beauty compels, whose voice entices, and in whose face (it may be by the kindly obliterations of time) there is no apparent evil; and the unprejudiced historian must find himself hard put to it to say whether his sympathies are ranged on the side of Cleopatra or on that of her Roman rival in the great struggle for the mastery of the whole earth which is recorded in the following pages.

CHAPTER II.

THE CITY OF ALEXANDRIA.

No study of the life of Cleopatra can be of true value unless the position of the city of Alexandria, her capital, in relationship to Egypt on the one hand and to Greece and Rome on the other, is fully understood and appreciated. The reader must remember, and bear continually in mind, that Alexandria was at that time, and still is, more closely connected in many ways with the Mediterranean kingdoms than with Egypt proper. It bore, geographically, no closer relation to the Nile valley than Carthage bore to the interior of North Africa. Indeed, to some extent it is legitimate in considering Alexandria to allow the thoughts to find a parallel in the relationship of Philadelphia to the interior of America in the seventeenth century or of Bombay to India in the eighteenth century, for in these cases we see a foreign settlement, representative of a progressive civilisation, largely dependent on transmarine shipping for its prosperity, set down on the coast of a country whose habits are obsolete. It is almost as incorrect to class the Alexandrian Queen Cleopatra as a native Egyptian as it would be to imagine William Penn as a Red Indian or Warren Hastings as a Hindoo. Cleopatra in Alexandria was cut off from Egypt. There is no evidence that she ever even saw the Sphinx, and it would seem that the single journey up the Nile of which the history of her reign gives us any record was undertaken by her solely at the desire of Cæsar. Bearing this fact in mind, I do not think it is desirable for me to refer at any length to the affairs, or to the manners and customs, of Egypt proper in this volume; and it will be observed that, in order to avoid giving to events here recorded an Egyptian character which in reality they did not possess in any very noticeable degree, I have refrained from introducing any account of the people who lived in the great country behind Alexandria over which Cleopatra reigned.

The topographical position of Alexandria, selected by its illustrious founder, seems to have been chosen on account of its detachment from Egypt proper. The city was erected upon a strip of land having the Mediterranean on the one side and the Mareotic lake on the other. It was thus cut off from the hinterland far more effectively even than was Carthage by its semicircle of hills. Alexander had intended to make the city a purely Greek settlement, the port at which the Greeks should land their goods for distribution throughout Egypt, and whence the produce of the abundant Nile should be shipped to the north and west. He selected a remote corner of the Delta for his site, with the plain intention of holding his city at once free of, and in dominion over, Egypt; and so precisely was the location suited to his purpose that until this day Alexandria is in little more than name a city of the Egyptians. Even at the present time, when an excellent system of express railway trains connects Alexandria with Cairo and Upper Egypt, there are many well-to-do inhabitants who have not seen more

that ten miles of Egyptian landscape; and the vast
majority have never been within sight of the Pyramids.
The wealthy foreigners settled in Alexandria often know
nothing whatsoever about Egypt, and Cairo itself is
beyond their ken. The Greeks, Levantines, and Jews,
who now, as in ancient days, form a very large part of
the population of Alexandria, would shed bitter tears of
gloomy foreboding were they called upon to penetrate
into the Egypt which the tourists and the officials know
and love. The middle-class Egyptians of Alexandria are
rarely tempted to enter Egypt proper, and even those
who have inherited a few acres of land in the interior
are often unwilling to visit their property.

Egypt as we know it is a *terra incognita* to the
Alexandrian. The towering cliffs of the desert, the
wide Nile, the rainless skies, the amazing brilliance
of the stars, the ruins of ancient temples, the great
pyramids, the decorated tombs, the clustered mud-huts
of the villages in the shade of the dom-palms and the
sycamores, the creaking *sakkiehs* or water-wheels, the
gracefully worked *shádufs* or water-hoists,—all these are
unknown to the inhabitants of Alexandria. They have
never seen the hot deserts and the white camel-tracks
over the hills, they have not looked upon the Nile
tumbling over the granite rocks of the cataracts, nor
have they watched the broad expanse of the inunda-
tion. That peculiar, undefined aspect and feeling which
is associated with the thought of Egypt in the minds
of visitors and residents does not tincture the impression of the Alexandrians. They have not felt the
subtle influence of the land of the Pharaohs: they are
sons of the Mediterranean, not children of the Nile.

The climate of Alexandria is very different from that

of the interior of the Delta, and bears no similarity to
that of Upper Egypt.   At Thebes the winter days are
warm and brilliantly sunny, the nights often extremely
cold.   The summer climate is intensely hot, and there
are times when the resident might there believe himself
an inhabitant of the infernal regions.   The temperature
in and around Cairo is more moderate, and the summer
is tolerable, though by no means pleasant.   In Alexandria, however, the summer is cool and temperate.
There is perhaps no climate in the entire world so
perfect as that of Alexandria in the early summer.   The
days are cloudless, breezy, and brilliant; the nights cool
and even cold.   In August and September it is somewhat damp, and therefore unpleasant; but it is never
very hot, and the conditions of life are almost precisely
those of southern Europe.

The winter days on the sea-coast are often cold and
rainy, the climate being not unlike that of Italy at the
same time of year.   People must needs wear thick
clothing, and must study the barometer before taking
their promenades.   While Thebes, and even the Pyramids, bask in more or less continual sunshine, the city
of Alexandria is lashed by intermittent rainstorms, and
the salt sea-wind buffets the pedestrians as it screams
down the paved streets.   The peculiar texture of the true
Egyptian atmosphere is not felt in Alexandria: the air is
that of Marseilles, of Naples, or of the Piræus.

In summer-time the sweating official of the south
makes his way seaward in the spirit of one who leaves
the tropics for northern shores.   He enters the north-
bound express on some stifling evening in June, the
amazing heat still radiating from the frowning cliffs of
the desert, and striking up into his eyes from the

parched earth around the station. He lies tossing and panting in his berth while the electric fans beat down the hot air upon him, until the more temperate midnight permits him to fall into a restless sleep. In the morning he arrives at Cairo, where the moisture runs more freely from his face by reason of the greater humidity, though now the startling intensity of the heat is not felt. Anon he travels through the Delta towards the north, still mopping his brow as the morning sun bursts into the carriage. But suddenly, a few miles from the coast, a change is felt. For the first time, perhaps for many weeks, he feels cool: he wishes his clothes were not so thin. He packs up his helmet and dons a straw hat. Arriving at Alexandria, he is amused to find that he actually feels chilly. He no longer dreads to move abroad in the sun at high noon, but, waving aside the importunate carriage-drivers, he walks briskly to his hotel. He does not sit in a darkened room with windows tightly shut against the heat, but pulls the chair out on to the verandah to take the air; and at night he does not lie stark naked on his bed in the garden, cursing the imagined heat of the stars and the moon, and praying for the mercy of sleep; but, like a white man in his own land, he tucks himself up under a blanket in the cool bedroom, and awakes lively and refreshed.

A European may live the year round at Alexandria, and may express a preference for the summer. The wives and children of English officials not infrequently remain there throughout the warmer months, not from necessity but from choice; and there are many persons of northern blood who are happy to call it their home. In Cairo such families rarely remain during the summer, unless under compulsion, while in Upper Egypt there is hardly a white woman in the land between May and October. Egypt is considered by them to be solely a winter residence, and the official is of opinion that he pays toll to fortune for the pleasures of the winter season by the perils and torments of the summer months. Even the middle and upper class Egyptians themselves, recruited, as they generally are in official circles, from Cairo, suffer terribly from the heat in the south—often more so, indeed, than the English; and I myself on more than one occasion have had to abandon a summer day's ride owing to the prostration of one of the native staff.

The Egyptian of Alexandria and the north looks with scorn upon the inhabitants of the upper country. The southerner, on the other hand, has no epithet of contempt more biting than that of "Alexandrian." To the hardy peasant of the Thebaid the term means all that "scalliwag" denotes to us. The northern Egyptian, unmindful of the relationship of a kettle to a saucepan, calls the southerner "black" in disdainful tones. A certain Alexandrian Egyptian of undiluted native stock, who was an official in a southern district, told me that he found life very dull in his provincial capital, surrounded as he was by "all these confounded niggers." And if the *Egyptians* of Alexandria are thus estranged from those who constitute the backbone of the Egyptian nation, it will be understood how great is the gulf between the Greeks or other foreign residents in that city and the bulk of the people of the Nile.

I am quite sure that Cleopatra spoke of the Egyptians of the interior as "confounded niggers." Her interests and sympathies, like those of her city, were directed across the Mediterranean. She held no more intimate relationship to Egypt than does the London millionaire to the African gold-mines which he owns. Alexandria at the present day still preserves the European character with which it was endowed by Alexander and the Ptolemies; or perhaps it were more correct to say that it has once more assumed that character. There are large quarters of the city, of course, which are native in style and appearance, but, viewed as a whole, it suggests to the eye rather an Italian than an Egyptian seaport. It has extremely little in common with the Egyptian metropolis and other cities of the Nile; and we are aware that there was no greater similarity in ancient times. The very flowers and trees are different. In Upper Egypt the gardens have a somewhat artificial beauty, for the grace of the land is more dependent upon the composition of cliffs, river, and fields. There are few wild-flowers, and little natural grass. In the gardens the flowers are evident importations, while the lawns have to be sown every autumn, and do not survive the summer. But in Alexandria there is always a blaze of flowers, and one notes with surprise the English hollyhocks, foxgloves, and stocks growing side by side with the plants of southern Europe. In the fields of Mariout, over against Alexandria, the wild-flowers in spring are those of the hills of Greece. Touched by the cool breeze from the sea, one walks over ground scarlet and gold with poppies and daisies; there bloom asphodel and iris; and the ranunculus grows to the size of a tulip. There is a daintiness in these fields and gardens wholly un-Egyptian, completely different from the more permanent grace of the south. One feels that Pharaoh walked not in fields of asphodel, that

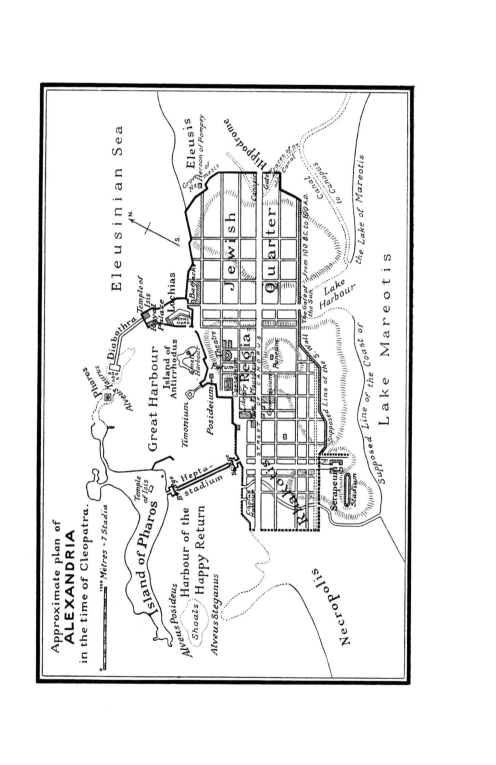

Approximate plan of
ALEXANDRIA
in the time of Cleopatra.

1300 Metres = 7 Stadia

E l e u s i n i a n   S e a

Eleusis

Grove of Nemesis
Heroon of Pompey

Hippodrome

Gate of the Sun
Faces of the Canal
Canopic Canal

Canals to Canopis

The Gate of the Sun
From 100 B.C. to 1870 A.D.

J e w i s h

Q u a r t e r

Wall

Lake
Harbour

the Lake of Mareotis

Temple of Isis
Diabathra
Royal Palace
Lochias
ROYAL HARB.
Barrack

Pharos
Taurus
Alveus

Great Harbour
Island of
Antirrhodus

Small Harbour
Theatre
Mausoleum
Forum
Canal
Timonium
Posideium

Library
Gymnasium
Museum

R e g i a

Paneium

STREET OF CANOPUS

Lake Harbour

Wall
Supposed Line of the

Supposed Line of the Coast of

L a k e   M a r e o t i s

Temple of Isis
Heptastadium

Bridge
Bridge
Cibotus Harbour

R h a c o t i s

Serapeum
Stadium

Alveus Posideus
Harbour of the
Happy Return
Shoals
Alveus Steganus

Island of Pharos

N e c r o p o l i s

Amon had no dominion here amidst the poppies by the sea. One is transplanted in imagination to Greece and to Italy, and the knowledge becomes the more apparent that Cleopatra and her city were an integral part of European life, only slightly touched by the very finger-tips of the Orient.

The coast of Egypt rises so little above the level of the Mediterranean that the land cannot be seen by those approaching it from across the sea, until but a few miles separate them from the surf which breaks upon the sand and rocks of that barren shore. The mountains of other East - Mediterranean countries — Greece, Italy, Sicily, Crete, Cyprus, and Syria—rising out of the blue waters, served as landmarks for the mariners of ancient days, and were discernible upon the horizon for many long hours before wind or oars carried the vessels in under their lee. But the Egyptian coast offered no such assistance to the captains of sea-going galleys, and they were often obliged to approach closely to the treacherous shore before their exact whereabouts became apparent to them. The city of Alexandria was largely hidden from view by the long, low island of Pharos, which lay in front of it and which was little dissimilar in appearance from the mainland.[1] Two promontories of land projected from the coast opposite either end of the island; and, these being lengthened by the building of breakwaters, the straits between Pharos Island and the mainland were converted into an excellent harbour, both it and the main part of the city being screened from the open sea. There was one tremendous landmark, however, which served to direct all vessels to their destination, namely, the far-famed Pharos lighthouse, standing upon the east end of

---

[1] This island has now become part of the mainland.

the island, and overshadowing the main entrance to the port.[1] It had been built during the reign of Ptolemy Philadelphus by Sostratus of Cnidus two hundred years and more before the days of Cleopatra, and it ranked as one of the wonders of the world. It was constructed of white marble, and rose to a height of 400 ells, or 590 feet. By day it stood like a pillar of alabaster, gleaming against the leaden haze of the sky; and from nightfall until dawn there shone from its summit a powerful beacon-light which could be seen, it is said,[2] for 300 stadia, *i.e.*, 34 miles, across the waters.

The harbour was divided into two almost equal parts by a great embankment, known as the Heptastadium, which joined the city to the island. This was cut at either end by a passage or waterway leading from one harbour to the other, but these two passages were bridged over, and thus a clear causeway was formed, seven stadia, or 1400 yards, in length. To the west of this embankment lay the Harbour of Eunostos, or the Happy Return, which was entered from behind the western extremity of Pharos Island; while to the east of the embankment lay the Great Harbour, the entrance to which passed between the enormous lighthouse and the Diabathra, or breakwater, built out from the promontory known as Lochias. This entrance was dangerous, owing to the narrowness of the fairway and to the presence of rocks, against which the rolling waves of the Mediterranean, driven by the prevalent winds of the north, beat with almost continuous violence.

A vessel entering the port of Alexandria from this side was steered towards the great lighthouse, around the foot

---

[1] For a restoration of the lighthouse, see the work of H. Thiersch.
[2] Josephus.

of which the waves leapt and broke in showers of white foam. Skirting the dark rocks at the base of this marble wonder, the vessel slipped through the passage into the still entrance of the harbour, leaving the breakwater on the left hand. Here, on a windless day, one might look down to the sand and the rocks at the bottom of the sea, so clear and transparent was the water and so able to be penetrated by the strong light of the sun. Seaweed of unaccustomed hues covered the sunken rocks over which the vessels floated; and anemones, like great flowers, could be seen swaying in the gentle motion of the under-currents. Passing on into the deeper water of the harbour, in which the sleek dolphins arose and dived in rhythmic succession, the traveller saw before him such an array of palaces and public buildings as could be found nowhere else in the world. There stood, on his left hand, the Royal Palace, which was spread over the Lochias Promontory and extended round towards the west. Here, beside a little island known as Antirrhodos, itself the site of a royal pavilion, lay the Royal Harbour, where flights of broad steps descended into the azure water, which at this point was so deep that the largest galleys might moor against the quays. Along the edge of the mainland, overlooking the Great Harbour, stood a series of magnificent buildings which must have deeply impressed all those who were approaching the city across the water. Here stood the imposing Museum, which was actually a part of another palace, and which formed a kind of institute for the study of the sciences, presided over by a priest appointed by the sovereign. The buildings seem to have consisted of a large hall wherein the professors took their meals; a series of arcades in which these men of learning walked and talked; a hall, or assembly rooms, in which their lectures were held; and, at the north end, close to the sea, the famous library, at this time containing more than half a million scrolls. On rising ground between the Museum and the Lochias Promontory stood the Theatre, wherein those who occupied the higher seats might look beyond the stage to the island of Antirrhodos, behind which the incoming galleys rode upon the blue waters in the shadow of Pharos. At the back of the Theatre, on still higher ground, the Paneum, or Temple of Pan, had been erected. This is described by Strabo as "an artificial mound of the shape of a fir-cone, resembling a pile of rock, to the top of which there is an ascent by a spiral path, from whose summit may be seen the whole city lying all around and beneath it." To the west of this mound stood the Gymnasium, a superb building, the porticos of which alone exceeded a stadium, or 200 yards, in length. The Courts of Justice, surrounded by groves and gardens, adjoined the Gymnasium. Close to the harbour, to the west of the Theatre, was the Forum; and in front of it, on the quay, stood a temple of Neptune. To the west of this, near the Museum, there was an enclosure called Sema, in which stood the tombs of the Ptolemaic Kings of Egypt, built around the famous Mausoleum wherein the bones of Alexander the Great rested in a sarcophagus of alabaster.[1]

These buildings, all able to be seen from the harbour, formed the quarter of the city known as the Regia, Brucheion, or Royal Area. Here the white stone structures reflected in the mirror of the harbour, the statues and monuments, the trees and brilliant flower-

---

[1] The first Ptolemy brought the body of Alexander to Alexandria, and deposited it, so it is said, in a golden sarcophagus; but this was believed to have been stolen, and the alabaster one substituted.

gardens, the flights of marble steps passing down to the sea, the broad streets and public places, must have formed a scene of magnificence not surpassed at that time in the whole world. Nor would the traveller, upon stepping ashore from his vessel, be disappointed in his expectations as he roamed the streets of the town. Passing through the Forum he would come out upon the great thoroughfare, more than three miles long, which cut right through the length of the city in a straight line, from the Gate of the Necropolis, at the western end, behind the Harbour of the Happy Return, to the Gate of Canopus, at the eastern extremity, some distance behind the Lochias Promontory. This magnificent boulevard, known as the Street of Canopus, or the Meson Pedion, was flanked on either side by colonnades, and was 100 feet in breadth.[1] On its north side would be seen the Museum, the Sema, the palaces, and the gardens; on the south side the Gymnasium with its long porticos, the Paneum towering up against the sky, and numerous temples and public places. Were the traveller to walk eastwards along this street he would pass through the Jewish quarter, adorned by many synagogues and national buildings, through the Gate of Canopus, built in the city walls, and so out on to open ground, where stood the Hippodromos or Racecourse, and several public buildings. Here the sun-baked soil was sandy, the rocks glaring white, and but little turf was to be seen. A few palms, bent southward by the sea wind, and here and there a cluster of acacias, gave shade to pedestrians; while between the road and the sea the Grove of Nemesis offered a pleasant foreground to the sandy beach and the blue expanse of the Mediterranean

[1] Surely not 200 feet, as is sometimes said.

beyond. Near by stood the little settlement of Eleusis, which was given over to festivities and merry-making. Here there were several restaurants and houses of entertainment which are said to have commanded beautiful views; but so noisy was the fun supplied, and so dissolute the manners of those who frequented the place, that better-class Alexandrians were inclined to avoid it. At a distance of some three miles from Alexandria stood the suburb of Nicopolis, where numerous villas, themselves "not less than a city," says Strabo,[1] had been erected along the sea-front, and the sands in summertime were crowded with bathers. Farther eastwards the continuation of the Street of Canopus passed on to the town of that name and Egypt proper.

Returning within the city walls and walking westwards along the Street of Canopus, the visitor would pass once more through the Regia and thence through the Egyptian quarter known as Rhakotis, to the western boundary. This quarter, being immediately behind the commercial harbour, was partly occupied by warehouses and ships' offices, and was always a very busy district of the town. Here there was an inner harbour called Cibotos, or the Ark, where there were extensive docks; and from this a canal passed, under the Street of Canopus, to the lake at the back of the city. On a rocky hill behind the Rhakotis quarter stood the magnificent Serapeum, or Temple of Serapis, which was approached by a broad street running at right angles to the Street of Canopus, which it bisected at a point not far west of the Museum, being a continuation of the Heptastadium. The temple is said to have been surpassed in grandeur by no other building in the world except the Capitol

---

[1] Some years later, after it had been popularised by Augustus.

at Rome; and, standing as it did at a considerable elevation, it must have towered above the hubbub and the denser atmosphere of the streets and houses at its foot, as though to receive the purification of the untainted wind of the sea. Behind the temple, on the open rocky ground outside the city walls, stood the Stadium; and away towards the west the Necropolis was spread out, with its numerous gardens and mausoleums. Still farther westward there were numerous villas and gardens; and it may be that the wonderful flowers which at the present day grow wild upon this ground are actually the descendants of those introduced and cultivated by the Greeks of the days of Cleopatra.

Along the entire length of the back walls of the city lay the Lake of Mareotis, which cut off Alexandria from the Egyptian Delta, and across this stretch of water vast numbers of vessels brought the produce of Egypt to the capital. The lake harbour and docks were built around an inlet which penetrated some considerable distance into the heart of the city not far to the east of the Paneum, and from them a great colonnaded thoroughfare, as wide as the Street of Canopus, which it crossed at right angles, passed through the city to the Great Harbour, being terminated at the south end by the Gate of the Sun, and at the north end by the Gate of the Moon. These lake docks are said to have been richer and more important even than the maritime docks on the opposite side of the town; for over the lake the traffic of vessels coming by river and canal from all parts of Egypt was always greater than the shipping across the Mediterranean. The shores of this inland sea were exuberantly fertile. A certain amount of papyrus grew at the edges of the lake, considerable stretches of water being covered by the densely-growing reeds. The Alexandrians were wont to use the plantations for their picnics, penetrating in small boats into the thickest part of the reeds, where they were overshadowed by the leaves, which, also, they used as dishes and drinking-vessels. Extensive vineyards and fruit gardens flourished at the edge of the water; and there are said to have been eight islands which rose from the placid surface of the lake and were covered by luxuriant gardens.

Strabo tells us that Alexandria contained extremely beautiful public parks and grounds, and abounded with magnificent buildings of all kinds. The whole city was intersected by roads wide enough for the passage of chariots; and, as has been said, the three main streets, those leading to the Gate of Canopus, to the Serapeum, and to the Lake Harbour, were particularly noteworthy both for their breadth and length. Indeed, in the Fifteenth Idyll of Theocritus, one of the characters complains most bitterly of the excessive length of the Alexandrian streets. The kings of the Ptolemaic dynasty, for nearly three centuries, had expended vast sums in the beautification of their capital, and at the period with which we are now dealing it had become the rival of Rome in magnificence and luxury. The novelist, Achilles Tatius, writing some centuries later, when many of the Ptolemaic edifices had been replaced by Roman constructions perhaps of less merit, cried, as he beheld the city, "We are vanquished, mine eyes"; and there is every reason to suppose that his words were no unlicensed exaggeration. In the brilliant sunshine of the majority of Egyptian days, the stately palaces, temples, and public buildings which reflected themselves in the waters of the harbour, or cast their shadows across

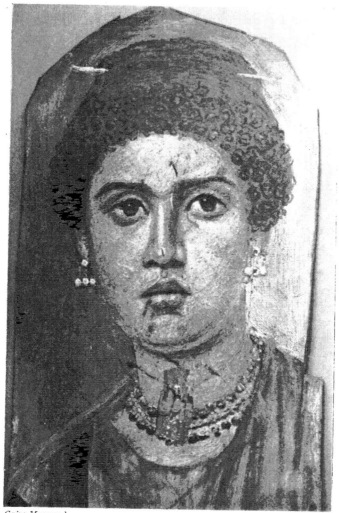

PORTRAIT OF A GREEK LADY.

THE PAINTING DATES FROM A GENERATION LATER THAN THAT OF CLEOPATRA,
BUT IT IS AN EXAMPLE OF THE WORK OF THE ALEXANDRIAN ARTISTS.

the magnificent Street of Canopus, must have dazzled the eyes of the spectator and brought wonder into his heart.

The inhabitants of the city were not altogether worthy of their splendid home. In modern times the people of Alexandria exhibit much the same conglomeration of nationalities as they did in ancient days; but the distinguishing line between Egyptians and Europeans is now more sharply defined than it was in the reign of Cleopatra, owing to the fact that the former are mostly Mohammedans and the latter Christians, no marriage being permitted between them. In Ptolemaic times only the Jews of Alexandria stood outside the circle of international marriages which was gradually forming the people of the city into a single type; for they alone practised that conventional exclusiveness which indicated a strong religious conviction. The Greek element, always predominant in the city, was mainly Macedonian; but in the period we are now studying so many intermarriages with Egyptians had taken place that in the case of a large number of families the stock was much mixed. There must have been, of course, a certain number of aristocratic houses, descended from the Macedonian soldiers and officials who had come to Egypt with Alexander the Great and the first Ptolemy, whose blood had been kept pure; and we hear of such persons boasting of their nationality, though the ruin of their fatherland and its subservience to Rome had left them little of which to be proud. In like manner there must have been many pure Egyptian families, no less proud of their nationality than were the Macedonians. The majority of educated people could now speak both the Greek and Egyptian tongues, and all official decrees and proclamations were published in both languages.   Many Greeks assumed Egyptian names in addition to their own; and it is probable that there were at this date Egyptians who, in like manner, adopted Greek names.

Besides Greeks and Egyptians, there were numerous Italians, Cretans, Phœnicians, Cilicians, Cypriots, Persians, Syrians, Armenians, Arabs, and persons of other nationalities, who had, to some extent, intermarried with Alexandrian families, thus producing a stock which must have been much like that to be found in the city at the present day and now termed Levantine. Some of these had come to Alexandria originally as respectable merchants and traders; others were sailors, and, indeed, pirates; yet others were escaped slaves, outlaws, criminals, and debtors who were allowed to enter Alexandria on condition that they served in the army; while not a few were soldiers of fortune who had been enrolled in the forces of Egypt.   There was a standing army of these mercenaries in Alexandria, and Polybius, writing of the days of Cleopatra's great - grandfather, Ptolemy IX., speaks of them as being oppressive and dissolute, desiring to rule rather than to obey.   A further introduction of foreign blood was due to the presence of the Gabinian Army of Occupation, the members of which had settled down in Alexandria and had married Alexandrian women.   These soldiers were largely drawn from Germany and Gaul; and though there had not yet been time for them to do more than add a horde of half-cast children to the medley, their own presence in the city contributed strikingly to the cosmopolitan character of the streets.   This barbaric force, with its Roman officers, must have been in constant rivalry with the so-called Macedonian Household Troops which guarded the palace; but when Cleopatra came to the throne the latter force had already been freely recruited from all the riff-raff of the world, and was in no way a match for the northerners.

The aristocracy of Alexandria probably consisted of the cosmopolitan officers of the mercenaries and Household Troops, the Roman officers of the Gabinian army, the Macedonian courtiers, the Greek and Egyptian officials, and numerous families of wealthy Europeans, Syrians, Jews, and Egyptians. The professors and scholars of the Museum constituted a class of their own, much patronised by the court, but probably not often accepted by the aristocracy of the city for any other reason than that of their learning. The mob was mainly composed of Greeks of mixed breed, together with a large number of Egyptians of somewhat impure stock; and a more noisy, turbulent, and excitable crowd could not be found in all the world, not even in riotous Rome. The Greeks and Jews were constantly annoying one another, but the Greeks and Egyptians seem to have fraternised to a very considerable extent, for there was not so wide a gulf between them as might be imagined. The Egyptians of Alexandria, and, indeed, of all the Delta, were often no darker-skinned than the Greeks. Both peoples were noisy and excitable, vain and ostentatious, smart and clever. They did not quarrel upon religious matters, for the Egyptian gods were easily able to be identified with those of Greece, and the chief deity of Alexandria, Serapis, was here worshipped by both nations in common. In the domain of art they had no cause for dissensions, for the individual art of Egypt was practically dead, and that of Greece had been accepted by cultivated Egyptians as the correct expression of the refinement in which they desired to live. Both peoples were industrious, and eager in the pursuit of wealth, and both were able to set their labours aside with ease, and to turn their whole attention to the amusements which the luxurious city provided. Polybius speaks of the Egyptians as being smart and civilised; and of the Alexandrian Greeks he writes that they were a poor lot, though he seems to have preferred them to the Egyptians.

The people of Alexandria were passionately fond of the theatre. In the words of Dion Chrysostom, who, however, speaks of the citizens of a century later than Cleopatra, "the whole town lived for excitement, and when the manifestation of Apis (the sacred bull) took place, all Alexandria went fairly mad with musical entertainments and horse-races. When doing their ordinary work they were apparently sane, but the instant they entered the theatre or the racecourse they appeared as if possessed by some intoxicating drug, so that they no longer knew nor cared what they said or did. And this was the case even with women and children, so that when the show was over, and the first madness past, all the streets and byways were seething with excitement for days, like the swell after a storm." The Emperor Hadrian says of them: "I have found them wholly light, wavering, and flying after every breath of a report. . . . They are seditious, vain, and spiteful, though as a body wealthy and prosperous." The impudent wit of the young Græco-Egyptian dandy was proverbial, and must always have constituted a cause of offence to those whose public positions laid them open to attack. No sooner did a statesman assume office, or

a king come to the throne, than he was given some scur-
rilous nickname by the wags of the city, which stuck
to him throughout the remainder of his life.   Thus,
to quote a few examples, Ptolemy IX. was called
"Bloated," Ptolemy X. "Vetch," Ptolemy XIII.
"Piper"; Seleucus they named "Pickled-fish Pedlar,"
and in later times Vespasian was named "Scullion."
All forms of ridicule appealed to them, and many are
the tales told in this regard.   Thus, when King Agrippa
passed through the city on his way to his insecure throne,
these young Alexandrians dressed up an unfortunate
madman whom they had found in the streets, put a
paper crown upon his head and a reed in his hand,
and led him through the town, hailing him as King of
the Jews: and this in spite of the fact that Agrippa
was the friend of Caligula, their Emperor.   Against
Vespasian they told with delight the story of how he
had bothered one of his friends for the payment of a
trifling loan of six obols, and somebody made up a song
in which the fact was recorded.   They ridiculed Cara-
calla in the same manner, laughing at him for dressing
himself like Alexander the Great, although his stature
was below the average; but in this case they had not
reckoned with their man, whose revenge upon them was
an act no less frightful than the total extermination of
all the well-to-do young men of the city, they being collected together under a false pretence and butchered in
cold blood.   These Alexandrians were famous for the
witty and scathing verses which they composed upon
topical subjects; and a later historian speaks of this
proficiency of theirs "in making songs and epigrams
against their rulers."   Such ditties were carried from
Egypt to Rome, and were sung in the Italian capital,

just as nowadays the latest American air is hummed and whistled in the streets of London. Indeed, in Rome the wit of Alexandria was very generally appreciated; and, a few years later, one hears of Alexandrian comedians causing Roman audiences to rock with laughter.

The Emperor Hadrian, as we have seen, speaks of the Alexandrians as being spiteful; and, no doubt, a great deal of their vaunted wit had that character. The young Græco-Egyptian was inordinately vain and self-satisfied; and no critic so soon adopts a spiteful tone as he who has thought himself above criticism. The conceit of these smart young men was very noticeable, and is frequently referred to by early writers. They appear to have been much devoted to the study of their personal appearance; and if one may judge by the habits of the upper-class Egyptians and Levantines of present-day Alexandria, many of them must have been intolerable fops. The luxury of their houses was probably far greater than that in Roman life at this date, and they had studied the culinary arts in an objectionably thorough manner. Dion Chrysostom says the Alexandrians of his day thought of little else but food and horse-racing. Both Greeks and Egyptians in Alexandria had the reputation of being fickle and easily influenced by the moment's emotion. "I should be wasting many words in vain," says the author of 'De Bello Alexandrino,' "if I were to defend the Alexandrians from the charges of deceit and levity of mind. . . . There can be no doubt that the race is most prone to treachery." They had few traditions, no feelings of patriotism, and not much political interest. They did not make any study of themselves, nor write histories of their city: they lived for the moment, and if the Government of the hour were distasteful to them they revolted against it with startling rapidity. The city was constantly being disturbed by street rioting, and there was no great regard for human life.

The population of Alexandria is said to have been about 300,000 during the later years of the Ptolemaic dynasty, which was not much less than that of Rome before the Civil War, and twice the Roman number after that sanguinary struggle.[1] In spite of its reputation for frivolity it was very largely a business city, and a goodly portion of its citizens were animated by a lively commercial spirit which quite outclassed that of the Italian capital in enterprise and bustle. This, of course, was a Greek and not an Egyptian characteristic, for the latter are notoriously unenterprising and conservative in their methods, while the Greeks, to this day, are admirable merchants and business men. Alexandria was the most important corn-market of the world, and for this reason was always envied by Rome. Incidentally I may remark that proportionally far more corn was consumed in Cleopatra's time than in our own; and Cæsar once speaks of the *endurance* of his soldiers in submitting to eat meat owing to the scarcity of corn.[2] The city was also engaged in many other forms of commerce, and in the reign of Cleopatra it was recognised as the greatest trading centre in the world. Here East and West met in the busy market-places; and at the time with which we are dealing the eyes of all men were beginning to be turned to this city as being the terminus of the new trade-route to India, along which such rich merchandise was already being conveyed.

[1] Plutarch : Cæsar.   [2] Bell. Civ. III. 47.

It was at the same time the chief seat of Greek learning, and regarded itself also as the leading authority on matters of art — a point which must have been open to dispute.   The great figure of Nilus, of which an illustration is given in this volume, is generally considered to be an example of Alexandrian art.   The famous "Alexandrian School," celebrated for its scientific work and its poetry, had existed for more than two hundred years, and was now in its decline, though it still attempted to continue the old Hellenic culture.[1] The school of philosophy, which succeeded it in celebrity, was just beginning to come into prominence. Thus the eyes of all merchants, all scientists, all men of letters, all scholars, and all statesmen, were turned in these days to Alexandria; and the Ptolemaic court, in spite of the degeneracy of its sovereigns, was held in the highest esteem.

[1] Susemihl. Geschichte der griechischen Litteratur in der Alexandrinerzeit.

CHAPTER III.

THE BIRTH AND EARLY YEARS OF CLEOPATRA.

CLEOPATRA was the last of the regnant Ptolemaic sovereigns of Egypt, and was the seventh Egyptian Queen of her name,[1] in her person all the rights and privileges of that extraordinary line of Pharaohs being vested. The Ptolemaic Dynasty was founded in the first years of the third century before Christ by Ptolemy, the son of Lagus, one of the Macedonian generals of Alexander the Great, who, on his master's death, seized the province of Egypt, and, a few years later, made himself King of that country, establishing himself at the newly-founded city of Alexandria on the sea-coast. For two and a half centuries the dynasty presided over the destinies of Egypt, at first with solicitous care, and later with startling nonchalance, until, with the death of the great Cleopatra and her son Ptolemy XVI. (Cæsarion), the royal line came to an end.

For the right understanding of Cleopatra's character it must be clearly recognised that the Ptolemies were in no way Egyptians. They were Macedonians, as I

---

[1] In hieroglyphs the name reads *Kleopadra.* It is a Greek name, meaning "Glory of her Race."

have already said, in whose veins flowed not one drop of Egyptian blood. Their capital city of Alexandria was, in the main, a Mediterranean colony set down upon the sea-coast of Egypt, but having no connection with the Delta and the Nile Valley other than the purely commercial and official relationship which of necessity existed between the maritime seat of Government and the provinces. The city was Greek in character; the temples and public buildings were constructed in the Greek manner; the art of the period was Greek; the life of the upper classes was lived according to Greek habits; the dress of the court and of the aristocracy was Greek; the language spoken by them was Greek, pronounced, it it is said, with the broad Macedonian accent. It is probable that no one of the Ptolemies ever wore Egyptian costume, except possibly for ceremonial purposes; and, in passing, it may be remarked that the modern conventional representation of the great Cleopatra walking about her palace clothed in splendid Egyptian robes and wearing the vulture-headdress of the ancient queens has no justification.[1] It is true that she is said to have attired herself on certain occasions in a dress designed to simulate that which was supposed by the priests of the time to have been worn by the mother-deity Isis; but contemporaneous representations of Isis generally show her clad in the Greek and not the Egyptian manner. And if she ever wore the ancient dress of the Egyptian queens, it must have been only at great religious festivals or on occasions where conformity to obsolete habits was required by the ritual.

The relationship of the royal house to the people was

[1] Representations of Cleopatra or other sovereigns of the dynasty dressed in Egyptian costume are probably simply traditional.

very similar to that existing at the present day between the Khedivial dynasty and the provincial natives of Egypt. The modern Khedivial princes are Albanians, who cannot record in their genealogy a single Egyptian ancestor. They live in the European manner, and dress according to the dictates of Paris and London. Similarly the Ptolemies retained their Macedonian nationality, and Plutarch tells us that not one of them even troubled to learn the Egyptian language. On the other hand the Egyptians, constrained by the force of circumstances, accepted the dynasty as the legal successor of the ancient Pharaonic line, and assigned to the Ptolemies all the titles and dignities of their great Pharaohs.

These Greek sovereigns, Cleopatra no less than her predecessors, were given the titles which had been so proudly borne by Rameses the Great and the mighty Thutmosis the Third, a thousand years and more before their day. They were named, " Living Image of the God Amon," " Child of the Sun," and " Chosen of Ptah," just as the great Memnon and the conquering Sesostris had been named when Egypt was the first power in the world. In the temples throughout the land, with the exception of those of importance at Alexandria, these Macedonian monarchs were pictorially represented in the guise of the ancient Pharaohs, crowned with the tall crowns of Upper and Lower Egypt, the horns and feathers of Amon upon their heads, and the royal serpent at their foreheads. There they were seen worshipping the old gods of Egypt, prostrating themselves in the presence of the cow Hathor, bowing before the crocodile Sobk, burning incense at the shrine of the cat Bast, and performing all the magical ceremonies hallowed by the usage of four thousand years. They were shown enthroned with the gods, embraced by Isis, saluted by Osiris, and kissed by Mout, the Mother of Heaven. Yet it is doubtful whether in actual fact any Ptolemy at any time identified himself in this manner with the traditional character of a Pharaoh.

Very occasionally one of these Greek sovereigns left his city of Alexandria to visit Egypt proper, and to travel up the Nile. At certain cities he honoured the local temple with a visit and performed in a perfunctory manner the prescribed ceremonies, just as a modern sovereign lays a foundation-stone or launches a battle-ship. But there is nothing to show that any member of the royal house regarded himself as an Egyptian in the traditional sense of the word. They were careful as a rule to placate the priesthood, and to allow them a free use of their funds in the building and decoration of the temples; and Egyptian national life was fostered to a very considerable extent. But in Alexandria one might hardly have believed oneself to be in the land of the Pharaohs, and the court was almost entirely European in character.

The Ptolemies as a family were extraordinarily callous in their estimate of the value of human life, and the history of the dynasty is marked throughout its whole length by a series of villainous murders. In this respect they showed their non-Egyptian blood; for the people of the Nile were, and now are, a kindly, pleasant folk, not predisposed to the arts of the assassin and not by any means regardless of the rights of their fellow-men. It may be of interest to record here some of the murders for which the Ptolemies are responsible. Ptolemy III., according to Justin, was murdered by his son Ptolemy IV., who also seems to have planned at one time and

another the murders of his brother Magas, his uncle
Lysimachus, his mother Berenice, and his wife Arsinoe.
Ptolemy V. is described as a cruel and violent monarch,
who seems to have indulged the habit of murdering those
who offended him.   Ptolemy VII. is said by Polybius
to have had the Egyptian vice of riotousness, although
on the whole averse to shedding blood.   Ptolemy VIII.
murdered his young nephew, the heir to the throne,
and married the dead boy's mother, the widowed queen
Cleopatra II., who shortly afterwards presented him with
a baby, Memphites, whose paternal parentage is doubtful.
Ptolemy later, according to some accounts, murdered
this child and sent his body in pieces to the mother.   He
then married his niece, Cleopatra III.; and she, on being
left a widow, appears to have murdered Cleopatra II.
This Cleopatra III. bore a son who later ascended the
throne as Ptolemy XI., whom she afterwards attempted
to murder, but the tables being turned she was murdered
by him.   Ptolemy X. was driven from the throne by his
mother, who installed Ptolemy XI. in his place, and
was promptly murdered by the new king for her pains.
Ptolemy XII., having married his stepmother, murdered
her, and himself was murdered shortly afterwards.
Ptolemy XIII., the father of the great Cleopatra,
murdered his daughter Berenice and also several other
persons.

The women of this family were even more violent than
the men.   Mahaffy describes their characteristics in the
following words: " Great power and wealth, which
makes an alliance with them imply the command of
large resources in men and money; mutual hatred; disregard of all ties of family and affection; the dearest
object fratricide—such pictures of depravity as make

any reasonable man pause and ask whether human nature had deserted these women and the Hyrcanian tiger of the poet taken its place." In many other ways also this murderous family of kings possessed an unenviable reputation. The first three Ptolemies were endowed with many sterling qualities, and were conspicuous for their talents; but the remaining monarchs of the dynasty were, for the most part, degenerate and debauched. They were, however, patrons of the arts and sciences, and indeed they did more for them than did almost any other royal house in the world. Ptolemaic Alexandria was to some extent the birthplace of the sciences of anatomy, geometry, conic sections, hydrostatics, geography, and astronomy, while its position in the artistic world was most important. The splendour and luxury of the palace was far-famed, and the sovereign lived in a chronic condition of repletion which surpassed that of any other court. When Scipio Africanus visited Egypt he found our Cleopatra's great-grandfather, Ptolemy IX., who was nicknamed Physkon, "the Bloated," fat, puffing, and thoroughly over-fed. As Scipio walked to the palace with the King, who, in too transparent robes, breathed heavily by his side, he whispered to a friend that Alexandria had derived at least one benefit from his visit—it had seen its sovereign taking a walk. Ptolemy X., Cleopatra's grandfather, obtained the nickname " Lathyros," owing, it is said, to the resemblance of his nose to a vetch or some such flowery and leguminous plant: a fact which certainly suggests that the King was not a man of temperate habits. Ptolemy XI. was so bloated by gluttony and vice that he seldom walked without crutches, though, under the influence of wine, he was able to skip about the room freely enough with his drunken comrades. Ptolemy XIII., Cleopatra's father, had such an objection to temperance that once he threatened to put the philosopher Demetrius to death for not being intoxicated at one of his feasts; and the unfortunate man was obliged the next day publicly to drink himself silly in order to save his life. Such glimpses as these show us the Ptolemies at their worst, and we are constrained to ask how it is possible that Cleopatra, who brought the line to a termination, could have failed to be a thoroughly bad woman. Yet, as will presently become apparent, there is no great reason to suppose that her sins were either many or scarlet.

Cleopatra's father, Ptolemy XIII., who went by the nickname of Auletes, "the Piper," was a degenerate little man, who passes across Egypt's political stage in a condition of almost continuous inebriety. We watch his drunken antics as he directs the Bacchic orgies in the palace; we see him stupidly plotting and scheming to hold his tottering throne; we hear him playing the livelong hours away upon his flute; and we feel that his deeds would be hardly worth recording were it not for the fact that in his reign is seen the critical development of the political relationship between Rome and Egypt, which, towards the end of the Ptolemaic dynasty, came to have such a complicated bearing upon the history of both countries. After the battle of Pydna (B.C. 167) Rome had obtained almost absolute control of the Hellenistic world, and she soon began to lay her hands on all the commerce of the eastern Mediterranean. Towards the close of the Ptolemaic period the great Republic turned eager eyes towards Egypt, watching for an opportunity to seize that wealthy land for her own enrichment.

Reference to the genealogy at the end of this volume will show the reader that the main line of the Lagidæ came to an end on the assassination (after a reign of nineteen days) of Ptolemy XII. (Alexander II.), who had been raised to the throne by Roman help. The only legitimate child of Ptolemy X. (Soter II.) was Berenice III., the cousin of Ptolemy XII., who had been married to him, the union, however, producing no heir to the throne. Ptolemy X. had two sons, the half-brothers of Berenice III., but they were both illegitimate, the name and status of their mother being now unknown. It is possible that they were the children of Cleopatra IV., who was divorced from their father at his accession ; or it is possible that the lady was not of royal blood. On the death of Ptolemy XII. one of these two young men proclaimed himself Pharaoh of Egypt, being known to us as Ptolemy XIII., and the other announced himself as King of Cyprus, also under the name of Ptolemy. The people of Alexandria at once accepted Ptolemy XIII. as their king, for, whether illegitimate or not, he was the eldest male descendant of the line, and their refusal to accept his rule would have brought the dynasty to a close, thereby insuring an immediate Roman occupation. Cicero speaks of the new monarch as *nec regio genere ortus*, which implies that whoever his mother might be, she was not a reigning queen at the time of his birth ; but the Alexandrian populace were in no mood to raise scruples in regard to his origin, when it was apparent that he alone stood between their liberty and the stern domination of Rome.

No sooner had he ascended the throne, however, with

Alexandria Museum.]

SERAPIS,

THE CHIEF GOD OF ALEXANDRIA.

the title of Ptolemy (XIII.) Neos Dionysos, than the discovery was made that Ptolemy XII., under his name of Alexander, had in his will appointed the Roman Republic his heir, thus voluntarily bringing his dynasty to a close. Such a course of action was not novel. It had already been followed in the case of Pergamum, Cyrene, and Bithynia, and it seems likely that Ptolemy XII. had taken this step in order to obtain the financial or moral support of the Romans in regard to his accession, or for some equally urgent reason. The Senate acknowledged the authenticity of the will, which, of course, the party of Ptolemy XIII. had denied. It had been suggested that the testator was not Ptolemy XII. at all, but another Alexander, Ptolemy XI. (Alexander I.), or an obscure person sometimes referred to as Alexander III. There is little question, however, that the will was genuine enough; but there is considerable doubt as to whether it was legally valid. In the first place, it was probably written before Ptolemy XII. succeeded to the kingdom; and, in the second place, such a will would only be valid were there no heir to the throne; but the people of Alexandria had accepted Ptolemy XIII. as the rightful heir. At all events the Senate, while seizing, by virtue of the document, as much of the private fortune of the testator as they could lay hands on, took no steps to dethrone the two new kings, either of Egypt or Cyprus, though, on the other hand, they did not officially recognise them.

In this attitude they were influenced also by the fact that a large party in Rome did not wish to see the Republic further involved in Oriental affairs, nor did they feel at the moment inclined to place in the hands of any one man such power as would accrue to the official who should be appointed as Governor of the new province. Egypt was regarded as a very wealthy and important country, second only to Rome in the extent of its power. It held the keys to the rich lands of the south, and to Arabia and India it seemed to be one of the main gateways. The revenues of the palace of Alexandria were quite equal to the public income of Rome at this time; and, indeed, even at a later date, after Pompey had so greatly augmented the yearly sum in the Treasury, the wealth of the Egyptian Court was not far short of this increased total.[1] Alexandria had succeeded Athens as the seat of culture and learning, and it was now regarded as the second city of the world. It was therefore felt that the armies and the generals sent over the sea to this distant land might well run the risk of being absorbed into the life of the country which they were holding, and might as it were inevitably set up an Eastern Empire which would be a menace, and even a terror, to Rome.

The new King of Egypt, whom we may now call by his nickname Auletes, was much disturbed by the existence of this will, and throughout his reign he was constantly making efforts to buy off the expected interference of Rome. He was an unhappy and unfortunate man. All he asked was to be allowed to enjoy the royal wealth in drunken peace, and not to be bothered by the haunting fear that he might be turned out of his kingdom. He was a keen enjoyer of good living, and there was nothing that pleased him so much as the participation in one of the orgies of Dionysos. He played the pipes with some proficiency, and, when he was sober, it would seem that he spent many a contented hour piping pleasantly in the

[1] Mommsen.

sun. Yet his reign was continuously overshadowed by
this knowledge that the Romans might at any moment
dethrone him; and one pictures him often giving vent to
an evening melancholy by blowing from his little flute
one of those wailing dirges of his native land, which
flutter upon the ears like the notes of a night-bird,
and drift at last upon a half-tone into silence.

In the fifth year of his reign, that is to say in B.C. 75,
his kinswoman, Selene, sent her two sons to Rome with
the object of obtaining the thrones of Egypt, Cyprus, and
Syria; and Auletes must have watched with anxiety
their attempts to oust him. He knew that they were
giving bribes right and left to the Senators, in order to
effect their purpose, and he was aware that in this manner
alone the heart of the Roman Republic could be touched;
yet for the time being he avoided these methods of ex-
pending his country's revenue, and, after a while, he had
the satisfaction of hearing that Selene had abandoned
her efforts to obtain recognition. In the thirteenth year
of his reign Pompey sent a fleet under Lentulus Marcel-
linus to clear the Egyptian coast of pirates, and when
Lentulus was made consul he caused the Ptolemaic eagle
and thunderbolt to be displayed upon his coins to mark
the fact that he had exercised an act of sovereignty in
connection with that country. Three years later another
Roman fleet was sent to Alexandria to impose the will of
the Senate in regard to certain disputed questions; and
once more Auletes must have suffered from the terrors of
imminent dethronement.

In B.C. 65 he was again disturbed from his bibulous
ease by the news that the Romans were thinking of
sending Crassus or Julius Cæsar to annex his kingdom;
but the scheme came to naught, and for a time Auletes

was left in peace. In B.C. 63 Pompey annexed Syria
to the Roman dominions, and thereupon Auletes sent
him a large present of money and military supplies in
order to purchase his friendship. At the same time he
invited him to come to Egypt upon a friendly visit, but
Pompey, while accepting the King's money, did not think
it necessary to make use of his hospitality.

At last, in B.C. 59, Auletes decided to go himself to
Rome, in the hope of obtaining, through the good offices
of Pompey, or of Cæsar, who was Consul in that year,
the official recognition by the Senate of his right to the
Egyptian throne. Being so degenerate and so worthless
a personage, there was no likelihood that the Romans
would confirm him in his kingdom unless they were well
paid to do so, and he therefore took with him all the
money he could lay his hands upon. In Rome, as
Mommsen says, "men had forgotten what honesty was.
A person who refused a bribe was regarded not as an
upright man, but as a personal foe." Auletes, therefore,
when he had arrived, gave huge bribes to various
Senators in order to obtain their support, and he
appears to have been most systematically fleeced by
the acute magnates of Rome. When for the moment
his Egyptian resources were exhausted, he borrowed a
large sum from the great financier, Rabirius Postumus,
who persuaded some of his friends also to lend the King
money. These men formed a kind of syndicate to finance
Auletes, on the understanding that if he were confirmed
in his heritage, they should each receive in return a sum
vastly greater than that which they had put in.

The visit of Auletes to Rome was made in the nick
of time. The Pirate and the Third Mithridatic wars
had left the Republic in pressing need of money, and

there was much talk in regard to the advantages of an immediate annexation of Egypt. Crassus, the tribune Rullus, and Julius Cæsar had shown themselves anxious to take the country without delay; and the unfortunate King of Egypt thus found himself in a most desperate position. At last, however, a bribe of 6000 talents (about a million and a half sterling) induced the nearly bankrupt Cæsar to give Auletes the desired recognition, and the disgraceful transaction came to a temporary conclusion with Cæsar's violent forcing of his "Julian Law concerning the King of Egypt" through the Senate, whereby Ptolemy was named the "ally and friend of the Roman people."

In the next year, B.C. 58, the Romans, still in need of money, prepared to annex Cyprus, over which Ptolemy, the brother of Auletes, was reigning. The annexation had been proposed by Publius Clodius, a scoundrelly politician, who bore a grudge against the Cyprian Ptolemy owing to the fact that once when Clodius was captured by pirates Ptolemy had only offered two talents for his ransom. Ptolemy would not now buy off the invaders as his brother had done, and in consequence Cato landed on the island and converted it into part of the Roman province of Cilicia. Ptolemy, with a certain royal dignity, at once poisoned himself, preferring to die than to suffer the humiliation of banishment from the throne which he had usurped. His treasure of 7000 talents (some £1,700,000) fell into the hands of Cato, who having, no doubt, helped himself to a portion of the booty,[1] handed the remainder over to the benign Senate.

No sooner had Auletes obtained the support of Rome,

---

[1] Or do I wrong the hero of Utica?

however, than his own people of Alexandria, incensed by
the increase of taxation necessary for paying off his debts,
and angry also at the King's refusal to seize Cyprus from
the Romans, rose in rebellion and drove him out of
Egypt.   While the wretched man was on his way to
Rome, he put in at Rhodes, where he had heard that
Cato was staying, in order to obtain some help from this
celebrated Senator; and, having had few personal dealings with Romans, he sent a royal invitation or command
to Cato to come to him.   The Senator, however, who
that day was suffering from a bilious attack, and had just
swallowed a dose of medicine, was in no mind to wait
upon drunken kings.   He therefore sent a message to
Auletes stating that if he wished to see him he had better
come to his lodgings in the town; and the King of Egypt
was thus obliged to humble himself and to find his way
to the Senator's house.   Cato did not even rise from his
seat when Auletes was ushered in; but straightway
bidding the King be seated, gave him a severe lecture
on the folly of going to Rome to plead his cause.   All
Egypt turned into silver, he declared, would hardly
satisfy the greed of the Romans whom he would
have to bribe, and he strongly urged him to return to
Egypt and to make his peace with his subjects.   The
Senator's bilious attack, however, seems to have cut
short the interview, and Auletes, unconvinced, set sail
for Italy.

Meanwhile the King's daughter, Berenice IV., had
seized the Egyptian throne, and was reigning serenely in
her father's place.   This princess and her sister, Cleopatra VI., who died soon afterwards, were the only two
children of Auletes' first marriage—namely, with Cleopatra V.   There were four young children in the Palace

nurseries who were born of a second marriage, but who their mother was, or whether she was at this time alive or dead, history does not record. Of these four children, two afterwards succeeded to the throne as Ptolemy XIV. and Ptolemy XV., a third was the unfortunate Princess Arsinoe, and the fourth was the great Cleopatra VII., the heroine of the present volume, at this time about eleven years of age, having been born in the winter of B.C. 69-68.

Auletes having fled to Rome, approached the Senate in the manner of one who had been unjustly evicted from an estate which he had purchased from them. Again he bribed the leading statesmen, and again borrowed money on all sides, though now it is probable that his Roman creditors were less sanguine than on the previous occasion. Cæsar was absent in Gaul at this time, and there-fore was not able to be bribed. Pompey, curiously enough, does not appear to have accepted the King's money, though he offered him the hospitality of his villa in the Alban district, a fact which suggests that the idea of restoring Auletes to his throne had made a strong appeal to the imagination of this impressionable Roman. He had already made himself a kind of patron of the Egyptian Court, and there can be little doubt that he hoped to obtain from Auletes, in return for his favours, the freedom to make use of the wealth and resources of that monarch's enormously valuable dominion.

The people of Alexandria, who were eagerly desirous that Auletes should not be reinstated, now sent an embassy of a hundred persons to Rome to lay before the Senate their case against the King; but the banished monarch, driven by despair to any lengths, hired assas-sins and caused the embassy to be attacked near Puteoli,

the modern Pozzuoli, many of them being slain. Those
who survived were heavily bribed, and thus the crime
was hushed up. The leader of the deputation, the
philosopher Dion, escaped on this occasion, but was
poisoned by Auletes as soon as he arrived in Rome; and
thereupon the desperate King was able to breathe once
more in peace. All might now have gone well with his
cause, and a Roman army might have been placed at his
disposal had not some political opponent discovered in
the Sibylline Books an oracle which stated that if the
King of Egypt were to come begging for help he should
be aided with friendship but not with arms. Thereat, in
despair, the unfortunate Auletes quitted Rome, and took
up his residence at Ephesus, leaving in the capital an
agent named Ammonios to keep him in touch with
events.

Three years later, in January B.C. 55, the King's
interests were still being discussed, and Pompey was
trying, in a desultory manner, to assist him back to his
throne; but so great were the fears of the Senate at
placing the task in the hands of any one man, that no
decision could be arived at. It was suggested that
Lentulus Spinther, the Governor of Cilicia, should evade
the Sibylline decree by leaving Auletes at Ptolemais
(Acre) and going himself to Egypt at the head of an
army; but the King no doubt saw in this an attempt
by the wily Romans simply to seize his country, and he
appears to have opposed the plan with understandable
vehemence. It was then proposed that Lentulus should
take no army, but should trust to the might of the Roman
name for his purpose, thereby following the advice of the
prophetic Books.

At last, however, Auletes offered the huge bribe of

10,000 talents (nearly two and a half millions sterling) for the repurchase of his kingdom; and, as a consequence, the Governor of Syria, Aulus Gabinius, himself a bankrupt in sore need of money, arranged to invade Egypt and to place Auletes upon the throne in spite of the Sibylline warnings. Gabinius, being so deeply in debt, and knowing that a large portion of the promised sum would pass to him, was extremely eager to undertake the war, though it is said that he feared the possibility of disaster. He therefore pushed forward the arrangements for the campaign with all despatch, and soon was prepared to set out across the desert to Egypt.

Meanwhile the Alexandrians had married Berenice IV. to Archelaus, the High Priest of Komana in Cappadocia, an ambitious man of great influence and authority, a protégé of Pompey the Great, who had been raised to the High Priesthood by him in B.C. 64, and who at once attempted, but without success, to obtain through him the support of Rome. Gabinius was not long in declaring war against Archelaus, under the pretext that he was encouraging piracy along the North African coast, and also that he was building a fleet which might be regarded as a menace to Rome; and soon his army was marching across the desert from Gaza to Pelusium. The cavalry, which was sent in advance of the main army, was commanded by Marcus Antonius, at this time a smart young soldier whose future lay all golden before him. The frontier fortress of Pelusium fell to his brilliant generalship, and soon the Roman legions were marching on Alexandria. The palace soldiery now joined the invaders, Archelaus was killed, and the city fell.

Auletes was at once restored to his throne, and Berenice IV. was put to death. A large number of

Roman infantry and Celtic and German cavalry, of whom we shall hear again, were left in the city to preserve order, and it would seem that for a short time Anthony remained in Alexandria. The young Princess Cleopatra was now a girl of some fourteen years of age, and already she is said to have attracted the Roman cavalry leader by her youthful beauty and charm. At the east end of the Mediterranean a girl of fourteen years is already mature, and has long arrived at what is called a marriageable age. There is probably little importance to be attached to this meeting, but it is not without interest as an earnest of future events.

The Romans now began to demand payment of the various sums promised to them by Auletes. Rabirius Postumus appears to have been one of the largest creditors, and the only way in which the King could pay him back was by making him Chancellor of the Exchequer, so that all taxes might pass through his hands. Rabirius also represented the interests of the importunate Julius Cæsar, and probably those of Gabinius. The situation was thus not unlike that which was found in Egypt in the 'seventies, when a European Commission was appointed to handle all public funds in order that the ruler's private debts might be paid off. In the case of Auletes, however, it was the leading Romans who were his creditors, and hence we find the shadow of the great Republic hanging over the Alexandrian court, and Rome is seen to be inextricably mixed up with Egyptian affairs. Roman money had been lent and had to be regained; Roman officials handled all the taxes; a Roman army occupied the city, and the King reigned by permission of the Roman Senate to whom his kingdom had been bequeathed.

In B.C. 54 the Alexandrians made an attempt to shake off the incubus, and drove Rabirius out of Egypt. Roman attention was at once fixed upon Alexandria, and it is probable that the country would have been annexed at once had not the appalling Parthian catastrophe in the following year, when Crassus was defeated and killed, diverted their minds to other channels. Auletes, however, did not live long to enjoy his dearly - bought immunity; for in the summer of B.C. 51 he passed away, leaving behind him the four children born to him of his second marriage with the unknown lady who was now probably dead. The famous Cleopatra, the seventh of the name, was the eldest of this family, being, at her father's death, about eighteen years of age. Her sister Arsinoe, whom she heartily disliked, was a few years younger. The third child was a boy of ten or eleven years of age, afterwards known as Ptolemy XIV.; and lastly, there was the child who later became Ptolemy XV., now a boy of seven or eight.[1] Auletes, warned by his own bitter experiences, had taken the precaution to write an explicit will in which he stated clearly his wishes in regard to the succession. One copy of the will was kept at Alexandria, and a second copy, duly attested and sealed, was placed in the hands of Pompey at Rome, who had befriended the King when he was in that city, with the request that it should be deposited in the *ærarium*. In this will Auletes decreed that his eldest surviving daughter and eldest surviving son should reign jointly; and he called upon the Roman people in the name of all their gods and in view of all their treaties made with him, to

---

[1] Porphyry says he died in the eighth year of Cleopatra's reign, and Josephus states that he was fifteen years of age at his death. This would make him about seven years old at Cleopatra's accession, which seems probable enough.

see that the terms of his testament were carried out.
He further asked the Roman people to act as guardian to
the new King, as though fearing that the boy might be
suppressed, or even put out of the way by his co-regnant
sister. At the same time he carefully urged them to
make no change in the succession, and his words have
been thought to suggest that he feared lest Cleopatra, in
like manner, might be removed in favour of Arsinoe. In
a court such as that of the Ptolemies the fact that two
sons and two daughters were living at the palace at the
King's death boded ill for the prospects of peace; and it
would seem that Auletes' knowledge that Cleopatra and
Arsinoe were not on the best of terms gave rise in his
mind to the greatest apprehension. Being aware of the
domestic history of his family, and knowing that his own
hands were stained with the blood of his daughter Berenice, whom he had murdered on his return from exile,
he must have been fully alive to the possibilities of internecine warfare amongst his surviving children; and, being
in his old age sick of bloodshed and desiring only a bibulous peace for himself and his descendants, he took every
means in his power to secure for them that pleasant
inertia which had been denied so often to himself.

His wish that his eighteen-year-old daughter should
reign with his ten-year-old son involved, as a matter of
course, the marriage of the sister and brother, for the
Ptolomies had conformed to ancient Egyptian customs to
the extent of perpetrating when necessary a royal marriage between a brother and sister in this manner. The
custom was of very ancient establishment in Egypt, and
was based originally on the law of female succession,
which made the monarch's eldest daughter the heiress
of the kingdom. The son who had been selected by his

father to succeed to the throne, or who aspired to the sovereignty either by right or by might, obtained his legal warrant to the kingdom by marriage with this heiress. When such an heiress did not exist, or when the male claimant to the throne had no serious rivals, this rule often seems to have been set aside; but there are few instances of its disuse when circumstances demanded a solidification of the royal claim to the throne.

When, therefore, according to the terms of the will of Auletes, his eldest daughter and eldest son succeeded jointly to the throne as Cleopatra VII. and Ptolemy XIV., their formal marriage was contemplated as a matter of course. There is no evidence of this marriage, and one may suppose that it was postponed by Cleopatra's desire, on the grounds of the extreme youth of the King. Marriages at the age of eleven or twelve years were not uncommon in ancient Egypt, but they were not altogether acceptable to Greek minds; and the Queen could not have found much difficulty in making this her justification for holding the power in her own hands. The young Ptolemy XIV. was placed in the care of the eunuch Potheinos, a man who appears to have been typical of that class of palace intriguers with whom the historian becomes tediously familiar. The royal tutor, Theodotos, an objectionable Greek rhetorician, also exercised considerable influence in the court, and a third intimate of the King was an unscrupulous soldier of Egyptian nationality named Achillas, who commanded the troops in the palace. These three men very soon obtained considerable power, and, acting in the name of their young master, they managed to take a large portion of the government into their own hands. Cleopatra, meanwhile, seems to have suffered something of an eclipse. She was still only a young girl, and her advisers appear to have been men of less strength of purpose than those surrounding her brother's person. The King being still a minor, the bulk of the formal business of the State was performed by the Queen; but it would seem that the real rulers of the country were Potheinos and his friends.

Some two or three years after the death of Auletes, Marcus Calpurnius Bibulus,[1] the pro-consular Governor of Syria, sent his two sons to Alexandria to order the Roman troops stationed in that city to join his army in his contemplated campaign against the Parthians. These Alexandrian troops constituted the Army of Occupation, which had been left in Egypt by Gabinius in B.C. 55 as a protection to Auletes. They were for the most part, as has been said, Gallic and German cavalry, rough men whose rude habits and bulky forms must have caused them to be the wonder and terror of the city. These *Gabiniani milites* had by this time settled down in their new home, and had taken wives to themselves from the Greek and Egyptian families of Alexandria. In spite of the presence amongst them of a considerable body of Roman infantry veterans who had fought under Pompey, the discipline of the army was already much relaxed; and when the Governor of Syria's orders were received there was an immediate mutiny, the two unfortunate sons of Bibulus being promptly murdered by the angry and probably drunken soldiers. When the affair was reported to the palace, Cleopatra issued orders for the immediate arrest of the

---

[1] He had been Consul with Julius Cæsar in 59.

murderers; and the army, realising that their position
as mutinous troops was untenable, handed over the
ringleaders apparently without further trouble. The
prisoners were then sent by the Queen in chains to
Bibulus; but he, being possessed of the best spirit of
the old Roman aristocracy, sent back these murderers
of his two sons to her with the message that the right
of inflicting punishment in such cases belonged only to
the Senate. History does not tell us what was the
ultimate fate of these men, and the incident is not of
great importance except in so far as it shows the first
recorded act of Cleopatra's reign as being one of tactful
deliberation and fair dealing with her Roman neighbours.

Shortly after this, in the year B.C. 49, Pompey sent
his son, Cnæus Pompeius, to Egypt to procure ships
and men in preparation for the civil war which now
seemed inevitable; and the Gabinian troops, feeling
that a war against Julius Cæsar offered more favourable possibilities than a campaign against the ferocious
Parthians, cheerfully responded to the call. Fifty warships and a force of 500 men left Alexandria with Cnæus,
and eventually attached themselves to the command of
Bibulus, who was now Pompey's admiral in the Adriatic.
It is said that Cnæus Pompeius was much attracted by
Cleopatra's beauty and charm, and that he managed
to place himself upon terms of intimacy with her; but
there is absolutely nothing to justify the suggestion that
there was any sort of serious intrigue. I am of opinion
that the stories of this nature which passed into circulation were due to the fact that the possibility of a marriage between Cleopatra and the young Roman had been
contemplated by Alexandrian politicians. The great
Pompey was master of the Roman world, and a union

with his son, on the analogy of that between Berenice
and the High Priest of Komana, was greatly to be desired.
The proposal, however, does not seem to have obtained
much support, and the matter was presently dropped.

In the following year, B.C. 48, when Cleopatra was
twenty-one years of age and her co-regnant brother
fourteen, important events occurred in Alexandria of
which history has left us no direct record. It would
appear that the brother and sister quarrelled, and that
the palace divided itself into two opposing¹ parties. The
young Ptolemy, backed by the eunuch Potheinos, the
rhetorician Theodotos, and the soldier Achillas, set
himself up as sole sovereign of Egypt; and Cleopatra
was obliged to fly for her life into Syria. We have
no knowledge of these momentous events: the struggle
in the palace, the days in which the young queen
walked in deadly peril, the adventurous escape, and
the flight from Egypt. We know only that when the
curtain is raised once more upon the royal drama, the
young Ptolemy is King of Egypt, and, with his army,
is stationed on the eastern frontier to prevent the
incursion of his exiled sister, who has raised an ex-
peditionary force in Syria and is marching back to
her native land to seize again the throne which she
had lost. There is something which appeals very
greatly to the imagination in the thought of this
spirited young Queen's rapid return to the perilous
scenes from which she had so recently escaped; and
the historian feels at once that he is dealing with a
powerful character in this woman who could so speedily
raise an army of mercenaries, and could dare to march
back in battle array across the desert towards the land
which had cast her out.

CHAPTER IV.

THE DEATH OF POMPEY AND THE ARRIVAL OF CÆSAR IN EGYPT.

THE fortress of Pelusium, near which the opposing armies of Ptolemy and Cleopatra were arrayed, stood on low desert ground overlooking the sea, not far east of the modern Port Said. It was the most easterly port and stronghold of the Delta; and, being built upon the much-frequented highroad which skirted the coast between Egypt and Syria, it formed the Asiatic gateway of the Ptolemaic kingdom. The young Ptolemy XIV. had stationed himself, with his advisers and his soldiers, in this fortress, in order to oppose the entrance of his sister Cleopatra, who, as we have already seen, had marched with a strong army back to Egypt from Syria, whither she had fled. On September 28th, B.C. 48, when Cleopatra's forces, having arrived at Pelusium, were preparing to attack the fortress, and were encamped upon the sea-coast a few miles to the east of the town, an event occurred which was destined to change the whole course of Egyptian history. Round the barren headland to the west of the little port a Seleucian galley hove into sight, and cast anchor a short distance from the shore. Upon the

E

deck of this vessel stood the defeated Pompey the
Great and Cornelia his wife, who, flying from the rout
of Pharsalia, had come to claim the hospitality of the
Egyptian King.   The young monarch appears to have
been warned of his approach, for Pompey had touched
at Alexandria, and there hearing that Ptolemy had gone
to Pelusium, had probably sent a messenger to him
overland and himself had sailed round by sea.   The
greatest flurry had been caused in the royal camp by
the news, and for the moment the invasion of Cleopatra
and the impending battle with her forces were quite
forgotten in the excitement of the arrival of the man
who for so long had been the mighty patron of the
Ptolemaic Court.

Egypt, like all the rest of the world, had been watching
with deep interest the warfare waged between the two
Roman giants, Pompey and Cæsar, confident in the success of the former; and the messenger of the defeated
general must have brought the first authentic news of the
result of the eagerly awaited battle.   The sympathies of
the Alexandrians were all on the side of the Pompeians,
for the fugitive, who now asked a return of his former
favours, had always been to them the gigantic representative of Roman patronage.   They knew little, if
anything, about Cæsar, who had spent so many years
in the far north-west; but Pompey was Rome itself to
them, and had always shown himself particularly desirous of acting, when occasion arose, in their behalf.
For many years he had been, admittedly, the most
powerful personage in Rome, and the civilised world
had grovelled at his feet.   Then came the inevitable
quarrel with Julius Cæsar, a man who could not tolerate
the presence of a rival.   Civil war broke out, and the

POMPEY THE GREAT.

two armies met on the plains of Pharsalia. It is not necessary to record here how Pompey's patrician cavalry, in whom he confidently trusted, was defeated by Cæsar's hardened legions; how the foreign allies were awed into inactivity by the spectacle of the superb contest between Romans and Romans; how the debonnaire Pompey, realising his defeat, passed, dazed, to his pavilion and sat there staring in front of him, until the enemy had penetrated to his very door, when, uttering the despairing cry, "What! even into the camp?" he galloped from the field; and how Cæsar's men found the enemy's tents decked in readiness for the celebration of their anticipated victory, the doorways hung with garlands of myrtle, the floors spread with rich carpets, and the tables covered with goblets of wine and dishes of food. Pompey had fled to Larissa and thence to the sea, where he boarded a merchantman and set sail for Mitylene. Here picking up his wife Cornelia, he made his way to Cyprus, where he transhipped to the galley in which he crossed to Egypt. He had expected, very naturally, to be received with courtesy by Ptolemy, who was to be regarded as his political protégé; and he had some undefined but cogent plans of gathering his forces together again and giving battle a second time to his enemies. At Pharsalia he had thought his power irrevocably destroyed, but on his way to Egypt he learnt that Cato had rallied a considerable number of his troops, and that his fleet, which had not come into action, was still loyal; and he therefore hoped that with Ptolemy's expected help he might yet regain the mastery of the Roman world.

As soon as his approach was reported to the Egyptian King, a council of ministers was called, in order to decide the manner in which they should receive the fallen general. There were present at this meeting the three scoundrelly advisers of the youthful monarch whom we have already met: Potheinos, the eunuch, who was a kind of prime minister; Achillas, the Egyptian, who commanded the King's troops; and Theodotos of Chios, the professional master of rhetoric, and tutor to Ptolemy. These three men appear to have organised the plot by which Cleopatra had been driven from Egypt; and, having the boy Ptolemy well under their thumbs, they seem to have been acting with zeal in his name for the advancement of their own fortunes. "It was, indeed, a miserable thing," says Plutarch, "that the fate of the great Pompey should be left to the determinations of these three men; and that he, riding at anchor at a distance from the shore, should be forced to wait the sentence of this tribunal."

Some of the councillors suggested that he should be politely requested to seek refuge in some other country, for it was obvious that Cæsar might deal harshly with them if they were to befriend him. Others proposed that they should receive him and cast in their lot with him, for it was to be supposed, and indeed such was the fact, that he still had a very good chance of recovering from the fiasco of Pharsalia; and there was the danger that, if they did not do so, he might accept the assistance of their enemy Cleopatra. Theodotos, however, pointing out, in a carefully reasoned speech, that both these courses were fraught with danger to themselves, proposed that they should curry favour with Cæsar by murdering their former patron, thus bringing the contest to a close, and thereby avoiding any risk of backing the wrong horse; "and," he added with a smile, "a dead man cannot bite." The councillors readily approved this method of dealing with the difficult situation, and they committed its execution to Achillas, who thereupon engaged the services of a certain Roman officer named Septimius, who had once held a command under Pompey, and another Roman centurion named Salvius. The three men, with a few attendants, then boarded a small boat and set out towards the galley.

When they had come alongside Septimius stood up and saluted Pompey by his military title; and Achillas thereupon invited him to come ashore in the smaller vessel, saying that the large galley could not make the harbour owing to the shallow water. It was now seen that a number of Egyptian battleships were cruising at no great distance, and that the sandy shore was alive with troops; and Pompey, whose suspicions were aroused, realised that he could not now turn back, but must needs place himself in the hands of the surly-looking men who had come out to meet him. His wife Cornelia was distraught with fears for his safety, but he, bidding her to await events without anxiety, lowered himself into the boat, taking with him two centurions, a freedman named Philip, and a slave called Scythes. As he bade farewell to Cornelia he quoted to her a couple of lines from Sophocles—

> " He that once enters at a tyrant's door
> Becomes a slave, though he were free before ; "

and so saying, he set out towards the shore. A deep silence fell upon the little company as the boat passed over the murky water, which at this time of year is beginning to be discoloured by the Nile mud brought down by the first rush of the annual floods;[1] and in the damp heat of an Egyptian summer day the dreary little town and the barren colourless shore must have appeared peculiarly uninviting. In order to break the oppressive silence Pompey turned to Septimius, and, looking earnestly upon him, said: "Surely I am not mistaken in believing you to have been formerly my fellow-soldier?" Septimius made no reply, but silently nodded his head; whereupon Pompey, opening a little book, began to read, and so continued until they had reached the shore. As he was about to leave the boat he took hold of the hand of his freedman Philip; but even as he did so Septimius drew his sword and stabbed him in the back, whereupon both Salvius and Achillas attacked him. Pompey spoke no word, but, groaning a little, hid his face with his mantle, and fell into the bottom of the vessel, where he was speedily done to death.

Cornelia, standing upon the deck of the galley, witnessed the murder, and uttered so great a cry that it was heard upon the shore. Then, seeing the murderers stoop over the body and rise again with the severed head held aloft, she called to her ship's captain to weigh anchor, and in a few moments the galley was making for the open sea and was speedily out of the range of pursuit. Pompey's decapitated body, stripped of all clothing, was now bundled into the water, and a short time afterwards was washed up by the breakers upon the sands of the beach, where it was soon surrounded by a crowd of idlers. Meanwhile Achillas and his accomplices carried the head up to the royal camp.

[1] The end of September, owing to irregularities in the calendar, of which we shall presently hear more, corresponded to the middle of July.

The freedman Philip was not molested, and, presently making his way to the beach, wandered to and fro along the desolate shore until all had retired to the town. Then, going over to the body and kneeling down beside it, he washed it with sea-water and wrapped it in his own shirt for want of a winding-sheet. As he was searching for wood wherewith to make some sort of funeral pyre, he met with an old Roman soldier who had once served under the murdered general; and together these two men carried down to the water's edge such pieces of wreckage and fragments of rotten wood as they could find, and placing the body upon the pile set fire to it.

Upon the next morning one of the Pompeian generals, Lucius Lentulus, who was bringing up the two thousand soldiers whom Pompey had gathered together as a body-guard, arrived in a second galley before Pelusium; and as he was being rowed ashore he observed the still smoking remains of the pyre. "Who is this that has found his end here?" he said, being still in ignorance of the tragedy, and added with a sigh, "Possibly even thou, Pompeius Magnus!" And upon stepping ashore, he too was promptly murdered.

A few days later, on October 2nd, Julius Cæsar, in hot pursuit, arrived at Alexandria, where he heard with genuine disgust of the miserable death of his great enemy. Shortly afterwards Theodotos presented himself to the conqueror, carrying with him Pompey's head and signet-ring; but Cæsar turned in distress from the gruesome head, and taking only the ring in his hand, was for a moment moved to tears.[1] He then appears to have dismissed the astonished Theodotos from his presence like

---

[1] According to Plutarch and others; but the incident is not mentioned in Cæsar's memoirs.

an offending slave: and it was not long before that disillusioned personage fled for his life from Egypt. For
some years, it may be mentioned, he wandered as a
vagabond through Syria and Asia Minor; but at last,
after the death of Cæsar, he was recognised by Marcus
Brutus, and, as a punishment for having instigated the
murder of the great Pompey, was crucified with every
possible ignominy. Cæsar seems to have arranged that
the ashes of his rival should be sent to his wife Cornelia,
by whom they were ultimately deposited at his country
house near Alba; and he also gave orders that the
piteous head should be buried near the sea, in the grove
of Nemesis, outside the eastern walls of Alexandria,
where, in the shade of the trees, a monument was set
up to him and the ground around it laid out. Cæsar
then offered his protection and friendship to all those
partisans of Pompey whom the Egyptians had imprisoned, and he expressed his great satisfaction at being
able thus to save the lives of his fellow-countrymen.

It is not difficult to appreciate the consternation
caused by Cæsar's attitude. Potheinos and Achillas
at once realised that the disgrace of Theodotos awaited
them unless they acted with the utmost circumspection,
biding their time until, as was expected, Cæsar should
take his speedy departure, or until they might deal with
this new disturber of their peace in the same manner in
which they had disposed of the old. But Cæsar had no
intention of leaving Egypt in any haste, nor did he
give them the desired opportunity of anticipating the
Ides of March. With that audacious nonchalance which
so often baffled his observers, he quietly decided to take
up his residence in the Palace upon the Lochias Promontory at Alexandria, at that moment occupied by only

two members of the Royal Family, the younger Ptolemy and his sister Arsinoe; and, as soon as sufficient troops had arrived to support him, he left his galley and landed at the steps of the imposing quay. Two amalgamated legions, 3200 strong, and 800 Celtic and German cavalry, disembarked with him, this small force having been considered by Cæsar sufficient for the rounding up of the Pompeian fugitives, and for the secondary purposes for which he had come to Egypt.[1]

Cæsar's object in hastening across the Mediterranean had been, primarily, the capture of Pompey and his colleagues, and the prevention of a rally under the shelter of the King of Egypt's not inconsiderable armaments. It appears to have been his opinion that speed of pursuit would be more effective than strength of arms, and that his undelayed appearance at Alexandria would more simply discourage the undetermined Egyptians from rendering assistance to their former friend than a display of force at a later date. Fresh from the triumph of Pharsalia, with the memory of that astounding victory to warm his spirits, he did not anticipate any great difficulty in subjecting the Ptolemaic Court to his will, nor in demonstrating to them that he himself, and not the defeated Pompey, represented the authentic might of Rome. It would seem that he expected speedily to frustrate any further resort to arms, and to manifest his authority by acting ostentatiously in the name of the Roman people. He himself should assume the prerogatives lately held by Pompey, and should play the part of benevolent patron to the court of Alexandria so

---

[1] I do not know any record of what became of the 2000 men of Pompey's bodyguard. They probably fled back to Europe on the death of their commanding officer.

admirably sustained by his fallen rival for so many
years.   There were several outstanding matters in
Egypt which, on behalf of his home government, he
could regulate and adjust: and there is little doubt that
he hoped by so doing to establish a despotic reputation
in that important country which would retain for him,
as apparent autocrat of Rome, a personal control of its
affairs for many years to come.   In spite of all that has
been said to the contrary, I am of opinion that his
return to Rome was not urgent; indeed it seems to me
that it could be postponed for a short time with advantage.   Pompey had been a great favourite with the
Italians, and it was just as well that the turmoil caused
by his defeat and death should be allowed to subside,
and that the bitter memories of a sanguinary war, which
had so palpably been brought about by personal rivalry,
should be somewhat forgotten before the victor made
his spectacular entry into Rome.   At this time he was
not at all popular in the capital, and indeed, six months
previously he had been generally regarded as a criminal
and adventurer; while, on the other hand, Pompey had
been the people's darling, and it would take some time
for public opinion to be reversed.

When, therefore, Cæsar heard that the treacherous
deeds of the Egyptian ministers had rendered his primary
action unnecessary, he determined to enter Alexandria
with some show of state, to take up his residence there
for a few weeks, and to interfere in its internal affairs
for his own advancement and for the consolidation of
his power.

With this object in view his four thousand troops were
landed, and he set out in procession towards the Royal
Palace, the lictors carrying the *fasces* and axes before

him as in the consular promenades at Rome.[1]   No
sooner, however, were these ominous symbols observed
by the mob than a rush was made towards them; and
for a time the attitude of the crowd became ugly and
menacing.   The young King and his Court were still at
Pelusium, where his army was defending the frontier
from the expected attack of Cleopatra's invading forces;
but there were in Alexandria a certain number of troops
which had been left there as a garrison, and both
amongst these men and amongst the heterogeneous
townspeople there must have been many who realised
the significance of the *fasces*.   The city was full of
Roman outlaws and renegades, to whom this reminder
of the length of her arm could but bring foreboding
and terror.   To them Cæsar's formal entry meant the
establishment of that law from which they had fled;
while to many a merry member of the crowd the stately
procession appeared to bring to Egypt at last that
dismal shadow of Rome [2] by which it had so long
been menaced.   On all sides it was declared that
this state entry into the Egyptian capital was an insult
to the King's majesty; and so, indeed, it was, though
little did that trouble Cæsar, who was well aware now
of his unassailable position in the councils of Rome.

The city was in a ferment, and for some days after
Cæsar had taken up his quarters at the Palace rioting
continued in the streets, a number of his soldiers being
killed in different parts of the town.   He therefore sent
post-haste to Asia Minor for reinforcements, and took

---

[1] As Consul he would have been entitled to twelve lictors, as Dictator to
twenty-four; but we are not told which number he employed on this occasion.

[2] I quote the telling phrase used by Warde Fowler in his 'Social Life at
Rome.'

such steps as were necessary for securing his position
from attack.   It is probable that he did not suppose the
Alexandrians would have the audacity to make war upon
him, or attempt to drive him from the city; but at the
same time he desired to take no risks, for he seems at
the moment to have been heartily sick of warfare and
slaughter.   The Palace and royal barracks in which his
troops were quartered, being built mainly upon the
Lochias Promontory, were easily able to be defended
from attack by land—for, no doubt, in so turbulent a
city, the royal quarter was protected by massive walls;
and at the same time the position commanded the
eastern half of the Great Harbour and the one side of
its entrance over against the Pharos Lighthouse.   His
ships lay moored under the walls of the Palace; and a
means of escape was thus kept open which, if the worst
came to the worst, might be used with comparative
safety upon any dark night.   I think the turbulence
of the mob, therefore, did not much trouble him, and
he was able to set about the task which he desired to
perform with a certain degree of quietude.   The Civil
War had been a very great strain upon his nerves, and
he must have looked forward to a few weeks of actual
holiday here in the luxurious royal apartments which
he had so casually appropriated.   Summer at Alexandria
is in many ways a delightful time of year; and one may
therefore picture Cæsar, at all times fond of luxury and
opulence, now heartily enjoying these warm breezy days
upon the beautiful Lochias Promontory.   The crisis
of his life had been passed; he was now absolute master
of the Roman world; and his triumphant entry into
the capital, when, in a few weeks' time, the passions
of the mob had cooled, was an anticipation pleasant

enough to set his restless heart at ease, while he applied himself to the agreeable little task of regulating the affairs in Egypt. He had sent a courier to Rome announcing the death of Pompey, but it does not seem that this messenger was told to proceed with any great rapidity, for he did not arrive in the capital until near the middle of November.[1]

His first action was to send messengers to Pelusium strongly urging both Ptolemy and Cleopatra to cease their warfare, and to come to Alexandria in order to lay their respective cases before him. He chose to regard the settlement of the quarrel between the two sovereigns as a particular obligation upon himself, for it was during his previous consulship that the late monarch, Auletes, had entrusted his children to the Roman people and had made the Republic the executors of his will; and, moreover, that will had been confided to the care of Pompey, whose position as patron of the Egyptian Court Cæsar was now anxious to fill. In response to the summons Ptolemy came promptly to Alexandria, with his minister Potheinos, arriving, I suppose, on about October 5th, in order to ascertain what on earth Cæsar was doing in the Palace; and meanwhile Achillas was left in command of the army at Pelusium. On reaching Alexandria they seem to have been invited by Cæsar to take up their residence in the Palace into which he had intruded, and which was now patrolled by his Roman troops; and, apparently upon the advice of the unctuous Potheinos, the two of them made themselves as pleasant as possible to

---

[1] In interpreting the situation thus, I am aware that I place myself at variance with the accepted view which attributes to Cæsar an eagerness to return quickly to Rome.

their new patron.   Cæsar at once asked Ptolemy to
disband his army, but to this Potheinos would not
agree, and immediately sent word to Achillas to bring
his forces to Alexandria.   Cæsar, hearing of this, obliged
the young King to despatch two officers, Dioscorides and
Serapion, to order Achillas to remain at that place.
These messengers, however, were intercepted by the
agents of Potheinos, one being killed and the other
wounded; and two or three days later Achillas arrived
at the capital at the head of the first batch of his army
of some twenty thousand foot and two thousand horse,[1]
taking up his residence in that part of the city unoccupied
by the Romans.   Cæsar thereupon fortified his position,
deciding to hold as much of the city as his small force
could defend—namely, the Palace and the Royal Area
behind it, including the Theatre, the Forum, and
probably a portion of the Street of Canopus.   The
Egyptian army presented a pugnacious but not extremely
formidable array,[2] consisting as it did of the Gabinian
troops, who had now become entirely expatriated,
and had assumed to some extent the habits and liberties
of their adopted country; a number of criminals and
outlaws from Italy who had been enrolled as mercenary
troops; a horde of Syrian and Cilician pirates and
brigands; and, probably, a few native levies.   But as
Cæsar now had with him in the Palace King Ptolemy,
the little Prince Ptolemy, the Princess Arsinoe, and the
minister Potheinos, who could be regarded as hostages
for his safety, and four thousand of his war-hardened
veterans, ensconced in a fortified position and supported

---

[1] It is not certain whether the 2000 horse are to be included or not in the
total of 20,000.

[2] In spite of the statement to the contrary in De Bello Alexandrino.

by a business-like little fleet of galleys, I cannot see that he had any cause at the moment for alarm. One serious difficulty, however, presented itself. Immediately on arriving in Egypt he had sent orders to Cleopatra to repair to the Palace ; and his task as arbiter in the royal dispute could not be performed until she arrived, nor could he expect to assert his authority until her presence completed the group of interested persons under his enforced protection. Yet she could not dare to place herself in the hands of Achillas, nor rely upon him for a safe escort through the lines; and thus Cæsar found himself in a dilemma.

The situation, however, was relieved by the pluck and audacity of the young Queen. Realising that her only hope of regaining her kingdom lay in a personal presentation of her case to the Roman arbiter, she determined, by hook or by crook, to make her entry into the Palace. Taking ship from Pelusium to Alexandria, probably at the end of the first week of October, she entered a small boat when still some distance from the city, and thus, about nightfall, slipped into the Great Harbour, accompanied only by one friend, Apollodorus the Sicilian. She seems to have been aware that her brother and Potheinos were in residence at the Palace, together with a goodly number of their own attendants and servants ; but there were no means of telling how far Cæsar controlled the situation. Being unaccustomed to the presence of a power more autocratic than that of her own royal house, she does not seem to have realised that Cæsar was in absolute command of the Lochias, and that not he but Ptolemy was the guarded guest ; and she felt that in landing at the Palace quays she was running the gravest risk of falling into the hands of her brother's party and of being murdered before she could reach Cæsar's presence. This fear indeed may well have been justified, for there is no doubt that Ptolemy and Potheinos had considerable liberty of action within the precincts of the Palace; and, if the rumour had spread that Cleopatra was come, neither of them would have hesitated to put a dagger into her ribs in the first dark corridor through which she had to pass. Waiting, therefore, upon the still water under the walls of the Palace until darkness had fallen, she instructed Apollodorus to roll her up in the blankets and bedding which he had brought for her in the boat as a protection against the night air, and around the bundle she told him to tie a piece of rope which, I suppose, they found in the boat. She was a very small woman, and Apollodorus apparently experienced no difficulty in shouldering the burden as he stepped ashore. Bundles of this kind were then, as they are now, the usual baggage of a common man in Egypt, and were not likely to attract notice. An Alexandrian native at the present day thus carries his worldly goods tied up in his bedding, the mat or piece of carpet which serves him for a bedstead being wrapped around the bundle and fastened with a rope, and in ancient times the custom was doubt-less identical. Apollodorus, who must have been a power-ful man, thus walked through the gates of the Palace with the Queen of Egypt upon his shoulders, bearing himself as though she were no heavier than the pots, pans, and clothing which were usually tied up in this manner; and when challenged by the sentries he probably replied that he was carrying the baggage to one of the soldiers of Cæsar's guard, and asked to be directed to his apartments.

Cæsar's astonishment when the bundle was untied in

his presence, revealing the dishevelled little Queen, must
have been unbounded; and Plutarch tells us that he was
at once "captivated by this proof of Cleopatra's bold wit."
One pictures her bursting with laughter at her adventure,
and speedily winning the admiration of the susceptible
Roman, who delighted almost as keenly in deeds of daring
as he did in feminine beauty. All night long they were
closeted together, she relating to him her adventures
since she was driven from her kingdom, and he listening
with growing interest, and already perhaps with awaken-
ing love. And here it will be as well to leave them while
some description is given of the appearance and character
of the man who now found himself looking forward to
the ensuing days of his holiday in Alexandria with an
eagerness which it must have been difficult for him to
conceal.

CHAPTER V.

CAIUS JULIUS CÆSAR.

WHEN Cæsar thus made the acquaintance of the adventurous young Queen of Egypt he was a man of advanced middle age. He had already celebrated his fifty-fourth birthday, having been born on July 12, B.C. 102, and time was beginning to mark him down. The appalling dissipations of his youth to some extent may have added to the burden of his years; and, though he was still active and keen beyond the common measure, his face was heavily lined and seamed, and his muscles, I suppose, showed something of that tension to which the suppleness of early manhood gives place. Yet he remained graceful and full of the quality of youth, and he carried himself with the air of one conscious of his supremacy in the physical activities of life. He was a lightly-built man, of an aristocratic type which is to be found indiscriminately throughout Europe, and which nowadays, by a convention of thought, is usually associated in the mind with the cavalry barracks or the polo-ground. He appeared to be, and was, a perfect horseman. It is related of him that in Gaul he bred and rode a horse which no other man in the army dared mount; and it was his habit to demonstrate the firmness of his seat by

clasping his hands behind his back and setting the horse
at full gallop. Though by no means a small man, he
must have scaled under ten stone, and in other days and
other climes he might have been mistaken for a gentleman jockey. He was an extremely active soldier, a
clever, graceful swordsman, a powerful swimmer, and an
excellent athlete. In battle he had proved himself brave,
gallant, and cool-headed; and in his earlier years he had
been regarded as a dashing young officer who was neither
restrained in the performance of striking deeds of bravery
nor averse to receiving a gallery cheer for his pains.
Already at the age of twenty-one he had won the civic
crown, the Victoria Cross of that period, for saving a
soldier's life at the storming of Mytelene. In action he
exposed himself bare-headed amongst his men, cheering
them and encouraging them by his own fine spirits; and
it is related how once he laid hands on a distraught
standard-bearer who was running to cover, turned him
round, and suggested to him that he had mistaken the
direction of the enemy.

His thin, clean-shaven face, his keen dark eyes, his
clear-cut features, his hard, firm mouth with its whimsical
expression, and his somewhat pale and liverish complexion, gave him at first sight the appearance of one who,
being by nature a sportsman and a man of the world, a
fearless rider and a keen soldier, had enjoyed every
moment of an adventurous life. He was particularly well
groomed and scrupulously clean, and his scanty hair was
carefully arranged over his fine, broad head. His toga
was ornamented with an unusually broad purple stripe,
and was edged with a long fringe. He loved jewellery,
and on one occasion bought a single pearl for £60,000,
which he afterwards gave to a lady of his acquaintance.

Indeed, it is said that he only invaded Britain because he had heard that fine pearls were to be obtained there. There was thus a certain foppishness in his appearance, and a slight suggestion of conceit and personal vanity marked his manner, which gave the impression that he was not unaware of his good looks, nor desirous of concealing the fact of his disreputable successes with the fair sex. Yet he was at this time by no means an old *roué*. His great head, the penetration of his dark eyes, and the occasional sternness of his expression were a speedy indication that much lay behind these inoffensive airs and graces; and all those who came into his presence must have felt the power of his will and brain, even though direct observation did not convey to them more than the pleasing outlines of an elderly cavalier's figure. Regarded in certain lights and on certain occasions, the expression of his furrowed face showed the imagination, the romantic vision, and the artistic culture of his mind; but usually the qualities which were impressed upon a visitor who conversed with him at close quarters were those of keenness, determination, and, particularly, gentlemanliness, combined with the rather charming confidence of a man of fashion. His manner at all times was quiet and gracious; yet there was a certain fire, a controlled vivacity in his movements, which revealed the creative soldier and administrator behind the ideal aristocrat. His voice though high, and sometimes shrill, was occasionally very pleasant to the ear; but notwithstanding the fact that he was a wonderful orator, there was a correctness in his choice of words which was occasionally almost pedantic. His manner of speech was direct and straightforward, and his honesty of purpose and loftiness of principle were not doubted save by those who chanced to be aware of his little regard for moral integrity.

Cæsar was, in fact, an extremely unscrupulous man. I do not find it possible to accept the opinion of his character held by most historians, or to suppose him to have been an heroic figure who lived and died for his lofty and patriotic principles. There was immense good in him, and he had the unquestionable merit of being a great man with vast ambitions for the orderly governance of the nations of the earth; but when he threw himself with such enthusiasm into the task of winning the heart of the harum-scarum young Queen of Egypt, it seems to me that he was very well qualified to deceive her, and to play upon her emotions with all the known arts and wiles of a wicked world. So notorious was his habit of leading women astray, that when he returned to Rome from his Gallic Wars his soldiers sang a marching song in which the citizens were warned to protect their ladies from him lest he should treat them as he had treated all the women of Gaul. "*Urbani, servate uxores*," they sang; "*Calvum moechum adducimus.*"

He had no particular religion, not much honour, and few high principles; and in this regard all that can be said in his favour is that he was perfectly free from cant, never pretended to be virtuous, nor attempted to hide from his contemporaries the multitude of his sins. As a young man he indulged in every kind of vice, and so scandalous was his reputation for licentiousness that it was a matter of blank astonishment to his Roman friends when, nevertheless, he proved himself so brave and strenuous a soldier. His relationship with the mother of Brutus, who was thought to be his own son, shows that he prosecuted love intrigues while yet a boy. At one time he passed through a phase of extreme effeminacy, with its attendant horrors; and there was a period when he used to spend long hours each day in the practice of the mysteries of the toilet, being scented and curled and painted in the manner prescribed by the most degenerate young men of the aristocratic classes. Indeed so effeminate was he, that after staying with his friend Nicomedes, the King of Bithynia, he was jestingly called Queen of Bithynia; and on another occasion in Rome a certain wag named Octavius saluted Pompey as King and Cæsar as Queen of Rome. His intrigues with the wives of his friends had been as frequent as they were notorious. No good-looking woman was safe from him, least of all those whom he had the opportunity of seeing frequently, owing to his friendship for their husbands or other male relatives. Not even political considerations checked his amorous inclinations, as may be judged from the fact that he made a victim of Mucia, the wife of Pompey, whose friendship he most eagerly desired at that time. "He was the inevitable co-respondent in every fashionable divorce," writes Oman; "and when we look at the list of the ladies whose names are linked with his, we can only wonder at the state of society in Rome which permitted him to survive unscathed to middle age. The marvel is that he did not end in some dark corner, with a dagger between his ribs, long before he attained the age of thirty." Being a brilliant opportunist he made use of his success with women to promote his own interests, and at one time he is said to have conducted love intrigues with the wives of Pompey, Crassus, and Gabinius, all leaders of his political party. Even the knowledge of the habits of the young fops of the period, which he had acquired while emulating their mode of life, was turned to good account by him in after years. At the battle of Pharsalia, which had been fought but a few weeks before his arrival in Egypt, he had told his troops who were to receive the charges of the enemy's patrician cavalry that they should not attempt to hamstring the horses or strike at their legs, but should aim their blows at the riders' faces, "in the hopes," as Plutarch says, "that young gentlemen who had not known much of battles and wounds, but came, wearing their hair long, in the flower of their age and height of their beauty, would be more apprehensive of such blows and not care for hazarding both a danger at present and a blemish for the future. And so it proved, for they turned about, and covered their faces to safeguard them."

In regard to money matters Cæsar was entirely without principle. In his early years he borrowed vast sums on all sides, spent them recklessly, and seldom paid his debts save with further borrowed money. While still a young man he owed his creditors the sum of £280,000; and though most of this had now been paid off by means of the loot from the Gallic Wars, there had been times in his life when ruin stared him in the face. Most of his debts were incurred in the first place in buying for himself a high position in Roman political life, and in the second place in paying the electioneering expenses of candidates for office who would be likely to advance his power. He engaged the favour of the people by giving enormous public feasts, and on one occasion twenty-two thousand persons were entertained at his expense at a single meal. While he was ædile he paid for three hundred and twenty gladiatorial combats; and innumerable fêtes and shows were given by him throughout his life, and were paid for by the tears and anguish of his conquered enemies.

He was one of the most ambitious men who have ever walked the stage of life, his devouring passion for absolute power being at all times abnormal; and he cared not one jot in what manner he obtained or expended money so long as his career was advanced by that means. He could not brook the thought of playing a secondary part in the world's affairs, and nothing short of absolute autocracy satisfied his aspirations. While crossing the Alps on one occasion the poverty of a small mountain village was pointed out to him, and he was heard to remark that he would rather be first man in that little community than second man in Rome. On another occasion he was seen to burst into tears while reading the life of Alexander the Great, for the thought was intolerable to him that another man should have conquered the world at an age when he himself had done nothing of the kind. This restless "passion after honour," as Plutarch terms it, was not apparent in his manner and was not noticed save by those who knew him well. He was too gentlemanly, too well dressed, too beautifully groomed, to give the impression of one who was seeking indefatigably for his own advancement, and at whose heart the demons of insatiate ambition were so continuously gnawing. " When I see his hair so carefully arranged," said Cicero, "and observe him adjusting it with one finger, I cannot imagine it should enter such a man's thoughts to subvert the Roman State." Yet this elegant soldier, whose manners were so quietly aristocratic, whose charm was so delectable, would sink to any depths of moral de-

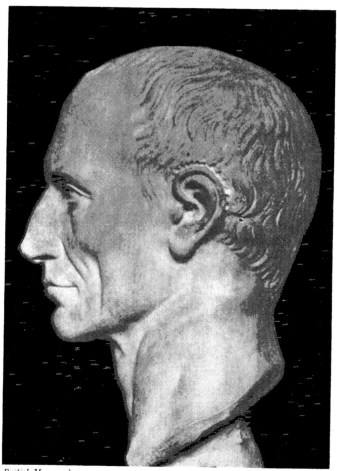

JULIUS CÆSAR.

pravity, whether financial or otherwise, in order to convert the world into his footstool. When he and Catullus were rival candidates for the office of Pontifex Maximus, the latter offered him a huge sum of money to retire from the contest; but Cæsar, spurning the proffered bribe with indignation, replied that he was about to *borrow* a larger sum than that in order to buy the votes for himself. At another period of his amazing career he desired to effect the downfall of Cicero, who was much in his way, and circumstances so fell out that this could best be accomplished by the appointment of a certain young scamp named Clodius as tribune. Now Clodius was the paramour of Cæsar's wife Pompeia, whom the Dictator had made co-respondent in the action for divorce which he had brought against that lady; yet, since it served his ambitious purpose, he did not now hesitate to obtain the appointment of this amorous rogue and use him for his infamous purposes. The story need not here be related of how Clodius had disguised himself as a woman, and had thus obtained admission to certain secret female rites at which Pompeia was officiating; how he had been discovered; how he had only escaped the death penalty for his sacrilege owing to the fact that the judges were afraid to condemn him since he was a favourite with the mob, and afraid to acquit him for fear of offending the nobility, and had therefore written their verdicts so illegibly that nobody could read them; and how Pompeia had been divorced by her husband, who had then made the famous remark that "Cæsar's wife must be above suspicion"; but it will be apparent that Plutarch is justified in regarding the man's appointment to the tribuneship as one of the most disgraceful episodes in the Dictator's career.

Cæsar's first wife was named Cossutia, and was a wealthy heiress whom he had married for her money's sake. Having, however, fallen in love with Cornelia, the daughter of Cinna, he divorced Cossutia, and wedded the woman of his heart, pluckily refusing to part with her when ordered to do so for political reasons by the terrible Sulla. Cornelia died in B.C. 68, and in the following year he married Pompeia, of whom we have just heard, in order to strengthen his alliance with Pompey, to whom she was related.

Cæsar's marriage to Calpurnia, after the dismissal of Pompeia, again showed his indifference to the moral aspect of political life. Calpurnia was the daughter of Calpurnius Piso, the pupil and disciple of Philodemus the Epicurean, a man whose verses in the Greek Anthology, and whose habits of life, were as vicious and poisonous as any in that licentious age. Cæsar at once obtained the consulship for his disreputable father-in-law, thereby causing Cato to protest that it was intolerable that the government should be prostituted by such marriages, and that persons should advance one another to the highest offices in the land by means of women. Cæsar went so far as to propose, shortly after this, that he should divorce Calpurnia and marry Pompey's daughter, who would have to be divorced from her husband, Faustus Sulla, for the purpose; and that Pompey should marry Octavia, Cæsar's niece, although she was at that time married to C. Marcellus, and also would have to be divorced.

There was a startling nonchalance in Cæsar's behaviour, a studied callousness, which was not less apparent to his contemporaries than to us. His wonderful ability to squander other people's money, his total disregard of principle, his undisguised satisfaction in political and domestic intrigue, revealed an uncon- cern which must inspire for all time the admiration of the criminal classes, and which, in certain instances, must appeal very forcibly to the imagination of all high - spirited persons. Who can resist the charm of the story of his behaviour to the pirates of Phar- macusa? For thirty-eight days he was held prisoner at that place by a band of most ferocious and blood- thirsty Cilicians, and during that time he treated his captors with a degree of reckless *insouciance* unmatched in the history of the world. When they asked him for a ransom of twenty talents (£5000) he laughed in their faces, and said that he was worth at least fifty (£12,500), which sum he ultimately paid over to them. He insisted upon joining in their games, jeered at them for their barbarous habits, and ordered them about as though they were his slaves. When he wished to sleep he demanded that they should keep absolute silence as they sat over their camp-fires; or, when the mood pleased him, he took part in their sing - songs, read them his atrocious Latin verses (for he was ever a poor poet), and abused them soundly if they did not applaud. A hundred times a day he told them that he would have them all hanged as soon as he was free, a pleasantry at which the pirates laughed heartily, thinking it a merry jest; but no sooner was he released than he raised a small force, attacked his former captors, and, taking most of them prisoners, had them all crucified. Crucifixion is a form of death by torture, the prolonged and frightful agony of which is not fully appreciated at the present day, owing to a complacent familiarity with the most notorious case of its application; but Cæsar being, on occasion, with all his indifference, a kind-hearted man, decided at the last moment mercifully to put an end to the agonies of his disillusioned victims, and with a sort of considerate nonchalance he therefore quietly cut their throats.

He was not by any means consistently a cruel man, and his kindness and magnanimity were often demonstrated. He shed tears, it will be remembered, upon seeing the signet-ring of his murdered enemy, Pompey; and in Rome he ordered that unfortunate soldier's statues to be replaced upon the pedestals from which they had been thrown. In warfare, however, he was often ruthless, and had recourse to wholesale massacres which could hardly be regarded as necessary measures. At Uxellodunum and elsewhere he caused thousands of prisoners to be maimed by the hacking off of their right hands; and his slaughter of the members of the Senate of the Veneti seems to have been an unnecessary piece of brutality. His behaviour in regard to the Usipetes and Tencteri will always remain the chief stain upon his military reputation. After concluding peace with these unfortunate peoples, he attacked them when they were disarmed, and killed 430,000 of them—men, women, and children. For this barbarity Cato proposed that he should be put in chains and delivered over to the remnant of the massacred tribes, that they might wreak their vengeance upon him.

During his ten years' campaigning in Gaul he took 800 towns by storm, subdued 300 states, killed a million men, and sent another million into slavery.[1] His cold-blooded execution of the brave Vercingetorix, after six years of captivity, seems more cruel to us, perhaps, than it did to

---

[1] So the early writers state.

his contemporaries; and it may be said in his favour that he treated the terrified remnant of the conquered peoples with justice and moderation. In spite of a kindly and even affable manner, his wit was caustic and his words often terribly biting. When a certain young man named Metellus, at that time tribune, had persistently questioned whether Cæsar had a right to appropriate treasury funds in the prosecution of his wars, Cæsar threatened to put him to death if any more was heard of his dissent. "And this you know, young man," said he, "is more disagreeable for me to say than to do." He associated freely with all manner of persons, and although so obviously an aristocrat, he was noted for his friendliness and tact in dealing with the lower classes. During his campaigns he shared all hardships with his men, and, consequently, was much beloved by them, in spite of their occasional objection to the heavy work or strenuous manœuvres which he required them to undertake. He was wont to travel in time of war at the rate of a hundred miles a day; and when a river or stream obstructed his progress he did not hesitate to dive straightway into the water and swim to the opposite shore. On the march he himself usually slept in his litter, or curled up on the floor of his chariot, and his food was of the coarsest description. At no time, indeed, was he a gourmet; and it is related how once he ate without a murmur some asparagus which had been treated with something very much like an ointment in mistake for sauce. In later life he drank no wine of any kind, an abstemiousness which was probably forced upon him by ill-health; and he who, in his early years, had been notorious for his dissipations and luxurious living, was, at the time with which we are now dealing, famous for his abstinence.

When Cæsar arrived in Alexandria he was come direct
from his great victory over Pompey at Pharsalia, and was
now absolute master of the Roman world.   His brilliant
campaigns in Gaul had raised him to the highest position
in the Republic, and now that Pompey was dead he was
without any appreciable rival.   He carried himself with
careful dignity, and presumed—quite correctly—that all
eyes were turned upon him.   He had, as Mommsen says,
"a pleasing consciousness of his own manly beauty";
and the thought of his many brilliant victories and
successful surmounting of all obstacles gave him
the liveliest satisfaction.   No longer was his elegant
frame shaken with sobs at the envious thought of the
exploits of Alexander the Great; but, since his insatiable
ambition still urged him to make use of his opportunities,
he was for the moment content to indulge his passion
for conquest by attempting to win the affections of the
charming, omnipotent, and fabulously wealthy Queen
of Egypt.

CHAPTER VI.

CLEOPATRA AND CÆSAR IN THE BESIEGED PALACE
AT ALEXANDRIA.

THERE can be little doubt that Cæsar's all-night interview with Cleopatra put an entirely new complexion
upon his conception of the situation. Until the Queen's
dramatic entry into the Palace, his main object in remaining for a short time at Alexandria, after he had been
shown the severed head of the murdered Pompey, had
been to assert his authority in that city of unrivalled
commercial opulence, and at the same time to make full
use of a favourable opportunity to rest his weary mind
and body in the luxury of its royal residence and the
perfection of its sun-bathed summer days, while Rome
should be quieted down and made ready for his coming.
But now a new factor had introduced itself. He had
found that the Queen of this desirable and important
country was a young woman after his own heart: a dare-
devil girl, whose manners and beauty had fired his imagination, and whose apparent admiration for him had set
him thinking of the uses to which he might put the
devotion he confidently expected to arouse. She seems
to have laid her case before him with frankness and
sincerity. She had shown him how her brother had

driven her from the throne, in direct opposition to the
will of her father, who had so earnestly desired the two
of them to reign jointly and in harmony.   And while she
had talked to him through the long hours of the night he
had found himself most willingly carried away by the
desire to obtain her love, both for the pleasure which it
might be expected to afford him and for the political
advantage which would accrue from such an intercourse.   Here was a simple means of bringing Egypt
under his control — Egypt which was the granary of
the world, the most important commercial market of
the Mediterranean, the most powerful factor in eastern
politics, and the gateway of the unconquered kingdoms
of the Orient.   He had made himself lord of the West;
Greece and Asia Minor were, since the late war, at his
feet; and now Alexandria, so long the support of
Pompey's faction, should come to him with the devotion of its Queen.   I do not hold with those who
suppose him to have been led like a lamb to the slaughter
by the wiles of Cleopatra, and to have succumbed to her
charms in the manner of one whose passions have confused his brain, causing him to forget all things save
only his desire.   In consideration of the fact that the
young Queen was at that time, so far as we know, a
woman of blameless character, and that he, on the contrary, was a man of the very worst possible reputation in
regard to the opposite sex, it seems, to say the least,
unfair that the burden of the blame for the subsequent
events should have been assigned for all these centuries
to Cleopatra.

Before the end of that eventful night Cæsar seems to
have determined to excite the passionate love of that wild
and irresponsible girl, whose personality and political im-

portance made a doubly powerful appeal to him ; and ere
the light of dawn had entered the room his decision to
restore her to the throne, and to place her brother in the
far background, had been irrevocably made.   As the sun
rose he sent for King Ptolemy, who, on entering Cæsar's
presence, must have been dismayed to be confronted with
his sister whom he had driven into exile and against
whom he had so recently been fighting at Pelusium.   It
would appear that Cæsar treated him with sternness,
asking him how he had dared to go against the wishes
of his father, who had entrusted their fulfilment to the
Roman people, and demanding that he should at once
make his peace with Cleopatra.   At this the young man
lost his temper, and, rushing from the room, cried out to
his friends and attendants who were waiting outside that
he had been betrayed and that his cause was lost.
Snatching the royal diadem from his head in his boyish
rage and chagrin, he dashed it upon the ground, and, no
doubt, burst into tears.   Thereupon an uproar arose,
and the numerous Alexandrians who still remained within
the Roman lines at once gathering round their King,
nearly succeeded in communicating their excitement to
the royal troops in the city, and arousing them to a
concerted attack upon the Palace by land and sea.
Cæsar, however, hurried out and addressed the crowd,
promising to arrange matters to their satisfaction; and
thereupon he called a meeting at which Ptolemy and
Cleopatra were both induced to attend, and he read out
to them their father's will wherein it was emphatically
stated that they were to reign together.   He reiterated
his right, as representative of the Roman people, to
adjust the dispute ; and at last he appears to have
effected a reconciliation between the brother and sister.

G

The unfortunate Ptolemy must have realised that from
that moment his ambitions and hopes were become dust
and ashes, for he would now always remain under the
scrutiny of his elder sister; and the liberty of action for
which he and his ministers had plotted and schemed was
for ever gone. According to Dion Cassius, he could
already see plainly that there was an understanding
between Cæsar and his sister; and Cleopatra's manner
doubtless betrayed to him her elation. She must have
been intensely excited. A few hours previously she had
been an exile, creeping back to her own city in imminent
danger of her life; now, not only was she Queen of Egypt
once more, but she had won the esteem and, so it
seemed, the heart also of the Autocrat of the world,
whose word was absolute law to the nations. One may
almost picture her making faces at her brother as they
sat opposite one another in Cæsar's improvised court of
justice, and the unhappy boy's distress must have been
acute.

Cæsar's dominant idea now was to control the politics
of Egypt by means of a skilled play upon the heart of
Cleopatra. He did not much care what happened to
King Ptolemy or to his minister Potheinos, for they
had forfeited their right to consideration by their attempt
to set aside the wishes of Auletes, and by their disgusting
behaviour to Pompey, who, though Cæsar's enemy, had
yet been his mighty fellow-countryman; but it was his
wish as soon as possible to placate the mob, and to
endear the people of Alexandria to him, so that in
three or four weeks' time he might leave the country
in undisturbed quiet. Now the control of Cyprus was
one of the most fervent aspirations of the city, and it
seems to have occurred to Cæsar that the presentation

of the island to their royal house would be keenly appreciated by them, and would go a long way to appease their hostile excitement. When the Romans annexed Cyprus in B.C. 58, the Alexandrians had risen in revolt against Auletes largely because he had made no attempt to claim the country for himself. It had been more or less continuously an appendage of the Egyptian crown, and its possession was still the people's dearest wish. Now, therefore, according to Dion, Cæsar made a present of the island to Egypt in the names of the two younger members of the royal house, Prince Ptolemy and Princess Arsinoe; and though we have no records definitely to show that they ever assumed control of their new possession, or that it ceased, at any rate for a year or two, to be regarded as a part of the Roman province of Cilicia, it is certain that a few years later, in B.C. 42, it had become an Egyptian dominion and was administered by a viceroy of that country.[1]

Having thus relieved the situation, Cæsar turned his attention to other matters. While Auletes was in Rome, in B.C. 59, he had incurred enormous debts in his efforts to buy the support of the Roman Senate in re-establishing himself upon the Ptolemaic throne, and in this fact Cæsar now saw a means both of showing his benevolence towards the Egyptians, and of making them pay for the upkeep of his small fleet and army at Alexandria. His claim on behalf of the creditors of Auletes he fixed at the very moderate sum of ten million denarii (£400,000), although it must have been realised by all that the original debts amounted to a much higher figure than this. At the same time he made no attempt to demand a war contribution from the Egyptians, although their

[1] Page 235.

original advocacy of the cause of Pompey would have
justified him in doing so.[1] In this manner, and by the
gift of Cyprus, he made a bid for the goodwill of the
Alexandrians; but, unfortunately, his efforts in this
direction were entirely frustrated by the intrigues of
Potheinos. There probably need not have been any
difficulty in the raising of £400,000; but Potheinos
chose to order the King's golden dishes and the rich
vessels in the temples to be melted down and converted
into money. He furnished the King's own table with
wooden or earthenware plates and bowls, and caused the
fact to be made known to the townspeople, in order
that they should be shown the straits to which Cæsar's
cupidity had reduced them. Meanwhile, he supplied
the Roman soldiers with a very poor quality of corn,
and told them, in reply to their complaints, that they
ought to be grateful that they received any at all, since
they had no right to it. Nor did he hesitate to tell
Cæsar that he ought not to waste his time in Alexandria,
or concern himself with the insignificant affairs of Egypt,
when urgent business should be calling him back to
Rome. His manner towards the Dictator was consistently rude and hostile, and there seems little doubt
that he was plotting against him and was keeping in
touch with Achillas.

Hostilities of a more or less sporadic nature soon
broke out, and it was not long before Cæsar made his
first hit at the enemy. Hearing that they were attempting to man their imprisoned ships, which lay still in the

---

[1] It is usually stated that Cæsar remained in Egypt chiefly because he was
in need of money, as is suggested by Dion, xlii. 9 and 34; Oros, vi. 15,
29, and Plutarch, 48. But the small sum which he took from the Egyptians
is against this theory.

western portion of the Great Harbour, and knowing that he was not strong enough either to hold or to utilise more than a few of them, he sent out a little force which succeeded in seting fire to, and destroying, the whole fleet, consisting of the fifty men-o'-war which, during the late hostilities, had been lent to Pompey, twenty-two guardships, and thirty-eight other craft, thus leaving in their possession only those vessels which lay in the Harbour of the Happy Return, beyond the Heptastadium. In this conflagration some of the buildings on the quay near the harbour appear to have been burnt, and it would seem that some portion of the famous Alexandrian library was destroyed; but the silence of contemporary writers upon this literary catastrophe indicates that the loss was not great, and, to my mind, puts out of account the statement of later authors that the burning of the entire library occurred on that occasion. Cæsar's next move was to seize the Pharos Lighthouse and the eastern end of the island upon which it was built, thus securing the entrance to the Great Harbour, and making the passage of his ships to the open sea a manœuvre which could be employed at any moment. At the same time he threw up the strongest fortifications at all the vulnerable points in his land defences, and thereby rendered himself absolutely secure from direct assault.

He was not much troubled by the situation. It is said that he was obliged more than once to keep awake all night in order to protect himself against assassination; but such a contingency did not interfere to any great extent with his enjoyments of the life in the Alexandrian Palace. From early youth he must have been accustomed to the thought of the assassin's knife.

His many love-affairs had made imminent each day the possibility of sudden death, and his political and administrative career also laid him open at all times to a murderous attack. The jealousy of the husbands whose wives he had stolen, the vengeance of the survivors of the massacres instigated by him, the resentment of the politicians whose ambitions he had thwarted, and the hatred of innumerable persons whom, in one way or another, he had offended, placed his life in continuous jeopardy. The machinations of Potheinos, therefore, left him undismayed, and he was able to prosecute what was, in plain language, the seduction of the Queen of Egypt with an undistracted mind.

Cleopatra appears to have been as strongly attracted to Cæsar as he was to her; and although at the outset each realised the advantage of winning the other's heart, and regulated their actions accordingly, there seems little doubt that, after a day or two of close companionship, a romantic attachment of a very genuine nature had been formed between them. In the case of Cleopatra, no doubt, her love held all the sweetness of the first serious affair of her life, and on the part of Cæsar there is apparent the passionate delight of a man past his prime in the vivacity and charm of a beautiful young girl. Though elderly, Cæsar was what a romanticist would call an ideal lover. His keen, handsome face, his athletic and graceful figure, the fascination of his manners, and the wonder of the deeds which he had performed, might be calculated to win the heart of any woman; and to Cleopatra he must have made a special appeal by reason of his reputation for bravery and reliability on all occasions, and his present display of *sang-froid* and light-heartedness.

Cæsar was, at this time, in holiday mood, and the life he led at the Palace was of the gayest description. He had cast from him the cares of state with an ease which came of frequent practice in the art of throwing off responsibilities; and when about October 25th he received news from Rome that he had been made Dictator for the whole of the coming year, 47, he was able to feel that there was no cause for anxiety. While the unfortunate young Ptolemy sulked in the background, Cæsar and Cleopatra openly sought one another's company and made merry together, it would seem, for a large part of every day. With such a man as Cæsar, the result of this intimacy was inevitable; nor was it to be expected that the happy-go-lucky and impetuous girl of but twenty years of age would act with much caution or propriety under the peculiar and exciting circumstances. It is possible that she had already gone through the form of marriage with her co-regnant brother, as was the custom of the Egyptian Court; but it is highly unlikely that this was anything more than the emptiest formality, and there is no reason to doubt that in actual fact she was, when she met Cæsar, still unwedded. The child which in due course she presented to the Dictator was her first-born; but had there been a previous marriage of more than a formal nature, it is at least probable, in view of her subsequent productivity, that she would already have been in enjoyment of the privileges of motherhood.

The gaiety of the life in the besieged Palace, and the progress of the romance which was there being enacted, were rudely disturbed by two consecutive events which led at once to the outbreak of really serious hostilities.

The little Princess Arsinoe, who, like all the women of this family, must have been endowed with great spirit and pluck, suddenly made her escape from the Roman lines, accompanied by her *nutritius* Ganymedes,[1] and joined the Egyptian forces under Achillas. The plot, organised no doubt by Ganymedes, had for its object the raising of the Princess to the throne, while Cleopatra and her two brothers were imprisoned in the Lochias, and no sooner had they reached the Egyptian head-quarters than they began freely to bribe all officers and officials of importance in order to accomplish their purpose. Achillas, however, who had his own game to play, thought it wiser to remain loyal to his sovereign, and to attempt to rescue him from Cæsar's clutches. It was not long before a quarrel arose between Ganymedes and Achillas, which ended in the prompt assassination of the latter, whose functions were at once assumed by his murderer, the war being thereupon prosecuted with renewed vigour. Previous to the death of Achillas, Potheinos had been in secret communication with him, apparently in regard to the possibility of murdering Cæsar and effecting the escape of King Ptolemy and himself from the Palace ere Arsinoe and Ganymedes obtained control of affairs. Information of the plot was given to Cæsar by his barber, "a busy, listening fellow, whose excessive timidity made him inquisitive into everything";[2] and, at a feast held to celebrate the reconciliation between Ptolemy and Cleopatra, Potheinos

---

[1] In ancient Egypt the princes and princesses often had male "nurses," the title being an exceedingly honourable one. The Egyptian phrase sometimes reads "great nurse and nourisher," and M. Lefebvre tells me that in a Fayoum inscription the tutor of Ptolemy Alexander is called τροφεὺς καὶ τιθηνὸς 'Αλεξάνδρου.

[2] Plutarch.

was arrested and immediately beheaded, a death which the poet Lucan considers to have been very much too good for him, since it was that by which he had caused the great Pompey to die. So far as one can now tell, Cæsar was entirely justified in putting this wretched eunuch out of the way of further worldly mischief. He belonged to that class of court functionary which is met with throughout the history of the Orient, and which invariably calls forth the denunciation of the more moral West; but it is to be remembered in his favour that, so far as we know, he schemed as eagerly for the fortunes of his young sovereign Ptolemy as he did for his own advancement, and his treacherous manœuvres were directed against the menacing intrusion of a power which was relentlessly crushing the life out of the royal houses of the accessible world. His crime against fallen Pompey was no more dastardly than were many other of the recorded acts of the Court he served; and the fact that he, like his two fellow-conspirators, Achillas and Theodotos, paid in blood and tears for the riches of the moment, goes far to exonerate him, at this remote date, from further execration.

The first act of the war which caused Cæsar any misgivings was the pollution of his water supply by the enemy, and the consequent nervousness of his men. The Royal Area obtained its drinking water through subterranean channels communicating with the lake at the back of the city; and no sooner had Cæsar realised that these channels might be tampered with than he attempted to cut his way southwards, probably along the broad street[1] which led to the Gate of the Sun and to the Lake Harbour. Here, however, he met with a

[1] See p. 31.

stubborn resistance, and the loss of life might have been very great had he persisted in his endeavour. Fortunately, however, the sinking of trial shafts within the besieged territory led to the discovery of an abundance of good water, the existence of which had not been suspected; and thus he was saved from the ignominy of being ousted from the city which he had entered in such solemn pomp, and of being forced to retire across the Mediterranean, his self-imposed task left uncompleted, and his ambitions for the future of Cleopatra unfulfilled.

Not long after this the welcome news was brought to him that the Thirty-seventh Legion had crossed from Asia Minor with food supplies, arms, and siege-instruments, and was anchored off the Egyptian coast, being for the moment unable to reach him owing to contrary winds. Cæsar at once sailed out to meet them, with his entire fleet, the ships being manned only by their Rhodian crews, all the troops having been left to hold the land defences. Effecting a junction with these reinforcements, he returned to the harbour, easily defeated the Egyptian vessels which had collected to the north of the Island of Pharos, and sailed triumphantly back to his moorings below the Palace.

So confident now was he in his strength that he next sailed round the island, and attacked the Egyptian fleet in its own harbour beyond the Heptastadium, inflicting heavy losses upon them. He then landed on the western end of Pharos, which was still held by the enemy, carried the forts by storm, and effected a junction with his own men who were stationed around the lighthouse at the eastern end. His plan was to advance across the Heptastadium, and thus, by holding both the island and the mole, to obtain possession of the western Harbour of the Happy Return and ultimately to strike a wedge into the city upon that side. But here he suffered a dangerous reverse. While he was leading in person the attack upon the south or city end of the Heptastadium, and his men were crowding on to it from the island and from the vessels in the Great Harbour, the Egyptians made a spirited attack upon its northern end, thus hemming the Romans in upon the narrow causeway, to the consternation of those who watched the battle from the Lochias Promontory. Fortunately vessels were at hand to take off the survivors of this sanguinary engagement, as the enemy drove them back from either end of the causeway; and presently they had all scrambled aboard and were rowing at full speed across the Great Harbour. Such numbers, however, jumped on to the deck of the vessel into which Cæsar had entered that it capsized, and we are then presented with the dramatic picture of the ruler of the world swimming for his life through the quiet waters of the harbour, holding aloft in one hand a bundle of important papers which he happened to be carrying at the moment of the catastrophe, dragging his scarlet military cloak along by his teeth, and at the same time constantly ducking his rather bald head under the water to avoid the missiles which were hurled at him by the victorious Egyptians, who must have been capering about upon the recaptured mole, all talking and shouting at once. He was, however, soon picked up by one of his ships; and thus he returned to the Palace, very cold and dripping wet, and having in the end lost the cloak which was the cherished mark of his rank. Four hundred legionaries and a number of seamen perished in this engagement, most of them being drowned; and now, perhaps for the first time, it began to appear to Cæsar that the warfare which he was waging was not the amusing game he had thought it. For at least four months he had entertained himself in the Palace, spending his days in pottering around his perfectly secure defences and his nights in enjoying the company of Cleopatra. Up till now he must have been in constant receipt of news from Rome, where his affairs were being managed by Antony, his boisterous but fairly reliable lieutenant, and it is evident that nothing had occurred there to necessitate his return. Far from being hemmed in within the Palace and obliged to fight for his life, as is generally supposed to have been the case, it seems to me that his position at all times was as open as it was secure. He could have travelled across the Mediterranean at any moment; and, had he thought it desirable, he could have sailed over to Italy for a few weeks and returned to Alexandria without any great risk. His fleet had shown itself quite capable of defending him from danger upon the high seas, as, for example, when he had sailed out to meet the Thirty-seventh Legion;[1] and, as on that occasion, his troops could have been left in security in their fortified position. Supplies from Syria were plentiful, and the Rhodian sailors, after escorting him as far as Cyprus, could have returned to their duties at Alexandria in order to ensure the safe and continuous arrival of these stores and provisions.

It is thus very apparent that he had no wish to abandon the enjoyments of his winter in the Egyptian capital, where he had become thoroughly absorbed both in the little Queen of that country and in the problems

---

[1] Note also (p. 112) Cæsar's departure with his army from the besieged Palace.

which were represented to him by her.   He was an
elderly man, and the weight of his years caused him to
feel a temporary distaste for the restless anxieties which
awaited him in Rome.   His ambitions in the Occident
had been attained; and now, finding himself engaged in
what, I would suggest, was an easily managed and not
at all dangerous war, he was determined to carry the
struggle through to its inevitable end, and to find in this
quite interesting and occasionally exciting task an excuse
for remaining by the side of the woman who, for the time
being, absorbed the attention of his wayward affections.
Already he was beginning to realise that the subjection
of Egypt to his will was a matter of very great political
importance, as will be explained hereafter; and he felt
the keenest objection to abandoning the Queen to her
own devices, both on this account and by reason of the
hold which she had obtained upon his heart.   In after
years he did not look back upon the fighting with an
interest sufficient to induce him to record its history, as
he had done that of other campaigns, but he caused an
official account to be written by one of his comrades;
and this author has been at pains to show that the
struggle was severe in character.   Such an interpretation
of the war, however, though now unanimously accepted,
is to be received with caution, and need not be taken
more seriously than the statement that, in the first instance, Cæsar's prolonged stay at Alexandria was due to
the Etesian winds which made it difficult for his ships to
leave the harbour.   These annual winds from the north
might have delayed his return for a week or two; but it
is obvious that he had no desire to set sail; and the
author of *De Bello Alexandrino* was doubtless permitted
to cover Cæsar's apparent negligence of important

Roman affairs by thus attributing his lengthy absence to the strength of the enemy and to the inclemency of the Fates.

Now, however, after the ignominious defeat upon the Heptastadium, Cæsar appears to have become fully determined to punish the Alexandrians and to prosecute the campaign with more energy. He seems soon to have received news that a large army was marching across the desert from Syria to his relief, under the joint leadership of Mithridates of Pergamum, a natural son of Mithridates the Great, the Jewish Antipater, father of Herod, and Iamblichus, son of Sampsiceramus, a famous Arab chieftain from Hemesa. With the advent of these forces he knew that he would be able to crush all resistance and to impose his will upon Egypt; and he now, therefore, took a step which clearly shows his determination to handle affairs with sternness and ruthlessness, in such a manner that Cleopatra should speedily become sole ruler of the country, and thus should be in a position to lay all the might of her kingdom in his hands.

The Princess Arsinoe had failed to make herself Queen of Egypt in spite of the efforts of Ganymedes, and the royal army was still endeavouring to rescue King Ptolemy and to fight under his banner. Cæsar, therefore, determined to hand the young man over to them, knowing, as the historian of the war admits, that there was little probability of such an action leading to a cessation of hostilities. His avowed object in taking this step was to give Ptolemy the opportunity of arranging terms of peace for him; but he did not hesitate to record officially his opinion that, in the event of a continuation of the war, it would be far more honourable for him to be fighting

against a king than against "a crowd of sweepings of the
earth and renegades." The truth of the matter, however, seems to me to be that Cæsar wished to rid himself
of the boy, who stood in the way of the accomplishment
of his schemes in regard to the sole sovereignty of Cleopatra; and by handing him over to the enemy at the
moment when the news of the arrival of the army from
Syria made the Egyptian downfall absolutely certain, he
insured the young man's inevitable death or degradation.
The miserable Ptolemy must have realised this, for when
Cæsar instructed him to go over to his friends beyond
the Roman lines, he burst into tears and begged to be
allowed to remain in the Palace. He knew quite well
that the Egyptians had not a chance of victory—that
when once he had taken up his residence with his own
people their conqueror would treat him as an enemy
and punish him accordingly. Cæsar, however, on his
part, was aware that if in the hour of Roman victory
Ptolemy was still under his protection, it would be
difficult not to carry out the terms of the will of Auletes
by making him joint-sovereign with Cleopatra. The
King's tears and paradoxical protestations of devotion
were therefore ignored; and forthwith he was pushed
out of the Palace into the welcoming arms of the Alexandrians, the younger brother, whom Cæsar had designed
for the safely distant throne of Cyprus, being left in the
custody of the Romans alone with Cleopatra.

The relieving army from Syria soon arrived at the
eastern frontier of Egypt, and, taking Pelusium by storm,
gave battle to the King's forces not far from the Canopic
mouth of the Nile. The Egyptians were easily defeated,
and the invaders marched along the eastern edge of the
Delta towards Memphis (near the modern Cairo), just

below which they crossed the Nile to the western bank. The young Ptolemy thereupon, expecting no mercy at Cæsar's hands, put himself boldly at the head of such troops as could be spared from the siege of the Palace at Alexandria, and marched across the Delta to measure swords with Mithridates and his allies. No sooner was he gone from the city than Cæsar, leaving a small garrison in the Palace, sailed out of the harbour with as many men as he could crowd into the ships at his disposal, and moved off eastwards as though making for Canopus or Pelusium. Under cover of darkness, however, he turned in the opposite direction, and before dawn disembarked upon the deserted shore some miles to the west of Alexandria. He thus out-manœuvred the Egyptian fleet with ease, and, incidentally, demonstrated that he had been throughout the siege perfectly free to come and go across the water as he chose. Marching along the western border of the desert, as his friends had marched along the eastern, he effected a junction with them at the apex of the Delta, not far north of Memphis, and immediately turned to attack the approaching Egyptian army. Ptolemy, on learning of their advance, fortified himself in a strong position at the foot of a *tell*, or mound, the Nile being upon one flank, a marsh upon the other, and a canal in front of him; but the allies, after a two-days' battle, turned the position and gained a complete victory. The turning movement had been entrusted to a certain Carfulenus, who afterwards fell at Mutina fighting against Antony, and this officer managed to penetrate into the Egyptian camp. At his approach Ptolemy appears to have jumped into one of the boats which lay moored upon the Nile; but the weight of the numbers of fugitives who followed his example sank the vessel, and the young king was never seen alive again. It is said that his dead body was recognised afterwards by the golden corselet which he wore, and which, no doubt, had caused by its weight his rapid death. His tragic end, at the age of fifteen, relieved Cæsar of the embarrassing necessity either of pardoning him and making him joint-sovereign with Cleopatra, according to the terms of his father's will, or of carrying him captive to Rome and putting him to death in the customary manner at the close of his triumph. The boy had foreseen the fate which would be chosen for him, when he had begged with tears to be allowed to remain in the Palace; and his sudden submersion in the muddy waters of the Nile must have terminated a life which of late had been intolerably overshadowed by the knowledge that his existence was an obstacle to Cæsar's relentless ambitions, and by the horror of the certainty of speedy death.

On March 27th, B.C. 47,[1] Cæsar, who had ridden on with his cavalry, entered Alexandria in triumph, its gates being now thrown open to him. The inhabitants dressed themselves in mourning garments, sending deputations to him to beg for his mercy and forgiveness, and bringing out to him the statues of their gods as a token of their entire submission. Princess Arsinoe and Ganymedes were handed over to him as prisoners: and in pomp he rode through the city to the Palace, where as a conquering hero and saviour he was received into the arms of Cleopatra.

[1] This was actually some time in January.

H

CHAPTER VII.

THE BIRTH OF CÆSARION AND CÆSAR'S DEPARTURE FROM EGYPT.

THE death of Ptolemy and the submission of Alexandria brought the war to a definite close; and Cæsar, once more in comfortable residence at the Palace, was enabled at last to carry out his plans for the regulation of Egyptian affairs, with the execution of which the campaign had so long interfered. Cleopatra's little brother, the younger Ptolemy, was a boy of only eleven years of age, who does not seem to have shown such signs of marked intelligence or strong character as would cause him to be a nuisance either to Cæsar or to his sister; and therefore it was arranged that he should be raised to the throne in place of his deceased brother, as nominal King and consort of Cleopatra. Cæsar, it will be remembered, had given Cyprus to this youth and to his sister Arsinoe; but now, since the latter was a prisoner in disgrace and the former was not old enough to cause trouble in Egypt, the island kingdom was not pressed upon them. To the Alexandrians, whose campaign against him had entertained him so admirably while he had pursued his intrigue with Cleopatra, Cæsar showed no desire to be other than lenient, and he preferred to regard the great havoc wrought in certain parts of their city as sufficient punishment for their misdeeds. He granted to the Jews, however, equal rights with the Greeks, in consideration of their assistance in the late war, a step which must have been somewhat irritating to the majority of the townsfolk. He then constituted a regular Roman Army of Occupation, for the purpose of supporting Cleopatra and her little brother upon the throne,[1] and to keep order in Alexandria and throughout the country. This army consisted of the two legions which had been besieged with him in the Palace, together with a third which presently arrived from Syria; and to the command of this force Cæsar appointed an able officer named Rufinus, who had risen by his personal merit from the ranks, being originally one of Cæsar's own freedmen. It is usually stated that in handing over the command to a man of this standing and not to a person belonging to the Senate, Cæsar was showing his disdain for Egypt; but I am of opinion that the step was taken deliberately to retain the control of the country entirely in his own hands, Rufinus being, no doubt, absolutely Cæsar's man. We do not hear what became of the Gabinian troops who had fought against Cæsar, but it is probable that they were drafted to legions stationed in other parts of the world.

It was now April,[2] and Cæsar had been in Egypt for more than six months. He had originally intended to return to Rome, it would seem, in the previous November; but his defiance by the Alexandrians, and later the siege of the Palace, had given him a reasonable excuse for

---

[1] Just as the British Army of Occupation now in Egypt was originally stationed there to support the Khedive upon his throne and to keep order.

[2] Corresponding to the actual season of February.

remaining with Cleopatra. Being by nature an opportunist, he had come during these months to interest
himself keenly in Egyptian affairs, and, as we have seen,
both they and his passion for the Queen had fully occupied his attention. The close of the war, however, did
not mean to him the termination of these interests, but
rather the beginning of the opportunity for putting his
schemes into execution. He must have been deeply impressed by the possibilities of expansive exploitation
which Egypt offered. Cleopatra, no doubt, had told
him much concerning the wonders of the land, wonders
which she herself had never yet found occasion to verify.
He had heard from her, and had received visible proof,
of the wealth of the Nile Valley; and his march through
the Delta must have revealed to him the richness of the
country. No man could fail to be impressed by the
spectacle of the miles upon miles of grain fields which
are to be seen in Lower Egypt; and reports had doubtless reached him of the splendours of the upper reaches
of the Nile, where a peaceful and law-abiding population
found time both to reap three crops a year from the
fertile earth, and to build huge temples for their gods and
palaces for their nobles. The yearly tax upon corn alone
in Egypt, which was paid in kind, must have amounted
to some twenty millions of bushels, the figure at which
it stood in the reign of Augustus; and this fact, if
no other, must have given Cæsar cause for much
covetousness.

He had probably heard, too, of the trade with India,
which was already beginning to flourish, and which, a
few years later, came to be of the utmost importance;[1]
and he had doubtless been told of the almost fabulous

[1] Pliny, vi. 26.

lands of Ethiopia, to which Egypt was the threshold, whence came the waters of the Nile. Egypt has always been a land of speculation, attracting alike the interest of the financier and the enthusiasm of the conqueror; and Cæsar's imagination must have been stimulated by those ambitious schemes which have fired the brains of so many of her conquerors, just as that of the great Alexander had been inspired three centuries before. Feeling that his work in Gaul and the north-west was more or less completed, he may, perhaps, have considered the expediency of carrying Roman arms into the uttermost parts of Ethiopia; of crossing the Red Sea into Arabia; or of penetrating, like Alexander, to India and to the marvellous kingdoms of the East. Even so, eighteen hundred years later, Napoleon Bonaparte dreamed of marching his army through Egypt to the lands of Hindustan; and so also England, striving to hold her beloved India (as the prophetic Kinglake wrote in 1844), fixed her gaze upon the Nile Valley, until, as though by the passive force of her desire, it fell into her hands. For long the Greeks had thought that the Nile came from the east and rose in the hills of India; and even in the days with which we are now dealing Egypt was regarded as the gateway of those lands. The trade-route from Alexandria to India was yearly growing in fame. The merchants journeyed up the Nile to the city of Koptos, and thence travelled by caravan across the desert to the seaport of Berenice, whence they sailed with the trade wind to Muziris, on the west coast of India, near the modern Calicut and Mysore. It is possible that Cæsar had succumbed to the fascination of distant conquest and exploration with which Egypt, by reason of her geographical situation, has inspired so

many minds, and that he was allowing his thoughts to
travel with the merchants along the great routes to the
East. He must always have felt that the unconquered
Parthians would cause a march across Asia to India to
be a most difficult and hazardous undertaking, and there
was some doubt whether he would be able to repeat the
exploits of Alexander the Great along that route; but
here through Egypt lay a road to the Orient which
might be followed without grave risk. The merchants
were wont to leave Berenice, on the Egyptian coast,
about the middle of July, when the Dog-star rose with
the Sun, reaching the west coast of India about the
middle of September;[1] and it would be strange indeed
if Cæsar had not given some consideration to the
possibility of carrying his army by that route to the
lands which Alexander, of whose exploits he loved to
read, had conquered.

Abundant possibilities such as these must have filled
his mind, and may have been the partial cause of his
desire to stay yet a little while longer in this fascinating
country; but there was another and a more poignant
reason which urged him to wait for a few weeks more
in Egypt. Cleopatra was about to become a mother.
Seven months had passed since those days in October
when Cæsar had applied himself so eagerly to the task of
winning the love of the Queen, and of procuring her surrender to his wishes; and now, in another few weeks,
the child of their romance would be placed in his arms.
Old profligate though he was, it seems that he saw something in the present situation different from those in
which he had found himself before. Cleopatra, by her
brilliant wit, her good spirits, her peculiar charm of

[1] Pliny, vi. 26.

manner, her continuous courage, and her boundless optimism, had managed to retain his love throughout these months of their close proximity; and an appeal had been made to the more tender side of his nature which could not be resisted. He wished to be near her in her hour of trial; and, moreover (for in Cæsar's actions there was always a practical as well as a sentimental motive), it is probable that he entertained high hopes of receiving from Cleopatra an heir to his worldly wealth and position, who should be in due course fully legitimised. His long intercourse with the Queen had much altered his point of view; and I think there can be little doubt that his mind was eagerly feeling forward to new developments and revolutionary changes in his life.

At Cleopatra's wish he was now allowing himself to be recognised by the Egyptians as the divine consort of the Queen, an impersonation of the god Jupiter-Amon upon earth. Some form of marriage had taken place between them, or, at any rate, the Egyptian people, if not the cynical Alexandrians, had been constrained to recognise their legal union. The approaching birth of the child had made it necessary for Cleopatra to disclose her relationship with Cæsar, and at the same time to prove to her subjects that she, their Queen, was not merely the mistress of an adventurous Roman. As soon, therefore, as her brother and formal husband Ptolemy XIV. had died, she had begun to circulate the belief that Julius Cæsar was the great god of Egypt himself come to earth, and that the child which was about to make its appearance was the offspring of a divine union. Upon the walls of the temples of Egypt, notably at Hermonthis, near Thebes, bas-reliefs were afterwards sculptured in which Cleopatra was represented in converse with the god Amon, who appears in human form, and in which the gods are shown assisting at the celestial birth of the child. A mythological fiction of a similar nature had been employed in ancient Egypt in reference to the births of earlier sovereigns, those of Hatshepsut (B.C. 1500) and of Amenophis III. (B.C. 1400) being two particular instances. In the known occasions of its use, the royal parentage of the child had been open to question, this being the reason why the story of the divine intercourse was introduced; and thus in the case of Cleopatra the myth had become familiar, by frequent use, to the priest-ridden minds of the Egyptians, and was not in any way startling or original. In the later years of the Queen's reign events were dated as from this supernatural occurrence, and there is preserved to us an epitaph inscribed in the "twentieth year of (or after) the union of Cleopatra with Amon."

Cæsar was quite willing thus to be reckoned in Egypt as a divinity. His hero Alexander the Great in like manner had been regarded as a deity, and had proclaimed himself the son of Amon, causing himself to be portrayed with the ram's horns of that god projecting from the sides of his head. Though his belief in the gods was conspicuously absent, Cæsar had always boasted of his divine descent, his family tracing their genealogy to Iulus, the son of Æneas, the son of Anchises and the goddess Venus; and there is every reason to suppose that Cleopatra had attempted to encourage him to think of himself as being in very truth a god upon earth. She herself ruled Egypt by divine right, and deemed it no matter for doubt that she was the representative of the Sun-god here below, the mediator between man and his creator. The

Egyptians, if not the Alexandrians, fell flat upon their faces when they saw her, and hailed her as god, in the manner in which their fathers had hailed the ancient Pharaohs. From earliest childhood she had been called a divinity, and she was named an immortal in the temples of Egypt as by undoubted right. Those who came into contact with her partook of the divine affluence, and her companions were holy in the sight of her Egyptian subjects. Cæsar, as her consort, thus became a god; and as soon as her connection with him was made public, he assumed *ex officio* the nature of a divine being. We shall see presently how, even in Rome, he came to regard himself as more than mortal, and how, setting aside in his own favour his disbelief in the immortals, before he died he had publicly called himself god upon earth. At the present period of his life, however, these startling assumptions were not clearly defined; and it is probable that he really did not know what to think about himself. Cleopatra had fed his mind with strange thoughts, and had so flattered his vanity, though probably without intention, that if he could but acknowledge the existence of a better world, he was quite prepared to believe himself in some sort of manner come from it. She knew that she herself was supposed to be divine; she loved Cæsar and had made him her equal; she was aware that he, too, was said to be descended from the gods: and thus, by a tacit assumption, it seems to me that she gradually forced upon him a sense of his divinity which, in the succeeding years, developed into a fixed belief.

This appreciation of his divine nature, which we see growing in Cæsar's mind, carried with it, of course, a feeling of monarchical power, a desire to assume the prerogatives of kingship. Cleopatra seems now to have been naming him her consort, and in Egypt, as we have said, he must have been recognised as her legal husband. He was already, in a manner of speaking, King of Egypt; and the fact that he was not officially crowned as Pharaoh must have been due entirely to his own objection to such a proceeding. The Egyptians must now have been perfectly willing to offer to him the throne of the Ptolemies, just as they had accepted Archelaus, the High Priest of Komana, as consort of Berenice IV., Cleopatra's half-sister;[1] and in these days when their young Queen was so soon to become a mother there must have been a genuine and eager desire to regularise the situation by such a marriage with Cæsar and his elevation to the throne. Nothing could be more happy politically than the Queen's marriage to the greatest man in Rome, and we have already seen how there was some idea of a union with Cnæus Pompeius in the days when that man's father was the ruler of the Republic. To the Egyptian mind the fact that Cæsar was already a married man, with a wife living in Rome, was no real objection. She had borne him no son, and therefore might be divorced in favour of a more fruitful vine. Cleopatra herself must have been keenly desirous to share her Egyptian throne with Cæsar, for no doubt she saw clearly enough that, since he was already autocrat and actual Dictator of Rome, it would not be long before they became sovereigns of the whole Roman world. If she could persuade him, like Archelaus of Komana, to accept the crown of the Pharaohs, there was good reason to suppose that he would try to induce Rome to offer him the sovereignty of his own country. The tendency towards

[1] Page 57.

monarchical rule in the Roman capital, thanks largely to Pompey, was already very apparent; and both Cæsar and Cleopatra must have realised that, if they played their game with skill, a throne awaited them in that city at no very distant date.

Cleopatra was a keen patriot, or rather she was deeply concerned in the advancement of her own and her dynasty's fortunes; and it must have been a matter of the utmost satisfaction to her to observe the direction in which events were moving. The man whom she loved, and who loved her, might at any moment become actual sovereign of Rome and its dominions; and the child with which she was about to present him, if it were a boy, would be the heir of the entire world. For years her dynasty had feared that Rome would crush them out of existence and absorb her kingdom into the Republic; but now there was a possibility that Egypt, and the lands to which the Nile Valley was the gateway, would become the equal of Rome at the head of the great amalgamation of the nations of the earth. Egypt, it must be remembered, was still unconquered by Rome, and was, at the time, the most wealthy and important nation outside the Republic. All Alexandrians and Egyptians believed themselves to be the foremost people in the world; and thus to Cleopatra the dream that Egypt might play the leading part in an Egypto - Roman empire was in no wise fantastic.

Her policy, then, was obvious. She must attempt to retain Cæsar's affection, and at the same time must nurse with care the growing aspirations towards monarchy which were developing in his mind. She must bind him to her so that, when the time came, she might ascend the throne of the world by his side; and she must make apparent to him, and keep ever present to his imagination, the fact of her own puissance and the splendour of her royal status, so that there should be no doubt in Cæsar's mind that her flesh and blood, and hers alone, were fitted to blend with his in the foundation of that single royal line which was to rule the whole Earth.

Approaching motherhood, it would seem, had much sobered her wild nature, and the glory of her ambitions had raised her thoughts to a level from which she must have contemplated with disdain her early struggles with the drowned Ptolemy, the decapitated Potheinos, the murdered Achillas, and the outlawed Theodotos. She, Cleopatra, was the daughter of the Sun, the sister of the Moon, and the kinswoman of the heavenly beings; she was mated to the descendant of Venus and the Olympian gods, and the unborn offspring of their union would be in very truth King of Earth and Heaven.

Historians both ancient and modern are agreed that Cleopatra was a woman of exceptional mental power. Her character, so often wayward in expression, was as dominant as her personality was strong; and she must have found no difficulty in making her appeal to the soaring ambitions of the great Roman. When occasion demanded she carried herself with dignity befitting the descendant of an ancient line of kings, and even in her escapades the royalty of her person was at all times apparent. The impression which she has left upon the world is that of a woman who was always significant of the splendour of monarchy; and her influence upon Cæsar in this regard is not to be overlooked. A man such as he could not live for six months in close contact with a queen without feeling to some extent the glamour of royalty. She represented monarchy in its most absolute form, and in Egypt her word was law. The very tone of her royal mode of life must have constituted new matter for Cæsar's mind to ruminate upon; and that trait in his character which led him to abhor the thought of subordination to any living man, must have caused him to watch the actions of an autocratic queen with frank admiration and restless envy. Tales of the Kings of Alexandria and stories of the ancient Pharaohs without doubt were narrated, and without doubt took some place in Cæsar's brain. Cleopatra's point of view, that of the most royal of the world's royal houses, must, by its very unfamiliarity, have impressed itself upon his thoughts.

Thus, little by little, under the influence of the Egyptian Queen and in the power of his own sleepless ambitions, Cæsar began to give serious thought to the possibilities of creating a world-empire over which he should rule as king, founding a royal line which should sit upon the supreme earthly throne for ages to come. Obviously it must have occurred to him that kings must rule by right of royal blood, and that his own blood, though noble and though said to be of divine origin, was not such as would give his descendants unquestionable command over the loyalty of their subjects. A man who is the descendant of many kings has a right to royalty which the son of a conqueror, however honourable his origin, does not possess. So thought Napoleon when he married the Austrian princess, founding a royal house in his country by using the royal blood of another land for the purpose. Looking around him with this thought in view, Cæsar could not well have chosen anybody but

Cleopatra as the foundress of his line. There was no Roman royal house extant, and therefore a Greek was the best, if not the only, possible alternative; and the Ptolemaic Kings of Egypt were pure Macedonians, deriving their descent, by popular belief, if not in actual fact, from the royal house of Cæsar's hero, Alexander the Great. He may well, then, have contemplated with enthusiasm the thought of the future monarchs of Rome sitting by inherited right upon the ancient throne of Macedonian Egypt; and Cleopatra on her part was no doubt inspired by the idea of future Pharaohs, blood of her blood and bone of her bone, ruling Rome by hereditary authority.

Cleopatra of necessity had to find a husband. Already she had postponed her marriage beyond the age at which such an event should take place; and any union with her co-regnant brother could but be of a formal nature. Cæsar now had come into her life, capturing her youthful affections and causing himself to be the parent of her child; and it is but natural to suppose that she would endeavour by every means in her power to make him her lifelong consort, thus adding to her own royal stock the worthiest blood of Rome. There can be no doubt that whether or not she might succeed in making Cæsar himself Pharaoh of Egypt, she intended to hand on the Egyptian throne to her child and his, adding to the name of Ptolemy that of the family of the Cæsars. Thus it may be said, though my assumption at first seems startling, that the Roman Empire to a large extent owes its existence to the Egyptian Queen, for the monarchy was in many respects the child of the union of Cæsar and Cleopatra.

These as yet undefined ambitions and hopes found

a very real and material expression in Cæsar's eagerness
to know whether the expected babe would be a girl, or a
son and heir; and it seems likely that his determination
to remain in Egypt was largely due to his unwillingness
to depart before that question was answered. This, and
the paternal responsibility which perhaps for the first
time in his sordid life he had ever felt, led him to postpone his return to Rome. He seems to have entertained
feelings of the greatest tenderness towards the Queen,
whom he was beginning to regard as his wife; and he
was, no doubt, anxious to be near her during the ordeal
through which the young and delicately-built girl had,
for the first time, to pass. It has been the custom for
historians to attribute Cæsar's prolonged residence in
Egypt, after the termination of the war and the settlement of Egyptian affairs, to the sensuous allurements of
Cleopatra, who is supposed to have held him captive by
the arts of love and by the voluptuous attractions of her
person; but here a natural fact of life has been overlooked. A woman who is about to render to mankind
the great service of her sex, has neither the ability nor
the desire to arouse the feverish emotions of her lover.
Her condition calls forth from him the more gentle
aspects of his affection. His responsibility is expressed
in consideration, in interest, in sympathy, and in a kind
of gratitude; but it is palpably absurd to suppose that a
mere passion, such as that by which Cæsar is thought to
have been animated, could at this time have influenced
his actions. If love of any kind held him in Egypt, it
was the love of a husband for his wife, the devotion of
a man who was about to become a parent to the woman
who would presently pay toll to Nature in response to
his incitement. Actually, as we have seen, there was

something more than love to keep him in Egypt; there was ambition, headlong aspiration, the intoxication of a conqueror turning his mind to new conquests, and the supreme interest of a would-be king constructing a throne which should be occupied not only by himself but by the descendants of his own flesh and blood for all time.[1]

While waiting for the desired event Cæsar could not remain inactive in the Palace at Alexandria.   He desired to ascertain for himself the resources of the land which was to be considered as his wife's dowry; and he therefore determined to conduct a peaceful expedition up the Nile with this subject in view.   The royal *dahabiyeh* or house-boat was therefore made ready for himself and Cleopatra, whose condition might be expected to benefit by the idle and yet interesting life upon the river; and orders were given both to his own legionaries and to a considerable number of Cleopatra's troops to prepare themselves for embarkation upon a fleet of four hundred Nile vessels.   The number of ships suggests that there were several thousand soldiers employed in the expedi-

---

[1] It has generally been stated that Cæsar left Egypt before the birth of Cæsarion, an opinion which, in view of the fact that Appian says he remained nine months in Egypt, has always seemed to me improbable; for it is surely more than a coincidence that he delayed his departure from Egypt until the very month in which Cleopatra's and his child was to be expected to arrive, he having met her in the previous October.   Plutarch's statement may be interpreted as meaning that Cæsar departed to Syria after the birth of his son.   I think that Cicero's remark, in a letter dated in June B.C. 47, that there was a serious hindrance to Cæsar's departure from Alexandria, refers to the event for which he was waiting.   Those who suggest that Cæsar did *not* remain in Egypt so long are obliged to deny that the authors are correct in stating that he went up the Nile; and they have to disregard the positive statement of Appian that the Dictator's visit lasted nine months.   Moreover, the date of the celebration of Cæsarion's seventeenth birthday (as recorded on p. 361) is a further indication that he was born no later than the beginning of July.

CLEOPATRA.

tion; and it appears to have been Cæsar's intention to penetrate far into the Sudan.[1] The royal vessel, or *thalamegos*, as it was called by the Greeks, was of immense size, and was propelled by many banks of oars.[2] It contained colonnaded courts, banqueting saloons, sitting-rooms, bedrooms, shrines dedicated to Venus and to Dionysos, and a grotto or "winter garden." The wood employed was cedar and cypress, and the decorations were executed in paint and gold-leaf. The furniture was Greek, with the exception of that in one dining-hall, which was decorated in the Egyptian style.[3] The rest of the fleet consisted, no doubt, of galleys and ordinary native transports and store-ships.

From the city of Alexandria the fleet passed into the nearest branch of the Nile, and so travelled southwards to Memphis, where Cleopatra perhaps obtained her first sight of the great Pyramids and the Sphinx. Thebes, the ancient capital, at that period much fallen into decay, was probably reached in about three weeks' time; and Cæsar must have been duly impressed by the splendid temples and monuments upon both banks of the Nile. Possibly it was at his suggestion that Cleopatra caused the great obelisk of one of her distant predecessors to be moved from the temple of Luxor at Thebes and to be transported down to Alexandria, where it was erected not far from the Forum,[4] an inscription recording its

[1] It has generally been thought that this was simply a pleasure cruise up the Nile; but the number of ships (given by Appian) indicates that many troops were employed, and the troops are referred to by Suetonius also.

[2] The *thalamegos* described by Athenæus was not that used on this occasion, but the description will serve to give an idea of its luxury.

[3] Athenæus, v. 37. The number of banks of oars and the measurements, as given by him, are probably exaggerated.

[4] It was presented to the British Government, and now stands on the Thames Embankment in London. It is known as "Cleopatra's Needle."

re-erection being engraved at the base.   The journey
was continued probably as far as Aswan and the First
Cataract, which may have been reached some four or
five weeks after the departure from Alexandria; and it
would seem that Cæsar here turned his face to the
north once more.   Suetonius states that he was anxious
to proceed farther up the Nile, but that his troops were
restive and inclined to be mutinous, a fact which is not
surprising, since the labour of dragging the vessels up
the cataract would have been immense, and the hot
south winds which often blow in the spring would have
added considerably to the difficulties.   The temperature at this time of year may rise suddenly from the
pleasant degree of an Egyptian winter to that of the
height of intolerable summer, and so remain for four or
five days.

Be this as it may, Cæsar turned about, having satisfied
himself as to the wealth and fertility of the country,
and, no doubt, having obtained as much information as
possible from the natives in regard to the trade-routes
which led from the Nile to Berenice and India, or to
Meroe, Napata, and the Kingdom of Ethiopia.   The
expedition arrived at Alexandria probably some nine or
ten weeks after its departure from that city—that is to
say, at the end of the month of June; and it would seem
that in the first week of July Cleopatra's confinement
took place.

The child proved to be a boy; and the delighted
father thus found himself the parent of a son and heir
who was at once accepted by the Egyptians as the
legitimate child of the union of their Queen with the
god Amon, who had appeared in the form of Cæsar.
He was named Cæsar, or more familiarly Cæsarion, a

Greek diminutive of the same word; but officially, of course, he was known also as Ptolemy, and ultimately was the sixteenth and last of that name. A bilingual inscription now preserved at Turin refers to him as "Ptolemy, who is also called Cæsar," this being often seen in Egyptian inscriptions in the words *Ptolemys zed nef Kysares,* "Ptolemy called Cæsar."

The Dictator waited no longer in Egypt. For the last few months he had put Roman politics from his thoughts and had not even troubled to write any despatches to the home Government.[1] But now he had to create the world-monarchy of which his winter with Cleopatra had led him to dream; and first there were campaigns to be fought on the borders of the Mediterranean; there was Parthia to be subdued; and finally India was to be invaded and conquered. Then, when all the known world had become dependent upon him, and only Egypt and her tributaries were still outside Roman dominion, he would, by one bold stroke, announce his marriage to the Queen of that country, incorporate her lands and her vast wealth with those of Rome, and declare himself sole monarch of the earth. It was a splendid ambition, worthy of a great man; and, as we shall presently see, there can be very little question that these glorious dreams would have been converted into actual realities had not his enemies murdered him on the eve of their realisation. Modern historians are unanimous in declaring that Cæsar had wasted his time in Egypt, and had devoted to a love intrigue the weeks and months which ought to have been spent in regulating the affairs of the world. Actually, however, these nine months, far from being wasted, were spent

[1] Cicero, A. xi. 17. 13.

in the very creation of the Roman Empire. True, Cæsar's schemes were frustrated by the knives of his assassins; but, as will be seen in the sequel, his plans were carried on by Cleopatra with the assistance of Antony, and finally were put into execution by Octavian.

As Cæsar sailed out of the Great Harbour of Alexandria he must have turned his keen grey eyes with peculiar interest upon the splendid buildings of the Palace, which towered in front of the city, upon the Lochias Promontory; and that quiet, whimsical expression must have played around his close-shut lips as he thought of the change that had been wrought in his mental attitude by the months spent amidst its royal luxuries. Enthusiasm for the work which lay before him must have burnt like a fire within him; but stamped upon his brain there must have been the picture of a darkened room in which the wild, happy-go-lucky, little Queen of Egypt, now so subdued and so gentle, lay clasping to her breast the new-born Cæsar, the sole heir to the kingdom of the whole world.

CHAPTER VIII.

CLEOPATRA AND CÆSAR IN ROME.

CÆSAR'S movements during the year after his departure from Egypt do not, for the purpose of this narrative, require to be recorded in detail. From Alexandria, which he may have left at about the middle of the first week in July, he sailed in a fast-going galley across the 500 miles of open sea to Antioch, arriving at that city a few days before the middle of that month.[1] There he spent a day or two in regulating the affairs of the country, and presently sailed on to Ephesus, some 600 miles from Antioch, which he probably reached at the end of the third week of July. At Antioch he heard that one of his generals, Domitius Calvinus, had been defeated by Pharnakes, the son of Mithridates the Great, and had been driven out of Pontus, and it seems that he at once sent three legions to the aid of the beaten troops with orders to await in north-western Galatia or Cappadocia for his coming. After a day or two at Ephesus, Cæsar travelled with extreme rapidity to the rendezvous, taking with him only a thousand cavalry; and arriving at Zela, 500 miles from Ephesus, on or before August 2nd, at once defeated the rebels. It had

---

[1] He could have performed the journey in five days or less with a favourable wind.

been his custom in Gaul to travel by himself at the rate
of a hundred miles a day, and even with a heavily laden
army he covered over forty miles a day, as for example in
his march from Rome to Spain, which he accomplished in
twenty-seven days, and he may thus have joined his main
army and commenced his preparations for the battle of
Zela as early as the last days of July. The crushing defeat
which he inflicted on the enemy so shortly after taking
over the command was thus a feat of which he might
justly be proud, and it so tickled his vanity that in
writing to a friend of his in Rome, named Amantius,
he described the campaign in the three famous words,
Veni, vidi, vici, "I came, I saw, I conquered," which so
clearly indicate that he was beginning to regard himself
as a sort of swift-footed, irresistible demigod.

Thence he sailed at last for Italy, and reached Rome
at the end of September, almost exactly a year after his
arrival in Egypt. He remained in Rome not more than
two and a half months, and about the middle of December he set out for North Africa, where Cato, Scipio, and
other fugitive friends of Pompey had established a pro-
visional government with the assistance of Juba, King
of Numidia, and were gathering their forces. Arriving
at Hadrumetum on December 28th, he at once began
the war, which soon ended in the entire defeat and
extermination of the enemy at Thapsus on April 6th.
Of the famous Pompeian leaders, Faustus Sulla, Lucius
Africanus, and Lucius Julius Cæsar were put to death;
and Lucius Manlius Torquatus, Marcus Petreius, Scipio,
and Cato committed suicide; while, according to Plutarch, some fifty thousand men were slain in the rout.
Arriving once more in Rome on July 25th, B.C. 46, Cæsar
at once began to prepare for his Triumph which was to

take place in the following month; and it would seem that he had already sent messengers to Cleopatra, who had spent a quiet year of maternal interests in Alexandria, to tell her to come with their baby to Rome.

According to Dion, the Queen arrived shortly *after* the Triumph, but several modern writers[1] are of opinion that she reached the capital in time for that event. I am disposed to think that she made the journey to Italy in company with the Egyptian prisoners who were to be displayed in the procession, Princess Arsinoe, the eunuch Ganymedes,[2] and others, whom Cæsar probably sent for in the late spring of this year soon after the battle of Thapsus. Cleopatra could not have been averse to witnessing the Triumph, for she must have regarded the late warfare in Alexandria not so much as a Roman campaign against the Egyptians as an Egypto-Roman suppression of an Alexandrian insurrection. The serious part of the campaign could be interpreted as having been waged by Cæsar on behalf of herself and her brother, Ptolemy XIV., against the rebels Achillas and Ganymedes, and later against this same Ptolemy who had gone over to the enemy; and the victory might thus be celebrated both by her and by her Roman champion. It would therefore be fitting that she should be a spectator of the degradation of Arsinoe and Ganymedes; and her presence in Rome at this time would obviously be desirable to her as indicating that she and her country had suffered no defeat. Cæsar, on his part, must have desired her presence that she might witness the dramatic demonstration of his power and popularity. He had just been made Dictator for the third time, and this appoint-

---

[1] Notably Dr Mahaffy.

[2] Judging by the remark of the commentator on Lucan, 'Pharsalia,' x. 521.

ment no doubt led him to feel the security of his position
and the imminence of that rise to monarchical power in
which Cleopatra and their son were to play so essential
a part. He was beginning to regard himself as above
criticism; and his two great victories, in Pontus and
Numidia, following upon his nine months of regal life
in Egypt, had somewhat turned his head, so that he no
longer considered the advisability of delaying his future
consort's introduction to the people of Rome. He had
yet much to accomplish before he could ascend with her
the throne of the world, but there can be no question
whatsoever that he now desired Cleopatra to begin to
make herself known in the capital; and, this being so,
it seems to me to be highly probable that he would
wish her to refute, by her presence as a witness of his
Triumph, any suggestion that she herself was to be included in that conquered Egypt[1] about which he was
so continuously boasting.

The Queen of Egypt's arrival in Rome must have
caused something of a sensation. Cartloads of baggage,
and numerous agitated eunuchs and slaves doubtless
heralded her approach and followed in her train. Her
little brother, Ptolemy XV., now eleven or twelve years
of age, whom she had probably feared to leave alone
in Alexandria lest he should follow the family tradition
and declare himself sole monarch, had been forced to
accompany her, and now added considerably to the
commotion of her arrival. The one-year-old heir of
the Cæsars and of the Ptolemies, surrounded by guards
and fussing nurses, must, however, have been the cyno-
sure of all eyes; for every Roman guessed its parentage,

---

[1] A coin inscribed with the words *Ægypto capta* was struck after his return
to Rome (Goltzius : de re Numm.)

knowing as they did the peculiarities of their Dictator. Cleopatra and her suite were accommodated in Cæsar's *transtiberini horti*, where a charming house stood amidst beautiful gardens on the right bank of the Tiber, near the site of the modern Villa Panfili; and it is to be presumed that his legal wife Calpurnia was left as mistress of another establishment within the city.

Cæsar's attitude towards Cleopatra at this time is not easily defined. It is not to be presumed that he was still very deeply in love with her; for natures such as his are totally incapable of continued devotion. During his residence in North Africa in the winter or early spring, he had been much attracted by Eunoe, the wife of Bogud, King of Mauretania, and had consoled himself for the temporary loss of Cleopatra by making her his mistress. Yet the Queen of Egypt still exercised a very considerable influence over him; and when she came to Rome it may be supposed that in his transpontine villa they resumed with some satisfaction the intimate life which they had enjoyed in the Alexandrian Palace. The first infatuation was over, however, and both Cæsar and Cleopatra must have felt that the basis of their relationship was now a business agreement designed for their mutual benefit. In all but name they were married, and it was the fixed intention of both that their marriage should presently be recognised in Rome as it already had been in Egypt. Cæsar, I suppose, took keen pleasure in the company of the witty, vivacious, and regal girl; and he was extremely happy to see her lodged in his villa, whither he could repair at any time of the day or night to enjoy her brilliant and refreshing society. Their baby son, too, was a source of interest and enjoyment to him. He was now

fourteen months old, and his likeness to Cæsar, so pronounced in after years, must already have been apparent.
Suetonius states that the boy came to resemble his father
very closely, and both in looks and in manners, notably
in his walk, showed very clearly his origin.   These
resemblances, already able to be observed, must have
delighted Cæsar, who took such careful pride in his
own appearance and personality; and they must have
formed a bond between himself and Cleopatra as nearly
permanent as anything could be in his progressive and
impatient nature.   The Queen, on her part, probably
still took extreme pleasure in the companionship of the
great Dictator, who represented an ideal both of manhood and of social charm.   She must have loved the
fertility of his mind, the autocratic power of his will,
and the energy of his personality; and though premature
age and ill-health were beginning to diminish his aptitude
for the *rôle* of ardent swain, she found in him, no doubt,
a lovable friend and husband, and one with whom the
intimacies of daily comradeship were a cause of genuine
happiness.   They were as well suited to one another as
two ambitious characters could be; and, moreover, they
were irrevocably bound to one another by the memory
of past passion not yet altogether in abeyance, by the
sympathy of mutual understanding, by the identity of
their worldly interests, and by the responsibilities of
correlative parentage.

The arrival of Cleopatra in Rome of course caused a
scandal, to which Cæsar showed his usual nonchalant
indifference.   People were sorry for the Dictator's legal
wife Calpurnia, who, since her marriage in B.C. 59, had
been left so much alone by her husband; and they were
shocked by the open manner in which the members of

the Cæsarian party paid court to the Queen. I find
no evidence to justify the modern belief[1] that Roman
society was at the time annoyed at the introduction of
an *eastern* lady into its midst;[2] for everybody must have
known that Cleopatra had not one drop of Egyptian
blood in her veins, and must have realised that she was
a pure Macedonian Greek, ruling over a city which
was the centre of Greek culture and civilisation. But
at the same time there is evidence to show that the
Romans did not like her. Cicero wrote that he detested
her;[3] and Dion says that the people pitied Princess
Arsinoe, her sister, whose degradation was a consequence
of Cleopatra's success with Cæsar. On the whole, however, her advent did not cause as much stir as might
have been expected, for she seems to have acted with
tactful moderation in the capital, and to have avoided
all ostentation.

The Triumph which Cæsar celebrated in August for
the amusement of Rome and for his own enjoyment
was fourfold in character, and lasted for four days.
Upon the first day Cæsar passed through the streets
of Rome in the *rôle* of conqueror of Gaul, and when
darkness had fallen ascended the Capitol by torchlight,
forty elephants carrying numerous torch-bearers to right
and left of his chariot. The unfortunate Vercingetorix,
who had been held prisoner for six miserable years, was
executed at the conclusion of this impressive parade—

---

[1] Houssaye, 'Aspasie, Cleopatre, Theodora,' p. 91, for example, says that
society was shocked at a Roman being in love with an Egyptian; and Sergeant,
'Cleopatra of Egypt,' writes: "It was as an Egyptian that Cleopatra offended
the Romans."

[2] Horace's Ode was written after the engineered talk of the "eastern peril"
had done its work—*i.e.*, after Actium.

[3] Ad Atticum, xv. 15.

an act of cold-blooded cruelty to an honourable foe
(who had voluntarily surrendered to Cæsar to save his
countrymen from further punishment) which, at the time,
may have been excused on the ground that such executions were customary at the end of a Triumph. Upon
the second day the conquest of the Dictator's Egyptian
enemies was celebrated, and the Princess Arsinoe was
led through the streets in chains, together, it would seem,
with Ganymedes, the latter perhaps being executed at
the close of the performance, and the former being spared
as a sort of compliment to Cleopatra's royal house. In
this procession images of Achillas and Potheinos were
carried along, and were greeted by the populace with
pleasant jeers; while a statue representing the famous
old Nilus, and a model of Pharos, the wonder of the
world, reminded the spectators of the importance of
the country now under Roman protection. African
animals strange to Rome, such as the giraffe, were led
along in the procession, and other wonders from Egypt
and Ethiopia were displayed for the delight of the
populace. On the third day the conquest of Pontus
was demonstrated, and a large tablet with the arrogant
words *Veni, Vidi, Vici* painted upon it was carried
before the conqueror. Finally, on the fourth day the
victories in North Africa were celebrated. In this last
procession Cæsar caused some offence by exhibiting
captured Roman arms; for the campaign had been
fought against Romans of the Pompeian party, a fact
which at first he had attempted to disguise by stating
that the Triumph was celebrated over King Juba of
Numidia, who had sided with the enemy. Still graver
offence was caused, however, when it was seen that
vulgar caricatures of Cato and other of Cæsar's personal

enemies were exhibited in the procession; and the populace must have questioned whether such a jest at the expense of honourable Romans whose bodies were hardly yet cold in their graves was in perfect taste. It would seem indeed that Cæsar's judgment in such matters had become somewhat warped during this last year of military and administrative success, and that he had begun to despise those who were opposed to him as though they could be but misguided fools. In this attitude one sees, perhaps, something of that same quality which led him blandly to accept in Egypt a sort of divinity as by personal right, and which persuaded him to aim always towards absolutism; for a man is in no wise normal who considers himself a being meet for worship and his enemy an object fit only for derision.

There seems, in fact, little doubt that Cæsar was not now in a normal condition of mind. For some years he had been subject to epileptic seizures, and now the distressing malady was growing more pronounced and the seizures were of more frequent occurrence. At the battle of Thapsus he is said to have been taken ill in this manner; and on other occasions he was attacked while in discharge of his duties. Such a physical condition may be accountable for much of his growing eccentricity, and, particularly, one may attribute to it his increasing faith in his semi-divine powers. Lombroso goes so far as to say that epilepsy is almost an essential factor in the personality of one who believes himself to be a Son of God or Messenger of the Deity. Akhnaton, the great religious reformer of Ancient Egypt, suffered from epilepsy; the Prophet Mohammed, to put it bluntly, had fits; and many other religious reformers suffered in like manner. One cannot tell what hallucinations and

strange manifestations were experienced by Cæsar under
the influence of this malady; but one may be sure that
to Cleopatra they were clear indications of his close
relationship to the gods, and that in explanation she
did not fail to remind him both of his divine descent
and her own inherited divinity, in which, as her consort,
he participated.

Towards the end of September Cæsar caused a sensation in Rome by an act which shows clearly enough his
attitude in this regard. He consecrated a magnificent
temple in honour of Venus Genetrix, his divine ances-
tress; and there, in the splendour of its marble sanctuary,
he placed a statue of Cleopatra, which had been executed
during the previous weeks by the famous Roman sculptor,
Archesilaus.[1] The significance of this act has been overlooked by modern historians. In placing in this shrine
of Venus, at the time of its inauguration, a figure of the
Queen of Egypt, who in her own country was the representative of Isis-Aphrodite upon earth,[2] Cæsar was demonstrating the divinity of Cleopatra, and was telling the
people, as it were in everlasting phrases of stone, that the
royal girl who now honoured his villa on the banks of the
Tiber was no less than a manifestation of Venus herself.
It will presently be seen how, in after years, Cleopatra
went to meet Antony decked in the character of Venus,
and how she was then and on other occasions hailed by
the crowd as the goddess come down to earth; and we
shall see how her mausoleum actually formed part of the
temple of that goddess. Both at this date and in later
times she was identified indiscriminately with Isis, with

---

[1] I think this fact may be regarded as an argument in favour of the opinion
that Cleopatra had been in Rome already several weeks.

[2] Venus and Isis were identified in Rome also.

Venus-Hathor, and with Venus-Aphrodite; and even after her death the tradition so far survived that one of her famous pearl earrings was cut into two parts, and, in this form, ultimately ornamented the ears of the statue of Venus in the Pantheon at Rome. Coins dating from this period have been found upon which Cleopatra is represented as Aphrodite, carrying in her arms the baby Cæsarion, who is supposed to be Eros. Cæsar was always boasting about the connection of his house with this goddess; and now the placing of this statue of Cleopatra in his new temple is, I think, to be interpreted as signifying that he wished the Roman people to regard the Queen as a "young goddess," which was the title given to her by the Greeks and Egyptians in her own country.

It is not altogether certain that Cæsar himself was actually beginning to regard Cleopatra in this light, though the increasing frequency of his epileptic attacks, and his consequent hallucinations, may have now made such an attitude possible even in the case of so hardened a sceptic as was the Dictator in former years. It seems more reasonable to suppose that he was at this time attempting to appeal to the imagination of the people in anticipation of the great *coup* which he was about to execute; and that, with this object in view, he allowed himself to be carried along by a kind of enthusiastic self-deception. He applied no serious analysis to his opinions in this regard; but, by means of a thoughtless vanity, he seems to have given rein to an undefined conviction, very suitable to his great purpose, that he himself was more than human, and that Cleopatra was not altogether a woman of mortal flesh and blood. Even so Alexander the Great had partially deluded himself when, on the one hand, he named himself the son of Jupiter-Ammon, and, on the other, was careful, once when wounded, to point out that ordinary mortal blood flowed from his veins.   And so, too, Napoleon Bonaparte, during his invasion of Egypt, declared that he was the Prophet of God, and, in after years, was willing to describe to a friend, as it were in jest, his vision of himself as the founder of a new Faith.

The inauguration of Cæsar's new temple, which was, one may say, the shrine of Cleopatra, was accompanied by amazing festivities, and the excitable population of this great city seemed, so to speak, to go mad with enthusiasm.   Great gladiatorial shows were organised, and a miniature sea-fight upon an artificial lake was enacted for the public entertainment.   The majority of the mob was ready enough to accept without comment the exalted position of the statue of Cleopatra.   At this time in Rome they were very partial to new and foreign deities, celestial or in the flesh; and actually the worship of the Egyptian goddess Isis, with whom Cleopatra, as Venus, was so closely connected, had taken firm hold of their imagination.   For the last few years the religion of Isis had been extremely popular with the lower classes in Rome; and when, in B.C. 58, a law which had been made forbidding foreign temples to be located within a certain area of the city, necessitated the destruction of a temple of Isis, not one man could be found who would touch the sacred building, and at last the Consul, Lucius Paullus, was obliged to tuck up his toga and set to work upon the demolition of the edifice with his own hands. Thus, this inaugural ceremony, so lavishly organised by Cæsar, was a marked success; and in spite of the indignation of Cicero, the statue of Cleopatra took its permanent place, with popular consent, in the sanctuary of Venus. No expense was spared on this or on any other occasion to please the people; and at one time twenty-two thousand persons partook of a sumptuous meal at Cæsar's expense. Such a courting of the people was, indeed, necessary at this time; for although the Dictator was at the moment practically omnipotent, and though there was talk of securing him in his office for a term of ten years, his party had not that solidity which was to be desired of it. Antony, the right-hand man of the Cæsarians, was, at the time, in some disgrace owing to a quarrel with his master; and there were rumours that he wished to revenge himself by assassinating Cæsar. It was already becoming clear that the Pompeian party, in spite of Pharsalia and Thapsus, was not yet dead, and still waited to receive its death-blow. Some of the Dictator's actions had given considerable offence, and there were certain people in Rome who made use of every opportunity to denounce him, and to offer their praise to the memory of his enemy Cato, whose tragic death after the battle of Thapsus, and the vilification of whose memory in the recent Triumph, had caused such a painful impression. Cicero wrote an encomium upon this unfortunate man, to which Cæsar, in self-defence, replied by publishing his Anti-Cato, which was marked by a tone of bitter and even venomous animosity. All manner of unpleasant remarks were being made in better-class circles in regard to Cleopatra; and when the Dictator publicly admitted the parentage of their child, and authorised him to bear the name of Cæsar, it began to be whispered that his legal marriage to the Queen was imminent.

The mixed population of Rome delighted in political

K

strife, and though Cæsar's position seemed unassailable, there were always large numbers of persons ready to make sporadic attacks upon it. There was at this time constant rioting in the Forum, and an almost continuous restlessness was to be observed in the streets and public places. In the theatres topical allusions were received with frantic applause;[1] and even in the Senate disturbances were not infrequent. The people had always to be humoured, and Cæsar was obliged at all times to play to the gallery. Fortunately for him he possessed in the highest degree the art of self-advertisement;[2] and his charm of manner, together with his striking and handsome appearance, made the desired appeal to the popular fancy. His relationship to Cleopatra stood, on the whole, in his favour amongst the lower classes, who had hailed him with coarse delight as the terror of the women of Gaul; and the fact that she was a foreigner mattered not in the least to the heterogeneous population of Rome. They themselves were largely a composition of the nations of the earth; and that Cæsar's mistress, and probable future wife, was a Greek, was to them in no wise a matter for comment. In any theatre in Rome at that date one might sit amidst an audience of foreigners to hear a drama given (at Cæsar's expense, by the way) in language such as Greek, Phœnician, Hebrew, Syrian, or Spanish. To them Cleopatra must have appeared as a wonderful woman, closely related to the gods, come from a famous city across the waters to enjoy the society of their own half-godlike Dictator; and they were quite

---

[1] As, for example, when the actor Diphilus alluded to Pompey in the words "Nostra miseria tu es—Magnus" (Cicero, Ad Att. ii. 19).

[2] I use the words of Oman.

prepared to accept her as a pleasant and romantic adjunct to the political situation.

Among the many reforms which Cæsar now introduced there was one which was the direct outcome of his visit to Egypt. For some time the irregularities of the calendar had been causing much inconvenience, and the Dictator, very probably at the Queen of Egypt's suggestion, now decided to invite some of Cleopatra's court astronomers to Rome in order that they might establish a new system based upon the Egyptian calendar of Eudoxus. Sosigenes was at that time the most celebrated astronomer in Alexandria, and it was to him, perhaps at Cleopatra's advice, that Cæsar now turned. After very careful study it was decided that the present year, B.C. 46, should be extended to fifteen months, or 445 days, in order that the nominal date might be brought round to correspond with the actual season. The so-called Julian calendar, which was thus established, is that upon which our present system is based; and it is not without interest to recollect that but for Cleopatra some entirely different set of months would now be used throughout the world.

Cæsar's mind at this time was full of his plans for the conquest of the East. In B.C. 65 Pompey had brought to Rome many details regarding the overland route to the Orient. This route started from the Port of Phasis on the Black Sea, ascended the river of that name to its source in Iberia, passed over to the valley of the river Cyrus (Kur), and so came to the coast of the Caspian Sea. Crossing the water the route thence led along the river Oxus, which at that time flowed into the Caspian, to its source, and thus through Cashmir into India.

There must then have been some talk of carrying the
eagles along this highway to the Orient; and while
Cæsar was in Egypt it seems probable, as we have seen,
that he had studied the question of leading Roman arms
thither by the great Egyptian trade route. Though this
latter road to the wonderful Orient, however, must have
seemed to him, after consideration, to be very suitable as
a channel for the despatch of reinforcements, he appears
to have favoured the land route across Asia for his
original invasion. This approach to the East was
blocked by the Parthians, and Cæsar now announced
his intention of conducting a campaign against these
people. There is no evidence to show that he desired
to follow Alexander's steps beyond Parthia into India,
but I am of opinion that such was his intention. In
view of the facts that the exploits of Alexander the Great
had been studied by him, that he publicly declared his
wish to rival them, that he must have heard from Pompey
of the overland route to India with which the Romans
had become acquainted during the war against Mithridates, that his love of distant conquest and exploration
was inordinate, that he had spent some months in
studying conditions in Egypt—a country which was in
those days full of talk of India and of the new trade with
the Orient, that after leaving Egypt he began at once to
prepare for a campaign against the one nation which
obstructed the overland route to the East, that no other
part of the known world, save poverty-stricken Germania,
remained to be brought by conquest under Roman sway,
that India offered possibilities of untold wealth, and that
Cleopatra herself ultimately made an attempt to reach
those far countries,—the inference seems to me to be
clear that Cæsar's designs upon Parthia were only

preliminary to a contemplated invasion of the East. The riches of those distant lands were already the talk of the age, and within the lifetime of young men of this period streams of Indian merchandise, comprising diamonds, precious stones, silks, spices, and scents, began to pour into Rome and were sold each year, according to the somewhat exaggerated account of Pliny, for some forty million pounds sterling.[1] Could Cæsar, the world's greatest spendthrift, the world's most eager plunderer, have resisted the temptation of making a bid for the loot which lay behind Parthia? Does the fact that he said nothing of such an intention preclude the possibility that thoughts of this kind now filled his mind, and formed a topic of conversation between him and the adventurous Cleopatra, the Ruler of the gateway of the Orient, who herself sent Cæsar's son to India, as we shall see in due course? Napoleon, when he invaded Egypt in 1798, said very little about his contemplated attack upon India; but it was none the less dominant in his mind for that. Egypt and Parthia in conjunction formed the basis of any attempt to capture the Orient: Egypt with its route across the seas, and Parthia with its highroad overland. Are we really to suppose that Cæsar did waste his time in Egypt, or was he then studying the same problem which now directed his attention to Parthia? By means of his partnership with Cleopatra he had secured one of the routes to India; and the merchants of Alexandria, if not his own great imagination, must have made clear to him the value of his possession in that regard; for ever since the discovery

---

[1] Pliny (vi. 26) says that some £400,000 in money was conveyed to India each year in exchange for goods which were sold for one hundred times that amount.

of the over-sea route to the East that value has been recognised. The Venetian Sanuto in later years told his compatriots of the effect on India which would follow from the conquest of the Nile Valley; the Comte Daru said that the possession of Egypt meant the opening up of India; Leibnitz told Louis XIV. of France that an invasion of Egypt would result in the capture of the Indian highroad; the Duc de Choiseul made a similar declaration to Louis XV.; Napoleon stated in his 'Memoirs' that his object in attacking Egypt was to lead an army of 60,000 men to India; and at the present day England holds the Nile Valley as being the gateway of her distant possessions. On the other side of the picture we see at the present time the attempts of Russia to establish her power in Northern Persia and Afghanistan, where once the Parthians of old held sway, in order to be ready for that day when English power in India shall decline. Was Cæsar, then, straining every nerve only for the possession of the two gateways of the Orient, or did his gaze penetrate through those gateways to the vast wealth of the kingdoms beyond? I am disposed to see him walking with Cleopatra in the gardens of the villa by the Tiber, just as Napoleon paced the parks of Passeriano, "frequently betraying by his exclamations the gigantic thoughts of his unlimited ambition," as Lacroix tells us of the French conqueror.

Such dreams, however, were rudely interrupted by the news that the Pompeian party had gathered its forces in Spain; and Cæsar was obliged to turn his attention to that part of the world. In the winter of B.C. 46, therefore, he set out for the south-west, impatient at the delay which the new campaign necessitated in his great schemes. He was in no mood to brook any opposition in Rome, and before leaving the capital he arranged that he should be made Consul without a colleague for the ensuing year B.C. 45, as well as Dictator, thus giving himself absolutely autocratic power. On his way to Spain he sent a despatch to Rome, appointed eight *praefecti urbi* with full powers to act in his name, thus establishing a form of cabinet government which should entirely over-ride the wishes of the Senate and of the people; and in this manner he secured the political situation to his own advantage. Naturally there was a very great outcry against this high-handed action; but Cæsar was far too deeply occupied by his vast schemes, and far too annoyed by this Spanish interruption of his course towards the great goal of his ambitions, to pay much attention to the outraged feelings of his political opponents.

The enemy in Spain were led by the two sons of the great Pompey, but at the battle of Munda, fought on March 17, B.C. 45, they were entirely defeated with a loss of some thirty thousand men. The elder of the two leaders, Cnæus Pompeius, who was said to have once been a suitor for Cleopatra's heart, was killed shortly after the battle, but the younger, Sextus, escaped. Cæsar then returned to Rome, being met outside the capital by Antony, with whom he was reconciled; and in the early summer he celebrated his Triumph. In this he offended a number of persons, owing to the fact that his victory had been won over his fellow-countrymen, whose defeat, therefore, ought not to have been the cause of more than a silent satisfaction. After Pharsalia Cæsar had cele-brated no triumph, since Romans had there fought Romans; and, indeed, as Plutarch says, "he had seemed rather to be ashamed of the action than to expect honour from it." But now he had come to feel that he himself was Rome, and that his enemies were not simply opposed to his party but were in arms against the State.

Knowing now that the Pompeians were at last crushed, Cæsar decided to attempt to appease any ill-feeling directed against himself by the friends of the fallen party; and for this purpose he caused the statues of Pompey the Great, which had been removed from their pedestals, to be replaced; and furthermore, he pardoned, and even gave office to, several leaders of the Pompeian party, notably to Brutus and Cassius, who afterwards were ranked amongst his murderers. He then settled down in Rome to prepare for his campaign in the East, and, in the meantime, to put into execution the many administrative reforms which were maturing in his restless brain. It appears that he lived for the most part of this time in the house of which his wife Calpurnia was mistress; but there can be little doubt that he was a constant visitor at his transpontine villa, and that he spent all his spare hours there in the society of Cleopatra, who remained in Rome until his death.

CHAPTER IX.

THE FOUNDATIONS OF THE EGYPTO-ROMAN MONARCHY.

THE people of Rome now began to heap honours upon
Cæsar, and the government which he had established did
not fail to justify its existence by voting him to a position
of irrevocable power. He was made Consul for ten years,
and there was talk of decreeing him Dictator for life.
The Senate became simply an instrument for the execution of his commands; and so little did the members
concern themselves with the framing of new laws at
home, or with the details of foreign administration, that
Cicero is able to complain that in his official capacity he
had received the thanks of Oriental potentates whose
names he had never seen before, for their elevation to
thrones of kingdoms of which he had never heard.
Cæsar's interests were world-wide, and the Government
in Rome carried out his wishes in the manner in which
an ignorant Board of Directors of a company with foreign
interests follows the advice of its travelling manager.
He had lived for such long periods in foreign countries,
his campaigns had carried him over so much of the
known world's surface, that Rome appeared to him to be
nothing more than the headquarters of his administration,
and not a very convenient centre at that. His intimacy

with Cleopatra, moreover, had widened his outlook, and had very materially assisted him to become an arbiter of universal interests. Distant cities, such as Alexandria, were no longer to him the capitals of foreign lands, but were the seats of local governments within his own dominions; and the throne towards which he was climbing was set at an elevation from which the nations of the whole earth could be observed.

In accepting as his own business the concerns of so many lands, he was assuming responsibilities the weight of which no man could bear; yet his dislike of receiving advice, and his uncontrolled vanity, led him to resent all interference, nor would he admit that the strain was too great for his weakened physique. Intimate friends of the Dictator, such as Balbus and Oppius, observed that he was daily growing more irritable, more self-opinionated; and the least suggestion of a decentralisation of his powers caused him increasing annoyance. He wished always to hold the threads of the entire world's concerns in his own hands. Now he was discussing the future of North African Carthage and of Grecian Corinth, to which places he desired to send out Roman colonists; now he was regulating the affairs of Syria and Asia Minor; and now he was absorbed in the agrarian problems of Italy. There were times when the weight of universal affairs pressed so heavily upon him that he would exclaim that he had lived long enough; and in such moods, when his friends warned him of the possibility of his assassination, he would reply that death was not such a terrible matter, nor a disaster which could come to him more than once. The frequency of his epileptic seizures was a cause of constant distress to him, and his gaunt, almost haggard, appearance must have indicated to his friends that the strain was becoming unbearable. Yet ever his ambitions held him to his self-imposed task; and always his piercing eyes were set upon that goal of all his schemes, the monarchy of the earth.

People were now beginning to discuss openly the subject of his elevation to the throne. It was freely stated that he proposed to make himself King and Cleopatra Queen, and, further, that he intended to transfer the seat of his government to Alexandria, or some other eastern city. The site of Rome was not ideal. It was too far from the sea ever to be a first-rate centre of commerce; nor had it any natural sources of wealth in the neighbourhood. The streets, which were narrow and crookedly built, were liable to be flooded at certain seasons by the swift-flowing Tiber.[1] Pestilence and sickness were rife amongst the congested quarters of the city; and in the middle ages, as Mommsen has pointed out, "one German army after another melted away under its walls and left it mysteriously victorious." After the battle of Actium, Augustus wished to change the capital to some other quarter of the globe, as, for example, to Byzantium; and it is very possible that the idea originated with Cæsar. At the period with which we are now dealing Rome was far less magnificent than it became a few years later, and it must have compared unfavourably with Alexandria and other cities. Its streets ascended and descended, twisted this way and that, in an amazing manner; and so narrow were they that Cæsar was obliged to pass a law prohibiting waggons from being driven along them in the daytime, all porterage being performed by men

[1] Horace, Od. 1, 2.

or beasts of burden. The great public buildings and palaces of the rich rose from amidst the encroaching jumble of small houses like exotic plants hemmed in by a mass of overgrown weeds; and Cæsar must often have given envious thought to Alexandria with its great Street of Canopus and its Royal Area.

Those who study the lives of Cleopatra and Cæsar in conjunction cannot fail to ask themselves how far the Queen influenced the Dictator's thoughts at this time. During these last years of his life—the years which mark his greatness and give him his unique place in history—Cleopatra was living in the closest intimacy with him; and, so far as we know, there was not another man or woman in the world who had such ample opportunities for playing an influential part in his career. If Cleopatra was interested, as we know she was, in the welfare of her country and her royal house, or in the career of herself and Cæsar, or in the destiny of their son, it is palpably impossible to suppose that she did not discuss matters of statecraft with the man who was, in all but name, her husband. At a future date Cleopatra was strong enough to play one of the big political *rôles* in history, dealing with kingdoms and armies as the ordinary woman deals with a house and servants; and in the light of the knowledge of her character as it is unfolded to us in the years after the Dictator's death, it is not reasonable to suppose that in Rome she kept aloof from all his schemes and plans, deeming herself capable of holding the attention of the master of the world's activities by the entertainments of the boudoir and the arts of the bedchamber. Her individuality does not dominate the last years of the Roman Republic, merely because of the profligacy of her life with Antony and the tragedy of their death, but because her personality was so irresistible that it influenced in no small degree the affairs of the world. I am of opinion that Cleopatra's name would have been stamped upon the history of this period even though the events which culminated at Actium had never occurred. The romantic tragedy of her connection with Antony has captured the popular taste, and has diverted the attention of historians from the facts of her earlier years. There is a tendency completely to overlook the influence which she exercised in the politics of Rome during the last years of Cæsar's life.[1] The eyes of historians are concentrated upon the Alexandrian drama, and the tale of Cleopatra's life in the Dictator's villa is overlooked. Yet who will be so bold as to state that a Queen, whose fortunes were linked by Cæsar with his own at the height of his power, left no mark upon the events of that time? When Cleopatra came to Rome her outlook upon life must have been in striking contrast to that of the Romans. The republic was still the accepted form of government, and as yet there was no definite movement towards monarchism. The hereditary emperors of the future were hardly dreamed of, and the kings of the far past were nigh forgotten. Now, although it may be supposed that Cleopatra, by contact with the world, had adopted a moderately rational view of her status, yet there can be no doubt that the sense of her royal

---

[1] Ferrero writes : "The Queen of Egypt plays a strange and significant part in the tragedy of the Roman Republic. . . . She desired to become Cæsar's wife, and she hoped to awaken in him the passion for kingship." But this is a passing comment.

and divine personality was far from dormant in her. Her education and upbringing, as I have already said, and now the adulation of Cæsar, must have influenced her mind, so that the knowledge of her royalty was at all times almost her predominant characteristic; and it would be strange indeed if the Dictator's thoughts had been proof against the insinuating influence of this atmosphere in which he chose to spend a great portion of his time. Did Rome herself supply Cæsar's stimulus, Rome which had not known monarchy for four hundred and fifty years? But admitting that Rome was ripe for monarchy, and that circumstances to some extent forced Cæsar towards that form of government, can we declare that the Dictator would, of his own accord, have embraced sovereignty and even divinity so rapidly had his consort not been a Queen and a goddess?

During the last months of his life—namely, from his return to Rome in the early summer after the Spanish campaign to his assassination in the following March—Cæsar vigorously pressed forward his schemes in regard to the monarchy. Originally, it would seem, he had intended to complete his eastern conquests before making any attempt to obtain the throne; but now the long delay in his preparations for the Parthian campaign had produced a feeling of impatience which could no longer be controlled. Moreover, his attention had been called to an old prophecy which stated that the Parthians would not be conquered until a *King* of Rome made war upon them; and Cæsar was sufficiently acute, if not sufficiently superstitious, to be influenced to an appreciable extent by such a declaration. Little by little, therefore, he assumed the prerogatives of kingship, daily adding to the royal character of his appearance, and daily assuming more autocratic and monarchical powers.

It was not long before he caused himself to be given the hereditary title of Imperator, a word which meant at that time "Commander-in-chief," and had no royal significance, though the fact that it was made hereditary gave it a new significance. It is to be observed that the persons who framed the decree must have realised that the son to whom the title would descend would probably be that baby Cæsar who now ruled the nurseries of the villa beside the Tiber; for there can be little doubt that the Dictator's legitimate marriage to Cleopatra at the first opportune moment was confidently expected by his supporters; and we are thus presented with the novel spectacle of enthusiastic Roman statesmen offering the hereditary office of Imperator to the future King of Egypt. There can surely be no clearer indication than this that the people of Rome took no exception to Cleopatra's foreign blood,[1] nor thought of her in any way as an Oriental. The attitude of the majority of modern historians suggests that they picture the Dictator at this time as living with some sort of African woman whom he had brought back with him from Egypt; but I must repeat that I am convinced that in actual fact the Romans regarded Cleopatra as a royal Greek lady whose capital city of Alexandria was the rival of the Eternal City in wealth, magnificence, and culture, bearing to Rome, to some extent, the relationship which New York bears to

---

[1] No Englishman is troubled by the knowledge that the mother of his king is a Dane, and no Spaniard is worried by the thought that his sovereign has married an Englishwoman. The kinship between Roman and Greek was as close as these.

London. It was rumoured at this time that a law was about to be introduced by one of the tribunes of the people which would enable Cæsar, if necessary, to have two wives — Calpurnia and Cleopatra — and that the new wife need not be a Roman. The people could have felt no misgivings at the thought of Cleopatra's son being Cæsar's heir; for already they knew well enough that Cæsar was to be King of Rome, and by his marriage with Cleopatra they realised that he was adding to Rome's dominions without force of arms the one great kingdom of the civilised world which was still independent, and was securing for his heirs upon the Roman throne the honourable appendage of the oldest crown in existence, and the vast fortune which went with it. In later years, when Cleopatra as the consort of Antony had become a public enemy, there was much talk of an East-Mediterranean peril, and the Queen came to represent Oriental splendour as opposed to Occidental simplicity; but at the time with which we are now dealing this attitude was entirely undeveloped, and Cleopatra was regarded as the most suitable mother for that son of Cæsar who should one day inherit his honours and his titles.

At about this date the baby actually became uncrowned King of Egypt, for Cleopatra's young brother, Ptolemy XV., mysteriously passes from the records of history, and is heard of no more. Whether Cleopatra and Cæsar caused him to be murdered as standing in the way of their ambitions, or whether he died a natural death, will now never be known. He comes into the story of these eventful days like a shadow, and like a shadow he disappears; and all that we know concerning his end is

JULIUS CÆSAR.

derived from Josephus,[1] who states that he was poisoned by his sister. Such an accusation, however, is only to be expected, and would certainly have been made had the boy died of a sudden illness. It is therefore not just to Cleopatra to burden her memory with the crime; and all that one may now say is that, while the death of the unfortunate young King may be attributed to Cleopatra without improbability, there is really no reason to suppose that she had anything to do with it.

Cæsar now caused a statue of himself to be erected in the Capitol as the eighth royal figure there, the previous seven being those of the old Kings of Rome. Soon he began to appear in public clad in the embroidered dress of the ancient monarchs of Alba; and he caused his head to appear in true monarchical manner upon the Roman coins. A throne of gold was provided for him to sit upon in his official capacity in the Senate and on his tribunal; and in his hand he now carried a sceptre of ivory, while upon his head was a chaplet of gold in the form of a laurel-wreath. A consecrated chariot, like the sacred chariot of the Kings of Egypt, was provided for his conveyance at public ceremonies, and a kind of royal bodyguard of senators and nobles was offered to him. He was given the right, moreover, of being buried inside

---

[1] Porphyry, writing several generations later, states that he died by Cleopatra's treachery; but he is evidently simply quoting Josephus. Porphyry says that he died in the eighth year of Cleopatra's reign and the fourth year of his own reign. This is confirmed by an inscription which I observed in Prof. Petrie's collection and published in 'Receuil de Traveaux.' This records an event which took place "In the ninth year of the reign of Cleopatra . . . [a lacuna] . . . Cæsarion." The lacuna probably reads, ". . . and in the first (or second) year of the reign of . . ." This inscription shows that in the Queen's ninth year Cæsarion was already her consort, which confirms Porphyry's statement.

L

the city walls, just as Alexander the Great had been laid to rest within the Royal Area at Alexandria. These marks of kingship, when observed in conjunction with the hereditary title of Imperator which had been conferred upon him, and the lifelong Dictatorship which was about to be offered to him, are indications that the goal was now very near at hand; and both Cæsar and Cleopatra must have lived at the time in a state of continuous excitement and expectation. Everybody knew what was in the air, and Cicero went so far as to write a long letter to Cæsar urging him not to make himself King, but he was advised not to send it. The ex-Consul Lucius Aurelius Cotta inserted the thin edge of the wedge by proposing that Cæsar should be made King of the Roman dominions *outside* Italy; but the suggestion was not taken up with much enthusiasm. Cæsar himself seems to have been undecided as to whether he should postpone the great event until after the Parthian war or not, and the settlement of this question must have given rise to the most anxious discussions.

There was no longer need for the Dictator to hide his intentions with any great care; and as a preliminary measure he did not hesitate to proclaim to the public his belief in the divinity of his person. He caused his image to be carried in the *Pompa circenis* amongst those of the immortal gods. A temple dedicated to Jupiter-Julius was decreed, and a statue in his likeness was set up in the temple of Quirinus, inscribed with the words, "To the Immortal God." A college of priestly *Luperci*, of whom we shall presently learn more, was established in his honour; and *flamines* were created as priests of his godhead, an institution which reminds one of the manner in which the Pharaoh of Egypt was worshipped by a body of priests. A bed of state was provided for him within the chief temples of Rome. In the formulæ of the political oaths in which Jupiter and the Penates of the Roman people had been named, the *Genius* of Cæsar was now called upon, just as in Egypt the *Ka*, or genius, of the sovereign was invoked. " The old national faith," says Mommsen, " became the instrument of a Cæsarian papacy "; and indeed it may be said that it became the instrument actually of a supreme Cæsarian deification.

By the end of the year B.C. 45 and the beginning of B.C. 44 there was no longer any doubt in the minds of the Roman people that Cæsar intended presently to ascend the throne; and the only question asked was as to whether the event would take place before or after the Eastern campaign.   Some time before February 15th he was made Dictator for life; and this, regarded in conjunction with the homage now paid to his person, and the hereditary nature of his title of Imperator, made the margin between his present status and that of kingship exceedingly narrow.   It is probable that Cæsar was not determined to introduce the old title of " King," although he affected the dress and insignia of those who had been " kings " of Rome.   It is more likely that he was seeking some new monarchical title; and when, on one occasion, he declared " I am Cæsar, and no ' King,' " he may already have decided to elevate his personal name to the significance of the royal title which it ultimately became, and still in this twentieth century continues to be.[1]

His arrogance was daily becoming more pronounced, and his ambition was now " swell'd so much that it did

---

[1] Kaiser, Czar, &c.

almost stretch the sides o' the world."[1] He severely
rebuked Pontius Aquila, one of the Tribunes, for not
rising when he passed in front of the Tribunician seats;
and for some time afterwards he used to qualify any
declaration which he made in casual conversation by
the sneering words, "By Pontius Aquila's kind permission." Once, when a deputation of Senators came
to him to confer new honours upon him, he, on the
other hand, received them without rising from his seat;
and he was now wont to keep his closest friends waiting
in an anteroom for an audience, a fact of which Cicero
bitterly complains. When his authority was questioned
he invariably lost his temper, and would swear in the
most horrible manner. "Men ought to look upon what
I say as *law*," he is reported by Titus Ampius to have
said; and, indeed, there were very few persons who had
the hardihood not to do so. On a certain occasion it
was discovered that some enthusiast had placed a royal
diadem upon the head of one of his statues, and, very
correctly, the two Tribunes caused it to be removed.
This so infuriated Cæsar, who declared the official act
to be a deliberate insult, that he determined to punish
the two men at the first convenient opportunity. On
January 26th of the new year this opportunity presented
itself. As he was walking through the streets some
persons in the crowd hailed him as King, whereupon
these zealous officials ordered them to be arrested and
flung into prison. Cæsar at once raised an appalling
storm, the result of which was that the two Tribunes
were expelled from the Senate.

Cleopatra's attitude could not well fail to be influenced
by that of the Dictator; and it is probable that she gave

[1] Cymbeline.

some offence by an occasional haughtiness of manner. Her Egyptian chamberlains and court officials must also have annoyed the Romans by failing to disguise their Alexandrian vanity; and there can be little doubt that many of Cæsar's friends began to regard the menage at the transpontine villa with growing dislike. A letter written by Cicero to his friend Atticus is an interesting commentary upon the situation. It seems that the great writer had been favoured by Cleopatra with the promise of a gift suitable to his standing, probably in return for some service which he had rendered her. " I detest the Queen," he writes, "and the voucher for her promises, Hammonios, knows that I have good cause for saying so. What she promised, indeed, were all things of the learned sort and suitable to my character, such as I could avow even in a public meeting. As for Sara (pion),[1] besides finding him an unprincipled rascal, I also found him inclined to give himself airs towards me. I only saw him once at my house; and when I asked him politely what I could do for him, he said that he had come in hopes of seeing Atticus. The Queen's insolence, too, when she was living in Cæsar's trans-tiberine villa,[2] I cannot recall without a pang. So I will not have anything to do with that lot."

The ill-feeling towards Cæsar, which was very decidedly on the increase, is sufficient to account for the growing unpopularity of Cleopatra; but it is possible that it was somewhat accentuated by a slight jealousy which must have been felt by the Romans owing to the Dictator's partiality for things Egyptian. Not only did it appear

---

[1] Both Hammonios and Sarapion are common Egyptian names.

[2] This may mean that Cleopatra had gone to some other part of Rome either permanently or temporarily.

to Cæsar's friends that he was modelling his future
throne upon that of the Ptolemies and was asserting his
divinity in the Ptolemaic manner; not only had he
been thought to desire Alexandria as the capital of the
Empire; but also he was employing large numbers of
Egyptians in the execution of his schemes. Egyptian
astronomers had reformed the Roman calendar; the
Roman mint was being improved by Alexandrian
coiners; the whole of his financial arrangements, it
would seem, were entrusted to Alexandrians;[1] while
many of his public entertainments, as, for example, the
naval displays enacted at the inauguration of the Temple
of Venus, were conducted by Egyptians. Cæsar's object
in thus using Cleopatra's subjects must have been due,
to some extent, to his desire to familiarise his countrymen
with those industrious Alexandrians who were to play
so important a part in the construction of the new
Roman Empire.

The great schemes and projects which were now
placed before the Senate by Cæsar must have startled
that institution very considerably. Almost every day
some new proposal was formulated or some new law
drafted. At one time the diverting of the Tiber from
its course occupied the Dictator's attention; at another
time he was arranging to cut a canal through the
Isthmus of Corinth. Now he was planning the construction of a road over the Apennines; and now he
was deep in schemes for the creation of a vast port at
Ostia. Plans of great public buildings to be erected
at Alexandria or in Rome were being submitted to him;
or, again, he was arranging for the establishment of
public libraries in various parts of the capital. Mean-

---

[1] Suetonius : Cæsar, 76.

while the preparations for the Parthian war must have occupied the greater part of his time; for the campaign was to be of a vast character. So sure was he that it would last for three years or more that he framed a law by virtue of which the magistrates and public officials for the next three years should be appointed before his departure. He thereby insured the tranquillity of Rome during his prolonged absence in the east, thus leaving himself free to carry his arms into remote lands where communication with the capital might be almost impossible. When we recollect that Cæsar's recent campaigns had all been of but a few months or weeks duration, and that the words *veni, vidi, vici* now represented his mature belief in his own capabilities, these plans for a three years' absence from Rome seem to me to indicate clearly that he had no intention of confining himself to the conquest of Parthia, but desired to follow in Alexander's footsteps to India, and thence to return to Rome laden with the loot of that vast country. He must have pictured himself entering the capital at the end of the war as the conqueror of the East, and there could have been no doubt in his mind that the delighted populace would then accept with enthusiasm his claim to the throne of the world.

As the weeks went by Cæsar's plans in regard to the monarchy became more clearly defined. He does not now seem to have considered it very wise to press forward the assumption of the sovereignty previous to the Parthian war, since his long absence immediately following his elevation to the throne might prove prejudicial to the new office. Moreover, a strong feeling had developed against his contemplated assumption of royalty, and Cæsar must have been aware that he could not put his plans into execution without considerable opposition. Plutarch tells us that "his desire of being King had brought upon him the most apparent and mortal hatred, —a fact which proved the most plausible pretence to those who had been his secret enemies all along." Much adverse comment had been made with reference to his not rising to receive the Senatorial deputation; and indeed he felt it necessary to make excuses for his action, saying that his old illness was upon him at the time. A report was spread that he himself would have been willing to rise, but that Balbus had said to him, "Will you not remember you are Cæsar and claim the honour due to your merit?" and it was further related that when the Dictator had realised the offence he had given, he had bared his throat to his friends, and had told them that he was ready to lay down his life if the public were angry with him. Incidents such as this showed that the time was not yet wholly favourable for his *coup;* and reluctantly Cæsar was obliged to consider its postponement. On the other hand, there was something to be said in favour of immediate action, and he must have been more or less prepared to accept the kingship if it were urged upon him before he set out for the East. The position of Cleopatra, however, must have caused him some anxiety. Without her and their baby son the creation of an hereditary monarchy would be superfluous. His own wife Calpurnia did not seem able to furnish him with an heir, and there was certainly no other woman in Rome who could be expected to act the part of Queen with any degree of success, even if she were proficient in the production of sons and heirs. Yet how, on the instant, was he to rid himself of Calpurnia and marry Cleopatra without offending public taste? If he were to accept the kingship at once and make Cleopatra his wife, was she capable of sustaining with success the *rôle* of Queen of Rome in solitude for three years while he was away at the wars? Would it not be much wiser to send her back to Egypt for this period, there to await his return, and then to marry her and to ascend the throne at one and the same instant? During his absence in the East Calpurnia might conveniently meet with a sudden and fatal illness, and no man would dare to attribute her death to his and the apothecary's ingenuity.

The will which he now made, or confirmed, in view of his departure, shows clearly that his desire for the monarchy was incompatible with his present marital conditions. Without a Queen and a son and heir there could be little point in creating a throne, since already he had been made absolute autocrat for his lifetime; for unless the office was to be handed on without dispute to his son Cæsarion, there was no advantage in striving for an immediate elevation to the kingship. By his will, therefore, which was made in view of his possible death before he had ascended his future throne, he simply divided his property, giving part of it to the nation and part to his relations, his favourite nephew, Octavian, receiving a considerable share. A codicil was added, appointing a large number of guardians for any offspring which might possibly be born to him by Calpurnia after his departure; but so little interest did he take in this remote contingency that he seems to have made no financial provision for such an infant. There was no need to leave money to Cleopatra or to her child, since she herself was fabulously wealthy. This will was, no doubt, intended to be destroyed if he were raised to the throne before his departure, and it was afterwards believed that he actually wrote another testament in favour of Cæsarion, which was to be used if a crown were offered to him; but if, as now seemed probable, that event were postponed until his return, the dividing of his property would be the best settlement for his affairs should he die while away in the East. So long as he remained uncrowned there was no occasion to refer either to Cleopatra or to Cæsarion in his testamentary wishes; for if he died in Parthia or India, still as Dictator, his hopes of founding a dynasty, his plans for his marriage to the Queen of Egypt, his scheme for training up Cæsarion to follow in his footsteps, indeed all his worldly ambitions, would have to be bundled into oblivion. Cæsar was not a man who cared much for the interests of other people; and, in the case of Cleopatra, he was quite prepared to leave her to fight for herself in Egypt, were he himself to be removed to those celestial spheres wherein he would have no further use for her. His passion for her appears now to have cooled; and though he must still have enjoyed her society, and, to a considerable extent, must have been open to her influence, her chief attraction for him in these latter days lay in the recognition of her suitability to ascend the new throne by his side. She, on her part, no doubt retained much of her old affection for him; and, in spite of his increasing irritability and eccentricity, she seems to have offered him the generous devotion of a warm-hearted young woman for a great and heroic old man.

Cæsar, indeed, was old before his time. The famous portrait of him, now preserved in the Louvre, shows him to have been haggard and worn. He was still under sixty years of age, but all semblance of youth had gone from him, and the burden of his years and of his illness weighed heavily upon his spare frame. His indomitable spirit, and the keen enthusiasm of his nature, held him to his appointed tasks; but it is very doubtful whether his constitution could now have borne the hardships of the campaign which lay before him. His ill-health must have caused Cleopatra the gravest anxiety, for all her hopes were centred upon him, and upon that day when he should make her Queen of the Earth. The fact that he was now considering the postponement of the creation of the monarchy until after the Parthian war must have been a heavy blow to her, for there was good reason to fear lest his strength should give out ere his task could be completed. For three years and more she had worked with Cæsar at the laying of the foundations of their throne; and now, partly owing to the undesirability of leaving Rome for so long a period immediately after accepting the crown, partly owing to the difficulty in regard to Calpurnia, and partly owing to the hostility of a large number of prominent persons to the idea of monarchy, Cæsar was postponing for three years that *coup* which seemed to her not only to mean the realisation of all her personal and dynastic ambitions, but actually to be the only means by which she could save Egypt from absorption into the Roman dominions or preserve a throne of any kind for her son. In the Second Philippic Cicero says of Cæsar that "after planning for many years his way to royal power, with great labour and with many dangers, he had effected his design. By public exhibitions, by monumental buildings, by bribes and by feasts, he had conciliated the unreflecting multitude. He had bound to

himself his own friends by favours, his opponents by a
show of clemency;" and yet, when in sight of his goal,
he hesitated, believing it better to wait to be carried
up to the throne by that wave of popular enthusiasm
which assuredly would burst over Rome when he should
lead back from the East his triumphant, loot-laden
legionaries, and should exhibit in golden chains in the
streets of the capital the captive kings of the fabulous
Orient. The delay must have been almost intolerable
to Cleopatra; and it may have been due to some arrangement made by her with the Dictator and Antony,
who now must have been a constant visitor at Cæsar's
villa, that an event took place which brought to a
head the question of the date of the establishment of
the monarchy.

On February 15th the annual festival of the Lupercalia
was celebrated in Rome; and upon this day all the populace, patrician and plebeian, were *en fête*. The Romans of
Cæsar's time do not seem to have known what was the
origin of this festival, nor what was the real significance
of the rites therein performed. They understood that
upon this day they paid their respects to the god
Lupercus; and, in a vague manner, they identified this
obscure deity with Faunus, or with Pan, in his capacity
as a producer of fertility and fecundity in all nature.
Two young men were selected from the honourable order
known as the College of the Luperci, and upon this day
these two men opened the proceedings by sacrificing a
goat and a dog. They were then "blooded," and the
ritual prescribed that as soon as this was done they
should both laugh. They next cut the skins of the
victims into long strips or thongs, known as *februa;*
and, using these as whips, they proceeded to run around

the city, striking at every woman with whom they came into contact. A thwack from the *februa* was believed to produce fertility, and any woman who desired to become a mother would expose herself to the blows which the two men were vigorously delivering on all sides. By reason of this strange old custom the day was known as the *Dies februatus*;[1] and from this is derived the name of the month of February in which the festival took place.

It seems to me certain that this ceremony was originally related to the Egyptian rites in connection with the god of fecundity, Min-Amon, the Pan of the Nile Valley. This god is usually represented holding in his hand a whip, perhaps consisting originally of jackal-skins tied to a stick;[2] and it has lately been proved that the hieroglyph for the Egyptian word indicating the reproduction of species[3] is composed simply of these three jackal-skins tied together, that is to say the *februa*. We know practically nothing of the ceremonies performed in Egypt in regard to the *februa*, but there is no reason to doubt that the rites were fundamentally similar to those of the Roman Lupercalia. The dog which was sacrificed in Rome had probably taken the place of the Egyptian jackal; and the goat is perhaps to be connected with the Egyptian ram which was sacred to Amon or Min-Amon.

Now it is very possible that in Alexandria Cleopatra and also Cæsar had become well acquainted with the Egyptian equivalent of the Roman Lupercalia, and it may be suggested, tentatively, that since Cæsar was regarded

[1] The action *februare* means "to purify," here used probably to signify the magical expurgation of the person struck and the banishing of the evil influences which prevented fertility.

[2] Compare also the whip carried by a Sixth Dynasty noble named Ipe, Cairo Museum, No. 61, which seems more than a simple fly-flap.

[3] The Egyptian word is *mes*.

in that country as the god Amon who had given fertility
to the Queen, he may, in Egypt, have been identified in
some sort of manner with these rites. One may certainly
imagine Cleopatra pointing out to Cæsar the similarity
between the two ceremonies, and suggesting to him that
he was, or had acted in the manner of, a kind of
Lupercus. He had practically identified Cleopatra with
Venus Genetrix, the goddess of fertility ; and he may
well have attributed to himself the faculties of that
corresponding god who carried on in Rome the traditions of the Egyptian Min, to whom already Cæsar had
been so closely allied by the priests of the Nile. The
Dictator certainly took great interest in the festival of
the Lupercalia in Rome, for he reorganised the proceedings, and actually founded an order known as the
Luperci Julii, a fact which could be regarded as indicating
a definite identification of himself with Lupercus. Indeed, if he was identified with Min-Amon in Egypt, and
if, as I have suggested, Min-Amon is originally connected
with the Lupercalia celebrations, it may be supposed that
Cæsar really assumed by right the position of divine head
of this order. Knowing the Dictator to have been so
careful an opportunist, one is almost tempted to suggest
that he found in this identification an excuse and a
justification for his behaviour to the many women to
whom he had lost his heart ; or perhaps it were better to
say that his unscrupulous attitude towards the opposite
sex, and the successful manner in which, as with
Cleopatra, he had succeeded in reproducing his kind,
appeared to fit him constitutionally for this particular
godhead.

Whether or no Cæsar, in the intolerable arrogance of
his last years, was now actually naming himself the

fruitful Lupercus in Rome as he was the fecund Amon in Egypt, it is a fact that upon this occurrence of the festival in the year B.C. 44 he was presiding over the ceremonies, while his lieutenant Antony was enacting the part of one of the two holders of the *februa*. On this day Cæsar, pale and emaciated, was seated in the Forum upon a golden throne, dressed in a splendid robe, in order to witness the celebrations, when suddenly the burly Antony, hot from his run, bounded into view, striking to right and left with the *februa*, and indulging, no doubt, in the horse-play which he always so much enjoyed. An excited and boisterous crowd followed him, and it is probable that both he and his companions thereupon did homage to the majestic figure of the Dictator, hailing him as Lupercus and king of the festivities. Profiting by the enthusiasm of the moment, and acting according to arrangements previously made with Cleopatra or with Cæsar himself, Antony now stepped forward and held out to the Dictator a royal diadem wreathed with laurels, at the same time offering him the kingship of Rome. Cæsar, as we have seen, had already been publicly hailed as a god upon earth, and now Antony seems to have addressed him in his Lupercalian character, begging him to accept this terrestrial throne as already he had received the throne of the heavens. No sooner had he spoken than a shout of approval was raised by a number of Cæsarians who had been posted in different parts of the Forum for this purpose; but, to Cæsar's dismay, the cheers were not taken up by the crowd, who, indeed, appear to have indulged in a little quiet booing; and the Dictator was thus obliged to refuse the proffered crown with a somewhat half-hearted show of disdain.

This action was received with general applause, and the temper of the crowd was clearly demonstrated. Again Antony held the diadem towards him, and again the isolated and very artificial cheers of his supporters were heard. Thereupon Cæsar, accepting the situation with as good a grace as possible, definitely refused to receive it; and at this the applause once more broke forth. He then gave orders that the diadem should be carried into the Capitol, and that a note should be inscribed in the official calendar stating that on this day the people had offered him the crown and that he had refused it. It seems probable that Antony, appreciating the false step which had been made, now rounded off the incident in as merry a manner as possible, beginning once more to strike about him with his magical whip, and leading the crowd out of the Forum with the same noise and horseplay with which they had entered it.

The chances now in regard to the immediate assumption of the kingship became more remote. Cæsar intended to set out for Parthia in about a month's time; and it must have been apparent to him that his hopes of a throne would probably have to be set aside until the coming war was at an end. In regard to Cleopatra nothing remained for him to do, therefore, but to bid her prepare to return to Egypt, there to await until the Orient was conquered; and during the next few weeks it seems that the disappointed and troubled Queen engaged herself in making preparation for her departure. Suetonius tells us that Cæsar loaded her with presents and honours in these last days of their companionship; and doubtless he encouraged her as best he could with the recitation of his great hopes and ambitions for the future. There was still a chance that the monarchy

would be created before the war, for there was some
talk that Antony and his friends would offer the crown
once more to Cæsar upon the Calends of March;[1] but
Cleopatra could not have dared to hope too eagerly for
this event in view of the failure at the Lupercalia. To
the Queen, who had expected by this time to be seated
upon the Roman throne, his reassuring words can have
been poor comfort; and an atmosphere of gloomy foreboding must have settled upon her as she directed the
packing of her goods and chattels and prepared herself
and her baby for the long journey across the Mediterranean to her now uneventful kingdom of Egypt.

[1] Plutarch : Brutus.

M

CHAPTER X.

THE DEATH OF CÆSAR AND THE RETURN OF CLEOPATRA TO EGYPT.

THERE can be little reason for doubt that Antony, who is to play so important a part in the subsequent pages of this history, saw Cleopatra in Rome on several occasions. After his reconciliation to Cæsar in the early summer of B.C. 45, he must have been a constant visitor at the Dictator's villa; and, as we shall presently see, his espousal of Cleopatra's cause in regard to Cæsar's will suggests that her charm had not been overlooked by him. It is said, as we have seen, that he had met her, and had already been attracted by her, ten years previously, when he entered Alexandria with Gabinius in order to establish her father Auletes upon his rickety throne. He was a man of impulsive and changeable character, and it is difficult to determine his exact attitude towards Cæsar at this time. While the Dictator was in Egypt Antony had been placed in charge of his affairs in Rome, but owing to a quarrel between the two men, Cæsar, on his return from Alexandria, had dismissed him from his service. Very naturally Antony had felt considerable animosity to the Dictator on this account, and it was even rumoured, as has been said, that he desired to assassinate him. After the Spanish war, however, the quarrel was forgotten; and, as we have just seen, it was Antony who had offered him the crown at the festival of the Lupercalia. In spite of this, Cæsar does not seem to have trusted him fully, although he now appears to have been recognised as the most ardent supporter of the Cæsarian party.

Cæsar had never excelled as a judge of men. Although unquestionably a genius and a man of supreme mental powers, the Dictator was ever open to flattery; and he collected around him a number of satellites who had won their way into his favour by blandishments and by countenance of their master's many eccentricities. Balbus and Oppius, Cæsar's two most intimate attendants, were men of mediocre standing; and Publius Cornelius Dolabella, who now comes into some prominence, was a young adventurer, whose desire for personal gain must have been concealed with difficulty. This personage, although only five-and-twenty years of age, had been appointed by Cæsar to the consulship which would become vacant upon his own departure for the East, a move that must have given grave offence to Antony; for Dolabella, a few years previously, had fallen in love with Antony's wife, Antonia, who had consequently been divorced, the outraged husband thereafter finding consolation in the marriage to his present wife Fulvia. The various favours conferred by Cæsar on this young scamp must therefore have caused considerable irritation to Antony; and it is not easy to suppose that the latter's apparent devotion to the cause of the Dictator was altogether genuine. Indeed, the rumour once more passed into circulation that Antony nursed designs upon Cæsar's life, this time, strange to say, in conjunction with Dolabella. On hearing this report the

Dictator remarked that he "did not fear such fat, luxurious men as these two, but rather the pale, lean fellows."

Of the latter type was Cassius, a sour, fanatical soldier and politician, who had fought against Cæsar at Pharsalia, and had been freely pardoned by him afterwards. From early youth Cassius entertained a particular hatred of any form of autocracy; and it is related of him that when at school the boy Faustus, the son of the famous Sulla, had boasted of his father's autocratic powers, Cassius had promptly punched his head. Cæsar's attempts to obtain the throne excited this man's ferocity, and he was probably the originator of the plot which terminated the Dictator's life. The plot was hatched in February B.C. 44, and, when Cassius and his friends had prevailed upon the influential and studious Marcus Brutus to join them, it rapidly developed into a widespread conspiracy. "I don't like Cassius," Cæsar was once heard to remark; "he looks so pale. What can he be aiming at?"

For Brutus, however, the Dictator entertained the greatest affection and esteem, and there was a time when he regarded him as his probable successor in office. One cannot view without distress, even after the passage of so many centuries, the devotion of the irritable old autocrat to this scholarly and promising young man who was now plotting against him; for, in spite of his manifold faults, Cæsar ever remains a character which all men esteem and with which all must largely sympathise. On one occasion somebody warned him that Brutus was plotting against him, to which the Dictator replied, "What, do you think Brutus will not wait out the appointed time of this little body of mine?" It is

probable that Cæsar thought it not at all unlikely that
Brutus was his own son, for his mother, Servilia, as
early as the year of his birth, and for long afterwards,
had been on such terms of intimacy with Cæsar as
would justify this belief.   Brutus, on the other hand,
thought himself to be the son of Servilia's legal husband,
and through him claimed descent from the famous Junius
Brutus who had expelled the Tarquins.   Servilia was the
sister of Cato, whose suicide had followed his defeat by
Cæsar in North Africa, and Porcia, the wife of Brutus,
was Cato's daughter.   It might have been supposed,
therefore, that Brutus would have felt considerable
antipathy towards the Dictator, more especially after
the publication of his venomous Anti - Cato.   There
was, however, equally reasonable cause for Brutus to
have sympathised with Cæsar, for his supposed father
had been put to death by Pompey, an execution which
Cæsar had, as it were, been instrumental in avenging.
As a matter of fact, Brutus was a young man who lived
upon high principles, as a cow does upon grass; and
such family incidents as the seduction of his mother, or
the destruction of his mother's brother and his wife's
father, or the bloodthirsty warfare between his father's
executioner and his father-in-law's enemy and calumniator,
were not permitted to influence his righteous brain.   In
his early years he had, very naturally, refused on principle
to speak to Pompey, but when the civil war broke out
he set aside all those petty feelings of dislike which, in
memory of his legal father, he had entertained towards
the Pompeian faction, and, on principle, he ranged
himself upon that side in the conflict, believing it to
be the juster cause.   Pompey is said to have been so
surprised at the arrival of this good young man in his

camp, whither nobody had asked him to come, and where nobody particularly desired his presence, that he stood up and embraced him as though he were a lost lamb come back to the fold.   Then followed the battle of Pharsalia, and Brutus had been obliged to fly for his life.   He need not, however, have feared for his safety, for Cæsar had given the strictest orders that nobody was to hurt him either in the battle or in the subsequent chase of the fugitives.   From Larissa, whither he had fled, he wrote, on principle, to Cæsar, stating that he was prepared to surrender; and the Dictator, in memory, it is said, of many a pleasant hour with Servilia, at once pardoned him and heaped honours upon him.   Brutus, then, on principle, laid information against Pompey, telling Cæsar whither he had fled; and thus it came about that the Dictator arrived in Egypt on that October morning of which we have read.

Brutus was an intellectual young man, whose writings and orations were filled with maxims and pithy axioms. He had, however, a certain vivacity and fire; and once when Cæsar had listened, a trifle bewildered, to one of his vigorous speeches, the Dictator was heard to remark, "I don't know what this young man means, but, whatever he means, he means it vehemently."   He believed himself to be, and indeed was, very firm and just, and he had schooled himself to resist flattery, ignoring all requests made to him by such means.   He was wont to declare that a man who, in mature years, could not say "no" to his friends, must have been very badly behaved in the flower of his youth.   Cassius, who was the brother-in-law of Brutus, deemed it very advisable to introduce this exemplary young man into the conspiracy, and he therefore invited him, as a preliminary

measure, to be present in the Senate on the Calends of
March, when it was rumoured that Cæsar would be
made king. Brutus replied that he would most certainly
absent himself on that day. Nothing daunted, Cassius
asked him what he would do supposing Cæsar insisted
on his being present. "In that case," said Brutus, in
the most approved style, "it will be my business not to
keep silent, but to stand up boldly, and die for the liberty
of my country." Such being his views, it was apparent
that there would be no difficulty in persuading him, on
principle, to assist in the murder of Cæsar, who had, it
is true, spared his life in Pharsalia, but who was, nevertheless, an enemy of the People. The conspirators,
therefore, dropped pieces of paper on the official chair
whereon he sat, inscribed with such words as "Wake
up, Brutus," or "You are not a true Brutus"; and on
the statue of Junius Brutus they scribbled sentences,
such as "O that we had a Brutus now!" or "O that
Brutus were alive!" In this way the young man's feelings were played upon, and, after a few days of solemn
thought, he came to the conclusion that it was his
painful duty, on principle, to bring Cæsar's life to a
close.

By March 1st the conspirators numbered in their
ranks some sixty or eighty senators, mostly friends of
the Dictator, and had Cæsar attempted then to proclaim
himself king he would at once have been assassinated.
There were too many rumours current of plots against
him, however, to permit him to take this step, and so
the days passed in uneventfulness. He had planned to
leave Rome for the East on March 17th, and it was
thought possible that his last visit to the Senate on
March 15th, or his departure from the capital, would

be the occasion of a demonstration in his favour which would lead to his being offered the crown as a parting gift. The conspirators therefore decided to make an end of Cæsar on March 15th, the Ides of March, upon which date he would probably come for the last time to the Senate as Dictator.

Brutus, of course, was terribly troubled as the day drew near. He was at heart a good and honourable man, but the weakness of his character, combined with his intense desire to act in a high-principled manner, led him often to appear to be a turncoat. Actually his motives were patriotic and noble, but he must have asked himself many a time whether what he believed to be his duty to his country was to be regarded as entirely abrogating what he *knew* to be his duty to his devoted patron. The tumult in his mind caused him at night to toss and turn in his sleep in a fever of unrest, and his wife, Porcia, observing his distress, implored him to confide his troubles to her. Brutus thereupon told her of the conspiracy, and thereby risked the necks of all his comrades.

A curious gloom seems to have fallen upon Rome at this time, and an atmosphere of foreboding, due perhaps to rumours that a plot was afoot, descended upon the actors in this unforgettable drama. Cæsar went about his preparations for the Oriental campaign in his usual business-like manner, and raised money for the war with his wonted unscrupulousness and acuteness; but it does not require any pressure upon the historical imagination to observe the depression which he now felt and which must have been shared by his associates. The majority of the conspirators were his friends and fellow-workers —men, many of them, whom he had pardoned for past offences during the Civil War and had raised to positions of trust in his administration.   At this time he appears to have been living with Calpurnia in his city residence, and so busy was he with his arrangements that he could not have found time to pay many visits to Cleopatra.[1] The Queen must therefore have remained in a state of distressing suspense.   The Calends of March, at which date the proclamation of the monarchy had been expected, had passed; and now the Dictator could have held out to her but one last hope of the realisation of their joint ambition previous to his departure.   Cæsar must have told her that, as far as the three-year-old Cæsarion was concerned, she could expect nothing until the throne had been created; for, obviously, this was no time in which to leave a baby as his heir.   His nephew Octavian, an active and energetic young man, would have to succeed him in office if he were to die before he had obtained the crown, and his vast property would have to be distributed.   The Dictator must have remembered the fact of the murder of the young son of Alexander the Great soon after his father's death, and he could have had no desire that his own boy should be slaughtered in like manner by his rapacious guardians.   Yet Cleopatra still delayed her departure, in the hope that the great event would take place on March 15th, so that at any rate she might return to Egypt in the knowledge that her position as Cæsar's wife was secured.

The prevailing depression acted strangely upon people's nerves, and stories began to spread of ominous premonitions of trouble, and menacing signs and wonders.   There

---

[1] According to Suetonius, the Queen had now been sent back to Egypt, but a letter from Cicero, written in the following month, shows that she was in Rome until then.

were unaccountable lights in the heavens, and awful
noises at dead of night.   Somebody said that he had
seen a number of phantoms, in the guise of men, fighting with one another, and that they were all aglow as
though they were red-hot; and upon another occasion
it was noticed that numerous strange birds of ill omen
had alighted in the Forum.   Once, when Cæsar was
sacrificing, the heart of the victim was found to be
missing, an omen of the worst significance; and at
other times the daily auguries were observed to be
extremely inauspicious.   An old soothsayer, who may
have got wind of the plot, warned the Dictator to
beware of the Ides of March; but Cæsar, whose
courage was always phenomenal, did not allow the
prediction to alter his movements.

Upon the evening of March 14th, the day before the
dreaded Ides, Cæsar supped with his friend Marcus
Lepidus, and as he was signing some letters which had
been brought to him for approval the conversation happened to turn upon the subject of death, and the
question was asked as to what kind of ending was to
be preferred.   The Dictator, quickly looking up from
his papers, said decisively, "A sudden one!" the significance of which remark was to be realised by his
friends a few hours later.   That night, Plutarch tells
us, as Cæsar lay upon his bed, suddenly, as though
by a tremendous gust of wind, all the doors and
windows of his house flew open, letting in the brilliant
light of the moon.   Calpurnia lay asleep by his side,
but he noticed that she was uttering inarticulate words
and was sobbing as though in the deepest distress;
and upon being awakened she said that she had thought
in her dreams that he was murdered.   Cæsar must have

realised that such a dream was probably due to her fears as to the truth of the soothsayer's prophecy; but, at the same time, her earnest request to him not to leave his house on the following day made a considerable impression upon him.

In the morning the conspirators collected in that part of the governmental buildings where the Senate was to meet that day. The place chosen was a pillared portico adjoining the theatre, having at the back a deep recess in which stood a statue of Pompey.[1] Some of the men were public officials whose business it was to act as magistrates and to hear cases which had been brought to them for judgment; and it is said that not one of them betrayed by his manner any nervousness or lack of interest in these public concerns. In the case of Brutus this was particularly noticeable; and it is related that upon one of the plaintiffs before him refusing to stand to his award and declaring that he would appeal to Cæsar, Brutus calmly remarked, "Cæsar does not hinder me, nor will he hinder me, from acting according to the laws."

This composure, however, began to desert them when it was found that the Dictator was delaying his departure from his house. The report spread that he had decided not to come to the Senate that day, and it was soon realised that this might be interpreted as meaning that he had discovered the plot. Their agitation was such that at length they sent a certain Decimus Brutus Albinus, a very trusted friend of the Dictator, to Cæsar's house to urge him to make haste. Decimus found him just preparing to postpone the meeting of the Senate, his feelings having been worked upon by

---

[1] The site is near the present Campo dei Fiori.

Calpurnia's fears, and also by the fact that he had received a report from the augurs stating that the sacrifices for the day had been inauspicious. In this dilemma Decimus made a statement to Cæsar, the truth of which is now not able to be ascertained. He told the Dictator that the Senate had decided unanimously to confer upon him that day the title of King of all the Roman Dominions outside Italy, and to authorise him to wear a royal diadem in any place on land or sea except in Italy.[1] He added that Cæsar should not give the Senate so fair a justification for saying that he had put a slight upon them by adjourning the meeting on so important an occasion owing to the bad dreams of a woman.

At this piece of news Cæsar must have been filled with triumphant excitement. The wished-for moment had come. At last he was to be made king, and the dominions to be delivered over to him were obviously but the first instalment of the vaster gift which assuredly he would receive in due course. The doubt and the gloom of the last few weeks in a moment were banished, for this day he would be monarch of an empire such as had never before been seen. What did it matter that in Rome itself he would be but Dictator? He would establish his royal capital elsewhere: in Alexandria, perhaps, or on the site of Troy. He would be able at once to marry Cleopatra and to incorporate her dominions with his own. Calpurnia might remain for the present the wife of the childless Dictator in Rome, and his nephew Octavian might be his official heir; but outside his fatherland, Queen Cleopatra should be his consort, and his own little son should be his heir and

[1] Plutarch : Cæsar.

successor. The incongruities of the situation would so
soon be felt that Rome would speedily acknowledge him
king in Italy as well as out of it. Probably he had
often discussed with Cleopatra the possibilities of this
solution of the problem, for the idea of making him
king outside Italy had been proposed some weeks previously;[1] and he must now have thought how amused
and delighted the Queen would be by this unexpected
decision of the Senate to adopt the rather absurd scheme.
As soon as he had married the Sovereign of Egypt and
had made Alexandria one of his capitals, his dominions
would indeed be an Egypto-Roman Empire; and when
at length Rome should invite him to reign also within
Italy, the situation would suggest rather that Egypt
had incorporated Rome than that Rome had absorbed
Egypt. How that would tickle Cleopatra, whose dynasty
had for so long feared extinction at the hands of the
Romans!

Rising to his feet, and taking Decimus by the hand,
Cæsar set out at once for the Senate, his forebodings
banished and his ambitious old brain full of confidence
and hope. On his way through the street two persons,
one a servant and the other a teacher of logic, made
attempts to acquaint him with his danger; and the
soothsayer who had urged him to beware of the Ides
of March once more repeated his warning. But Cæsar
was now in no mood to abandon the prospective excite-
ments of the day; and the risk of assassination may,
indeed, have been to him the very element which delighted him, for he was ever inspired by the presence
of danger.

Meanwhile the conspirators paced the Portico of

[1] Page 162.

Pompey in painful anxiety, fearing every moment to hear that the plot had been discovered. It must have been apparent to them that there were persons outside the conspiracy who knew of their designs; and when a certain Popilius Laena, a senator, not of their number, whispered to Brutus and Cassius that the secret was out, but that he wished them success, their feelings must have been hard to conceal. Then came news that Porcia had fallen into an hysterical frenzy caused by her suspense; and Brutus must have feared that in this condition she would reveal the plot.

At length, however, Cæsar was seen to be approaching; but their consequent relief was at once checked when it was observed that Popilius Laena, who had said that he knew all, entered into deep and earnest conversation with the Dictator. The conversation, however, proved to be of no consequence, and Cæsar presently walked on into the Curia where the Senate was to meet. A certain Trebonius was now set to detain Antony in conversation outside the doorway; for it had been decided that, although the latter was Cæsar's right-hand man, he should not be murdered, but that, after the assassination, he should be won over to the side of the so-called patriots by fair words.

When Cæsar entered the building the whole Senate rose to their feet in respectful salutation. The Dictator having taken his seat, one of the conspirators, named Tullius Cimber, approached him ostensibly with the purpose of petitioning him to pardon his exiled brother. The others at once gathered round, pressing so close upon him that Cæsar was obliged to order them to stand back. Then, perhaps suspecting their design, he sprang suddenly to his feet, whereupon Tullius caught hold of his toga and pulled it from him, thus leaving his spare frame covered only by a light tunic. Instantly a senator named Casca, whom the Dictator had just honoured with promotion, struck him in the shoulder with his dagger, whereupon Cæsar, grappling with him, cried out in a loud voice, "You villain, Casca! what are you doing?" A moment later, Casca's brother stabbed him in the side. Cassius, whose life Cæsar had spared after Pharsalia, struck him in the face; Bucolianus drove a knife between his shoulder-blades, and Decimus Brutus, who so recently had encouraged him to come to the Senate, wounded him in the groin. Cæsar fought for his life like a wild animal.[1] He struck out to right and left with his *stilus*, and, streaming with blood, managed to break his way through the circle of knives to the pedestal of the statue of his old enemy Pompey. He had just grasped Casca once more by the arm, when suddenly perceiving his beloved Marcus Brutus coming at him with dagger drawn, he gasped out, "You, too, Brutus—*my son!*" and fell, dying, upon the ground.[2] Instantly the pack of murderers was upon him, slashing and stabbing at his prostrate form, wounding one another in their excitement, and nigh tumbling over him where he lay in a pool of blood.

As soon as all signs of life had left the body, the conspirators turned to face the Senate; but, to their surprise, they found the members rushing madly from the building. Brutus had prepared a speech to make to them as soon as the murder should be accomplished; but in a few moments nobody was left in the Curia for him to address.

[1] Appian.
[2] Some authors state that he cried "Et tu, Brute"; others that the words "my son" were added; while yet others do not record any words at all.

He and his companions, therefore, were at a loss to know what to do; but at length they issued forth from the building, somewhat nervously brandishing their daggers and shouting catch-words about Liberty and the Republic. At their approach everybody fled to their homes; and Antony, fearing that he, too, would be murdered, disguised himself and hurried by side-streets to his house. They therefore took up their position in the Capitol, and there remained until a deputation of senators induced them to come down to the Forum. Here, standing in the rostra, Brutus addressed the crowd, who were fairly well-disposed towards him; but when another speaker, Cinna, made bitter accusations against the dead man, the people chased the conspirators back once more to the Capitol, where they spent the night.

When darkness had fallen and the tumult had subsided, Antony made his way to the Forum, whither, he had heard, the body of Cæsar had been carried; and here, in the light of the moon, he looked once more upon the face of his arrogant old master. Here, too, he met Calpurnia, and, apparently at her request, took charge of all the Dictator's documents and valuables.

Upon the next day, at Antony's suggestion, a general amnesty was proclaimed, and matters were amicably discussed. It was then decided that Cæsar's will should be opened, but the contents must have been a surprise to both parties. The dead man bequeathed to every Roman citizen 300 *sesterces*, giving also to the Roman people his vast estates and gardens on the other side of the Tiber, where Cleopatra was, at the time, residing. Three-quarters of the remainder of his estate was bequeathed to Octavian, and the other quarter was divided between his two nephews, Lucius Pinarius and

Quintus Pedius. In a codicil he added that Octavian should be his official heir ; and he named several guardians for his son, should one be born to him after his death.

The dead body lay in state in the Forum for some five days, while the ferment in the city continued to rage unabated. The funeral was at length fixed for March 20th,[1] and towards evening Antony went to the Forum, where he found the crowd wailing and lamenting around the corpse, the soldiers clashing their shields together, and the women uttering their plaintive cries. Antony at once began to sing a dirge-like hymn in praise of Cæsar ; pausing in his song every few moments to stretch his hands towards the corpse and to break into loud weeping. In these intervals the crowd took up the funeral chant, and gave vent to their emotional distress in the melancholy music customary at the obsequies of the dead, reciting monotonously a verse of Accius which ran, " I saved those who have given me death." Presently Antony held up on a spear's point the robes pierced by so many dagger-thrusts ; and standing beside this gruesome relic of the crime, he pronounced his famous funeral oration over the body of the murdered Dictator. When he had told the people of Cæsar's gifts to them, and had worked upon their feelings by exhibiting thus the blood-stained garments, the mob broke into a frenzy of rage against the conspirators, vowing vengeance upon one and all. Somebody recalled the speech made by Cinna on a previous day, and immediately howls were raised for that orator's blood. A minor poet, also called Cinna, happened to be standing in the crowd ; and when

---

[1] Ferrero has shown that March 19th was a day of *feriae publicae*, when the funeral could not take place. It could not well have been postponed later than the next day after this.

N

a friend of his had addressed him by that hated name, the people in the immediate vicinity thought that he must be the villain for whose life the mob was shouting. They therefore caught hold of the unfortunate man, and, without further inquiries, tore him limb from limb. They then seized benches, tables, and all available wood-work; and there, in the midst of the public and sacred buildings, they erected a huge pyre, upon the top of which they placed the Dictator's body, laid out upon a sheet of purple and gold. Torches were applied and speedily the flames arose, illuminating the savage faces of the crowd around the pyre, and casting grotesque shadows upon the gleaming walls and pillars of the adjoining buildings, while the volume of the smoke hid from view the moon now rising above the surrounding roofs and pediments. Soon the mutilated body disappeared from sight into the heart of the fire; and thereupon the spectators, plucking flaming brands from the blaze, dashed down the streets, with the purpose of burning the houses of the conspirators. The funeral pyre continued to smoulder all night long, and it must have been many hours before quiet was restored in the city. The passions of the mob were appeased next day by the general co-operation of all those concerned in public affairs, and the Senate passed what was known as an Act of Oblivion in regard to all that had occurred. Brutus, Cassius, and the chief conspirators, were assigned to positions of importance in the provinces far away from Rome; and the affairs of the capital were left, for the most part, in the hands of Antony. On March 18th, three days after Cæsar's death, Antony and Lepidus calmly invited Brutus and Cassius to a great dinner-party, and so, for the moment, peace was restored.

Meanwhile, Cleopatra's state of mind must have been appalling. Not only had she lost her dearest friend and former lover, but, with his death, she had lost the vast kingdom which he had promised her. No longer was she presumptive Queen of the Earth, but now, in a moment, she was once more simply sovereign of Egypt, seated upon an unfirm throne. Moreover, she must have fancied that her own life was in danger, as well as that of the little Cæsar. The contents of the Dictator's will must have been a further shock to her, although she probably already knew their tenor; and she must have thought with bitterness of the difference that even one day more might have made to her in this regard. It was perhaps true that the Senate had been about to offer him the throne of the provinces on the fatal Ides; and in that case Cæsar would most certainly have altered his will to meet the new situation, if indeed he had not already done so, as some say. There was reason to suppose that such a will, in favour of Cæsarion, had actually been made,[1] but if this were so, it was nowhere to be found, and had perhaps been destroyed by Calpurnia. What was she to do? When would Octavian appear to claim such property and honours as Cæsar had bequeathed to him? Should she at once proclaim her baby son as the rightful heir, or should she fly the country?

In this dilemma there seems to me to be no doubt that she must have consulted with Antony, the one man who had firmly grasped the tangled strings of the situation, and must have implored him to support the claims of her son. If the public would not admit that Cæsarion was Cæsar's son, then the boy would, with-

[1] Page 170.

out doubt, pass into insignificance, and ultimately be deprived, in all probability, even of his Egyptian throne. If, on the other hand, with Antony's support, he were officially recognised to be the Dictator's child, then there was a good chance that the somewhat unprepossessing Octavian might be pushed aside for ever. Cæsar had taken a fancy to this obscure nephew of his during the Spanish War. The young man, although still weak after a severe illness, had set out to join the Dictator in Spain with a promptitude which had won his admiration. He had suffered shipwreck, and had ultimately made his way to his uncle's camp by roads infested with the enemy, and thereafter had fought by his side. He was now following his studies in Apollonia, and intended to join Cæsar on his way to the East. If he could be prevented from coming to Rome the game would be in the Queen's hands; and I am of opinion that she must now have approached Antony with some such suggestion for the solution of the difficulty. Antony, on his part, probably realised that with the establishment of Octavian in Cæsar's seat his own power would vanish; but that, were he to support the baby Cæsarion, he himself would remain the all-powerful regent for many years to come. He might even take the dead man's place as Cleopatra's husband, and climb to the throne by means of the right of his stepson.[1]

It would seem, therefore, that he persuaded Cleopatra to remain for the present in Rome; and not long afterwards he declared in the Senate that the little Cæsarion had been acknowledged by Cæsar to be his rightful son. This was denied at once by Oppius, who favoured the

---

[1] Which, as will be seen, he ultimately attempted to do.

claims of Octavian, and ultimately this personage took the trouble to write a short book to refute Antony's statement.

The young Dolabella now seized the consulship in Rome, and, being on bad terms with Antony, at once showed his hostility to the friends of the late Dictator by various acts of violence against them. Cæsar, before his death, had assigned the province of Syria to Dolabella and that of Macedonia to Antony; but now the Senate, in order to rid Rome of the troublesome presence of the Dictator's murderers, had given Macedonia and Syria to Marcus Brutus and Cassius, and these two men were now collecting troops with which to enter their dominions in safety. There was thus a political reason for Antony and Dolabella to join forces; and presently we find the two of them working together for the overthrow of Brutus and Cassius.

Into these troubled scenes in Rome the news presently penetrated of the approach of the young Octavian, now nearly nineteen years of age, who was coming to claim his rights; and thereupon the city, setting aside the question of the conspirators, formed itself into two factions, the one supporting the newcomer, the other upholding Antony's attitude. It is usually stated by historians that Antony was fighting solely in his own interests, being desirous of ousting Octavian and assuming the dignities of Cæsar by force of arms. If this be so, why did he make a point of declaring in the Senate that Cæsarion was the Dictator's child? With what claims upon the public did he oppose those of Octavian if not by the supporting of Cæsar's son? We shall see that in after years he always claimed the Roman throne

on behalf of the child Cæsarion; and I find it difficult
to suppose that that attitude was not already assumed,
to some extent, by him.

There now began to be grave fears of the immediate
outbreak of civil war; and so threatening was the situation that Cleopatra was advised to leave Rome and to
return to Egypt with her son, there to await the outcome of the struggle. It is probable, indeed, that Antony
urged her to return to her own country in order to raise
troops and ships for his cause. Be this as it may, the
Queen left Rome a few days before April 15th, upon
which date Cicero wrote to Atticus, from Sinuessa, not
far from Rome, commenting on the news that she had
fled.

As she sailed over the Mediterranean back to Egypt
her mind must have been besieged by a hundred schemes
and plans for the future. The despair which she had
experienced, after the death of the Dictator, at the
demolition of all her vast hopes, may now have given
place to a spirited desire to begin the fight once more.
Cæsar was dead, but his great personality would live
again in his little son, whom Antony, she believed, would
champion, since in doing so he would further his own
ambitions. The legions left at Alexandria by the Dictator would, no doubt, stand by her; and she would
bring all the might and all the wealth of Egypt against
the power of Octavian. The coming warfare would be
waged by her for the creation of that throne for the
establishment of which Cæsar had indeed given his life;
and her arms would be directed against that form of
democratic government which the Dictator, perhaps at
her instance, had endeavoured to overthrow, but which
a man of Octavian's character, she supposed, would be

contented to support. Her mighty Cæsar would look down from his place amidst the stars to direct her, and to lead their son to the goal of their ambitions; for now he was in very truth a god amongst the gods. Recently during seven days a comet had been seen blazing in the sky, and all men had been convinced that this was the soul of the murdered Dictator rushing headlong to heaven. Even now a strange haze hung over the sun, as though the light of that celestial body were dimmed by the approach of the Divine Cæsar. Before the Queen left Rome she had heard the priests and public officials name him God in very truth; and maybe she had already seen his statues embellished by the star of divinity which was set upon his brow after his death. Surely now he would not desert her, his Queen and his fellow-divinity; nor would he suffer their royal son to pass into obscurity. From his exalted heights he would defend her with his thunderbolts, and come down to her aid upon the wings of the wind. Thus there was no cause for her to despair; and with that wonderful optimism which seems to have characterised her nature, she now set her active brain to thoughts of the future, turning her mature intellect to the duties which lay before her. When Cæsar had met her in Egypt she had been an irresponsible girl. Now she was a keen-brained woman, endowed with the fire and the pluck of her audacious dynasty, and prepared to fight her way with all their unscrupulous energy to the summit of her ambitions. And, moreover, now she held the trump card in her hands in the person of her little boy, who was by all natural laws the rightful heir to the throne of the earth.

PART II.

CLEOPATRA AND ANTONY

CHAPTER XI.

WHEN Antony and Octavian first met after the death
of Cæsar, the former was in possession of popular confidence; and he did not hesitate to advise Octavian to
make no attempt to claim his inheritance. He snubbed
the young man, telling him that he was mad to think
himself capable of assuming the responsibilities of the
Dictator's heir at so early an age; and as a result of
this attitude dissensions speedily broke out between
them. A reconciliation, however, was arrived at in the
following August, B.C. 44; but early in October there
was much talk in regard to a supposed attempt by
Octavian upon the life of Antony, and, as a result of
this, the inevitable quarrel once more broke out. Antony
now spread the story that his young rival had only been
adopted by Cæsar in consequence of their immoral relations, and he accused him of being a low-born adventurer.
Towards the end of the year Antony left Rome, and all
men believed that yet another civil war was about to
break out. He was now proclaiming himself the avenger
of the late Dictator, and I think it possible that he had
decided definitely to advance the claims of Cleopatra's
son, Cæsarion, against those of Octavian. After many

vicissitudes he was attacked and hunted as an enemy
of Rome, and the triumph of Octavian, thanks to the
assistance of Cicero, seemed to be assured; but, owing
to a series of surprising incidents, which we need not
here relate, a reconciliation was at last effected between
the combatants in October, B.C. 43. The two men, who
had not met for many months, regarded one another
with such extreme suspicion that when at length they
were obliged to exchange the embrace of friendship,
they are each said to have taken the opportunity of
feeling the other's person to ascertain that no sword
or dagger was concealed under the folds of the toga.

As soon as the reconciliation had been established,
Antony, Octavian, and a certain Lepidus formed a
Triumvirate, which was to have effect until December 31,
B.C. 38, it being agreed that Rome and Italy should be
governed jointly by the three, but that the provinces
should fall under distinctive controls, Antony and Lepidus
sharing the larger portion and Octavian receiving only
Africa, Numidia, and the islands. It was then decided
that they should each rid themselves of their enemies
by a general proscription and massacre. A list was
drawn up of one hundred senators and about two
thousand other rich and prominent men, and these were
hunted down and murdered in the most ruthless fashion,
amidst scenes of horror which can hardly have been
equalled in the world's history. Cicero was one of the
victims who suffered for his animosity to Antony, who
was now the leading Triumvir, and was in a position
to refuse to consider Octavian's plea for mercy for the
orator. The property of the proscribed persons was
seized, and upon these ill-gotten riches the three men
thrived and conducted their government.

Brutus and Cassius, the two leaders of the conspiracy which had caused Cæsar's death, had now come to blows with Antony and Octavian, and were collecting an army in Macedonia. Cassius, at one time, thought of invading Egypt in order to obtain possession of Cleopatra's money and ships; but the Queen, who was holding herself in readiness for all eventualities, was saved from this misfortune. She was, of course, the bitter enemy of Brutus and Cassius, the murderers of her beloved Cæsar; but, on the other hand, she could not well throw in her lot with the Triumvirate, since it included Octavian, who was the rival of her son Cæsarion in the heirship of the Dictator's estate. She must have been much troubled by the reconciliation between Octavian and Antony, for it seemed to show that she could no longer rely on the latter to act as her champion.

Presently Dolabella, who was now friendly to Antony and opposed to Brutus and Cassius, asked Cleopatra to send to his aid the legions left by the Dictator in Alexandria, and at about the same time a similar request came from Cassius. Cleopatra very naturally declined the latter, accepting Dolabella's request. Cassius, however, managed to obtain from Serapion, the Queen's viceroy in Cyprus, a number of Egyptian ships, which were handed over without her permission.[1] Dolabella was later defeated by Cassius, but the disaster did not seriously affect Cleopatra, for her legions had not managed to reach him in time to be destroyed. The Queen's next move was naturally hostile to her enemy

---

[1] See page 235, where I suggest that Serapion had possibly decided to throw in his lot with Arsinoe, who perhaps claimed the kingdom of Cyprus, and to assist the party of Brutus and Cassius against that of Antony which Cleopatra would probably support.

Cassius. She made an attempt to join Antony. This manœuvre, however, was undertaken half-heartedly, owing to her uncertainty as to his relations with Octavian, her son's rival; and when a serious storm had arisen, wrecking many of her ships and prostrating her with seasickness, she abandoned the attempt.

In October of B.C. 42 Antony defeated Brutus and Cassius at the battle of Philippi, Cassius being killed and Brutus committing suicide. Octavian, who was ill, took little part in the battle, and all the glory of the victory was given to Antony. The unpopularity of Octavian was clearly demonstrated after the fight was over, for the prisoners who were led before the two generals saluted Antony with respect, but cursed Octavian in the foulest language. It was decided that Antony should now travel through the East to collect money and to assert the authority of the Triumvirate, while Octavian should attempt to restore order in Italy, the African provinces being handed over to the insignificant Lepidus. The fact that Antony chose for his sphere of influence the eastern provinces, is a clear indication that Octavian was still in the background; for these rich lands constituted the main part of the Roman dominions. With a large army Antony passed on his triumphal way through Greece, and thence through Asia Minor; and at length, in the late summer of B.C. 41, he made his temporary headquarters at Tarsus.

From Tarsus Antony sent a certain officer named Dellius to Alexandria to invite Cleopatra to meet him in order to discuss the situation. It was suggested by Antony that she had given some assistance to the party of Brutus; but she, on the other hand, must have accused Antony of abandoning her by his league with Octavian.

She could not afford to quarrel with him, however, for he was now the most powerful man in the world; and she therefore determined to sail across to Tarsus at once.

She knew already the kind of man he was. She had seen him in Rome on many occasions, though no direct record is left of any such event, and she had probably made some sort of alliance with him; while she must constantly have heard of his faults and his virtues both from Julius Cæsar and from her Roman friends. The envoy Dellius, whom he had sent to her, had told her of his pacific intentions, and had described him as the gentlest and kindest of soldiers, while, as she well knew, a considerable part of the world called him a good fellow. He was at that time the most conspicuous figure on the face of the earth, and his nature and personality must have formed a subject of interested discussion in the palace at Alexandria as in every other court. Renan has called Antony a "colossal child, capable of conquering a world, incapable of resisting a pleasure"; and already this must have been the popular estimate of his character. The weight of his stature stood over the nations, dominating the incident of life; and, with a kind of boisterous divinity, his hand played alike with kings and common soldiers. To many men he was a good-natured giant, a personification of Bacchus, the Giver of Joy; but in the ruined lands upon which he had trampled he was named the Devourer, and the fear of him was almighty.

He was a man of remarkable appearance. Tall, and heavily built, his muscles developed like those of a gladiator, and his thick hair curling about his head, he reminded those who saw him of the statues and paintings of Hercules, from whom he claimed lineal descent. His forehead was broad, his nose aquiline, and his mouth and chin, though somewhat heavy, were strong and well formed. His expression was open and frank; and there was a suggestion of good-humour about his lips and eyes (as seen in the Vatican bust)[1] which must have been most engaging. His physical strength and his noble appearance evoked an unbounded admiration amongst his fellow-men, whilst to most women his masculine attraction was irresistible: a power of which he made ungoverned use. Cicero, who was his most bitter enemy, described him as a sort of butcher or prize-fighter, with his heavy jaw, powerful neck, and mighty flanks; but this, perhaps, is a natural, and certainly an easy, misinterpretation of features that may well have inspired envy.

His nature, in spite of many gross faults, was unusually lovable. He was adored by his soldiers, who, it is said, preferred his good opinion of them to their very lives. This devotion, says Plutarch, was due to many causes: to the nobility of his family, his eloquence, his frank and open manners, his liberal and magnificent habits, his familiarity in talking with everybody, and his kindness in visiting and pitying the sick and joining in all their pains. After a battle he would go from tent to tent to comfort the wounded, himself breaking into a very passion of grief at the sufferings of his men; and they, with radiant faces, would seize his hands and call him their emperor and their general. The simplicity of his character commanded affection; for, amidst the deep complexities and insincerities of human life, an open and intelligible nature is always most eagerly appreciated.

---

[1] Found at Tor Sapienza, outside the Porta Maggiore. The best gold and silver coins of Antony, issued by Cnæus Domitius Ahenobarbus, correspond with the bust in all essentials.

ANTONY.

The abysmal intellect of the genius gives delight to the highly cultured, but to the average man the child-like frankness of an Antony makes a greater appeal. Antony was not a genius: he was a gigantic commonplace. One sees in him an ordinary man in extraordinary circumstances, dominating success and towering above misfortune, until at the end he gives way unmeritoriously to the pressure of events.

The naturalness and ingenuousness of his character are surprisingly apparent in some of the anecdotes related by Plutarch. His wife, Fulvia, is described as a matron " not born for spinning or housewifery, nor one who could be content with ruling a private husband, but a woman prepared to govern a first magistrate or give orders to a commander-in-chief." To keep this strong-minded woman in a good-humour the guileless Antony was wont to play upon her all manner of boyish pranks; and it would seem that he took delight in bouncing out at her from dark corners of the house and the like. When Cæsar was returning from the war in Spain a rumour spread that he had been defeated and that the enemy were marching on Rome. Antony had gone out to meet his chief, and found in this rumour an opportunity for another practical joke at his stern wife's expense. He therefore disguised himself as a camp-follower and made his way back to his house, to which he obtained admittance by declaring that he had a terribly urgent letter from Antony to deliver into Fulvia's hands. He was shown into the presence of the agitated matron, and stood there before her, a muffled, mysterious figure, no doubt much like a Spanish brigand in a modern comic opera. Fulvia asked dramatically if aught had befallen her husband, but, without replying, the silent figure

o

thrust a letter at her; and then, as she was nervously opening it, he suddenly dashed aside the cloak, took her about the neck, and kissed her. After which he returned to Cæsar, and entered Rome in the utmost pomp, riding in the Dictator's chariot with all the solemnity befitting the occasion.

In later years he was constantly playing such tricks at Alexandria, and in the company of Cleopatra he was wont to wander about the city at night, disguised as a servant, and used to disturb and worry his friends by tapping at their doors and windows, for which, says Plutarch, he was often scurvily treated and even beaten, though most people guessed who he was. Antony remained a boy all his days; and it must have been largely this boisterous inconsequence during the most anxious periods that gave an air of Bacchic divinity to his personality. His friends must have thought that there was surely a touch of the divine in one who could romp through times of peril as he did.

He allowed little to stand in the way of his pleasures; and he played at empire-making as it were between meals. On a certain morning in Rome it was necessary for him to make an important public speech while he was yet suffering from the effects of immoderate drinking all night at the wedding of Hippias, a comedian, who was a particular friend of his. Standing unsteadily before the eager political audience, he was about to begin his address when he was overcome with nausea, and outraged nature was revenged upon him in the sight of all men. Incidents of this kind made him at times, as Cicero states, absolutely odious to the upper classes in Rome; but it is necessary to state that the above-mentioned accident occurred when he was still a young man, and that his excesses were not so crude in later years. During the greater part of his life his feasting and drinking were intemperate; but there is no reason to suppose that he was, except perhaps towards the end of his life, besotted to a chronic extent. One does not picture him imbibing continuously or secretly in the manner of an habitual drunkard; but at feasts and ceremonies he swallowed the wine with a will and drank with any man. When food and wine were short, as often happened during his campaigns, Antony became abstemious without effort. Once when Cicero had caused him and his legions to be driven out of Rome, he gave, in Plutarch's words, "a most wonderful example to his soldiers. He who had just quitted so much luxury and sumptuous living, made no difficulty now of drinking foul water and feeding on wild fruits and roots."

Antony was, of course, something of a barbarian, and his excesses often put one in mind of the habits of the Goths or Vikings. He drank hard, jested uproariously, was on occasion brutal, enjoyed the love of women, brawled like a schoolboy, and probably swore like a trooper. But with it all he retained until some two years before his death a very fair capacity for hard work, as is evidenced by the fact that he was Julius Cæsar's right-hand man, and afterwards absolute autocrat of the East. His nature was so forceful, and yet his character so built up of the magnified virtues and failings of mankind, that by his very resemblance to the ordinary soldier, his conformity to the type of the average citizen, he won an absolute ascendancy over the minds of normal men. It touched the vanity of every individual that a man, by the exercise of brains and faculties no greater than his own, was become lord

of half the world. It was no prodigious intellectual
genius who ruled the earth with incomprehensible
ability, but a burly, virile, simple, brave, vulgar man.
It was related with satisfaction that when Antony was
shown the little senate-house at Megara, which seems
to have been an ancient architectural gem of which the
cultured inhabitants were justly proud, he told them
that it was "not very large, but extremely *ruinous*"—
a remark which recalls the comment of the American
tourist in Oxford, that the buildings were very much
out of repair. A little honest Philistinism is a very
useful thing.

A touch of purple, too, as Stevenson has reminded
us, is not without its value. Antony was always something of an actor, and enjoyed a display in a manner
as theatrical as it was unforced. When he made his
public orations, he attempted to attract the eye of his
audience at the same time that he tickled their ears.
In his famous funeral oration after the death of Cæsar,
we have seen how he exhibited, at the psychological
moment, the gory clothes of the murdered Dictator,
showing to the crowd the holes made by the daggers
of the assassins and the stains of his blood. Desiring
to make a profound effect upon his harassed troops
during the retreat from Media, he clothed himself in a
dismal mourning habit, and was only with difficulty
persuaded by his officers to change it for the scarlet
cloak of a general. He enjoyed dressing himself to
suit the part of a Hercules, for which nature, indeed,
had already caused him to be cast; and in public as-
semblies he would often appear with "his tunic girt
low about his hips, a broadsword at his side, and over
all a large, coarse mantle," cutting, one may suppose,

a very fine figure. In cultured Athens he thought it was perhaps more fitting to present himself in a pacific guise, and we find him at the public games clad in the gown and white shoes of a steward, the wands of that gentle office carried before him. On this occasion, however, he introduced the herculean *rôle* to this extent, that he parted the combatants by seizing the scruff of their necks and holding them from one another at arm's length. In later life his love of display led him into strange habits; and, while he was often clothed in the guise of Bacchus, his garments for daily use were of the richest purple, and were clasped with enormous jewels.

The glamour of the stage always appealed to his nature, and he found, moreover, that the society of players and comedians held peculiar attractions for him. The actor Sergius was one of his best friends in Rome; and he was so proud of his acquaintance with an actress named Cytheris that he often invited her to accompany him upon some excursion, and assigned to her a litter not inferior to that of his own mother, which might have been extremely galling to the elder lady. On these journeys he would cause pavilions to be erected, and sumptuous repasts prepared under the trees beside the Tiber, his guests being served with priceless wines in golden cups. When he made his more public progress through the land a very circus-show accompanied him, and the populace were entertained by the spectacle of buffoons, musicians, and chariots drawn by lions. On these journeys Cytheris would often accompany him, as though to amuse him, and a number of dancing-girls and singers would form part of his retinue. At the night's halt, the billeting of these somewhat surprising young women in the houses of "serious fathers and mothers of families," as Plutarch puts it, caused much resentment, and suggested an attitude of mind in Antony which cannot altogether be attributed to a boyish desire to shock. There can be no doubt that he enjoyed upsetting decorum, and took kindly to those people whom others considered to be outcasts. Like Charles Lamb, he may have expressed a preference for "man as he ought *not* to be," which, to a controlled and limited extent, may be an admirable attitude. But it is more probable that actions such as that just recorded were merely thoughtless, and were not tempered by much consideration for the feelings of others until those outraged feelings were pointed out to him, whereupon, so Plutarch tells us, he could be frankly repentant.

He cared little for public opinion, and had no idea of the annoyance and distress caused by his actions. He was much in the hands of his courtiers and friends, and so long as all about him appeared to be happy and jolly, he found no reason for further inquiry. While in Asia he considered it needful to the good condition of his army to levy a tax upon the cities which had already paid their tribute to him, and orders were given to this effect, without the matter receiving much consideration by him. In fact, it would seem that the first tribute had slipped his memory. A certain Hybreas, therefore, complained to him in the name of the Asiatic cities, reminding him of the earlier tax. "If it has not been paid to you," he said, "ask your collectors for it; if it has, and is all gone, we are ruined men." Antony at once saw the sense of this, realised the suffering he was about to cause, and being, so it is said, touched to the

quick, promptly made other arrangements. Having a
very good opinion of himself, and being in a rough
sort of manner much flattered by his friends, he was
slow to see his own faults; but when he was of
opinion that he had been in the wrong, he became
profoundly repentant, and was never ashamed of asking the pardon of those he had injured. With boyish
extravagance he made reparation to them, lavishing
gifts upon them in such a manner that his generosity
on these occasions is said to have exceeded by far his
severity on others.

He was at all times generous, both to his friends and
to his enemies. He seems to have inherited this quality
from his father, who, from the brief reference to him in
Plutarch, appears to have been a kindly old man, somewhat afraid of his wife, and given to making presents to
his friends behind her back. Antony's "generous ways,"
says Plutarch, "his open and lavish hand in gifts and
favours to his friends and fellow-soldiers, did a great
deal for him in his first advance to power; and after
he had become great, long maintained his fortunes,
when a thousand follies were hastening their overthrow." So lavish were his presents to his friends and
his hospitality that he was always in debt, and even in
his early manhood he owed his creditors a huge fortune.
He had little idea of the value of money, and his extravagances were the talk of the world. On one occasion he ordered his steward to pay a certain large sum
of money to one of his needy friends, and the amount
so shocked that official that he counted it out in small
silver *decies*, which he caused to be piled into a heap
in a conspicuous place where it should catch the donor's
eye, and, by its size, cause him to change his mind. In

due course Antony came upon the heap of money, and
asked what was its purpose. The steward replied in a
significant tone that it was the amount which was to be
given to his friend. "Oh," said Antony, quite unmoved,
"I should have thought the *decies* would have been much
more. It is too little: let the amount be doubled."

He was as generous, moreover, in his dealings as in
his gifts. After his Alexandrian Triumph he did not put
to death the conquered Armenian King Artavasdes, who
had been led in golden chains through the streets, although such an execution was customary according to
Roman usage. Just previous to the battle of Actium,
the consul Domitius Ahenobarbus deserted and went
over to Octavian, leaving behind him all his goods and
chattels and his entire retinue. With a splendid nobility
Antony sent his baggage after him, not deigning to
enrich himself at the expense of his treacherous friend,
nor to revenge himself by maltreating any of those
whom the consul had left in such jeopardy. After the
battle of Philippi, Antony was eager to take his enemy,
Brutus, alive; but a certain officer named Lucilius heroically prevented this by pretending to be the defeated
general, and by giving himself up to Antony's soldiers.
The men brought their captive in triumph to Antony,
but as soon as he was come into his presence he explained that he was not Brutus, and that he had pretended to be so in order to save his master, and was
now prepared to pay with his life the penalty for his
deception. Thereupon Antony, addressing the angry
and excited crowd, said: "I see, comrades, that you
are upset, and take it ill that you have been thus
deceived, and think yourselves abused and insulted by
it; but you must know that you have met with a prize

better than that you sought. For you were in search of an enemy, but you have brought me here a friend. And of this I am sure, that it is better to have such men as this Lucilius our friends than our enemies." [1] And with these words he embraced the brave officer, and gave him a free pardon. Shortly after this, when Brutus, the murderer both of his old friend Julius Cæsar and of his own brother Caius, had committed suicide, he did not revenge himself upon the body by exposing it to insult, as was so often done, but covered it decently with his own scarlet mantle, and gave orders that it should be buried at his private expense with the honours of war. Similarly, after the capture of Pelusium and the defeat and death of Archelaus, Antony sought out the body of his conquered enemy and buried it with royal honours. In his earlier years, his treatment of Lepidus, whose army he had won over from him, was courteous in the extreme. Although absolute master of the situation, and Lepidus a prisoner in his hands, he insisted upon the fallen general remaining commander of the army, and always addressed him respectfully as Father.

Many of his actions were due to a kind of youthful impulsiveness. He gave his cook a fine house in Magnesia—the property, by the way, of somebody else—in reward for a single successful supper. This impetuosity was manifest in other ways, for, by its nature, which allowed of no delay in putting into action the thought dominant in his mind, it must be defined as a kind of impatience. As a young man desiring rapid fame, he had suddenly thrown in his lot with Clodius, "the most

[1] It is satisfactory to read that Lucilius remained his devoted friend until the end.

insolent and outrageous demagogue of the time," leading
with him a life of violence and disorder; and as suddenly
he had severed that partnership, going to Greece to study
with enthusiasm the polite arts.   In later years his sudden
invasion of Media, with such haste that he was obliged
to leave behind him all his engines of war, is the most
notable example of this impatience.   The battle of
Actium, which ended his career, was lost by a sudden
impulse on his part; and, at the last, the taking of his
own life was to some extent the impatient anticipation
of the processes of nature.

This trait in his character, combined with an inherent
bravery, caused him to cut a very dashing figure in warfare, and when fortune was with him, made of him a
brilliant general.   He stood in fear of nothing, and
dangers seem to have presented themselves to him as
pleasant relaxations of the humdrum of life.   In the
battle which opened the war against Aristobulus he
was the first man to scale the enemy's works; and in
a pitched battle he routed a force far larger than his
own, took Aristobulus and his son prisoners, and, like
an avenging deity, slaughtered almost the entire hostile
army.   At another time his dash across the desert to
Pelusium, and his brilliant capture of that fortress,
brought him considerable fame.   Again, in the war
against Pompey, "there was not one of the many
battles," says Plutarch, "in which he did not signalise
himself: twice he stopped the army in its full flight,
led them back to a charge, and gained the victory, so
that . . . his reputation, next to Cæsar's, was the greatest
in the army."   In the disastrous retreat from Media he
showed the greatest bravery; and it was no common
courage that allowed him, after the horrors of the

march back to Armenia, to prepare for a second campaign.

His generalship was not extraordinarily skilful, though
it is true that at Pharsalia Cæsar placed him in command of the left wing of the army, himself taking the
right; but his great courage, and the confidence and
devotion which he inspired in his men, served to make
him a trustworthy commander. His popularity amongst
his soldiers, as has been said, was unbounded. His
magnificent, manly appearance appealed to that sense
of the dramatic in which a soldier, by military display,
is very properly trained. His familiarity with his men,
moreover, introduced a very personal note into their
devotion, and each soldier felt that his general's eye
was upon him. He would sometimes go amongst them
at the common mess, sit down with them at their tables,
and eat or drink with them. He joined with them in
their exercises, and seems to have been able to run,
wrestle, or box with the best. He jested with high
and low, and liked them to answer him back. "His
raillery," says Plutarch, "was sharp and insulting, but
the edge of it was taken off by his readiness to submit
to any kind of repartee; for he was as well contented
to be rallied as he was pleased to rally others." In a
word, he was "the delight and pleasure of the army."

His eloquence was very marked, a faculty which he
seems to have inherited from his grandfather, who was
a famous pleader and advocate. As a young man he
studied the art at Athens, and took to a style known
as the Asiatic, which was somewhat flowery and ostentatious. When Pompey's power at Rome was at its
height, and Cæsar was in eclipse, Antony read his chief's
letters in the Senate with such effect that he obtained

many adherents to their cause. His public speech at
the funeral of Cæsar led to the downfall of the assassins.
When he himself was driven out of Rome he made such
an impression by his words upon the army of Lepidus,
to which he had fled, that an order was given to sound
the trumpets in order to drown his appealing voice.
" There was no man of his time like him for addressing
a multitude," says Plutarch, " or for carrying soldiers
with him by the force of words." It was in eloquence,
perhaps, that he made his nearest approach to a diver-
sion from the ordinary; though even in this it is possible
to find no more than an exalted mediocrity. A fine
presence, a frank utterance, and a vigorous delivery make
a great impression upon a crowd; and common sincerity
is the most electrifying agent in man's employment.

Yet another of the causes of his popularity both
amongst his troops and with his friends was the sympathy which he always showed with the intrigues and
troubles of lovers. " In love affairs," says Plutarch,
" he was very agreeable; he gained friends by the assistance he gave them in theirs, and took other people's
raillery upon his own with good-humour." He used to
lose his heart to women with the utmost ease and the
greatest frequency; and they, by reason of his splendid
physique and noble bearing, not infrequently followed
suit. Amongst serious - minded people he had an ill
name for familiarity with other men's wives; but the
domestic habits of the age were very irregular, and his
own wife Antonia had carried on an intrigue with his
friend Dolabella for which Antony had divorced her,
thereafter marrying the strong-minded Fulvia. Antony
was a full-blooded, virile man, unrestrained by any strong
principles of morality and possessed of no standard of

domestic constancy either by education or by inclination.
He was not ashamed of the consequences of his promiscuous amours, but allowed nature to have her will
with him.   Like his ancestor Hercules, he was so proud
of his stock that he wished it multiplied in many lands,
and he never confined his hopes of progeny to any one
woman.

There was a certain brutality in his nature, and of
this the particular instance is the murder of Cicero.
The orator had incurred his bitter hostility in the first
place by putting to death, and perhaps denying burial
to Antony's stepfather, Cornelius Lentulus.   Later he
was the cause of Antony's ejection from Rome and of
his privations while making the passage of the Alps.
The traitorous Dolabella was Cicero's son-in-law, which
must have added something to the family feud.   Moreover, Cicero's orations and writings against Antony were
continuous and full of invective.   It is perhaps not to be
wondered at, therefore, that when Octavian, Antony,
and Lepidus decided to rid the State of certain unde-
sirable persons, as we have already seen, Cicero was
proscribed and put to death.   Plutarch tells us that
his head and right hand were hung up above the
speaker's place in the Forum, and that Antony laughed
when he saw them, perhaps because, in his simple way,
he did not know what else to do to carry off a situation
of which he was somewhat ashamed.

As a rule, however, Antony was kind - hearted and
humane, and, as has already been shown, was seldom
severe or cruel to his enemies.   To many people he
embodied and personified good - nature, jollity, and
strength : he seemed to them to be a blending of
Bacchus with Hercules ; and if his morals were not

of a lofty character, it may be said in his defence that
they were consistent with the part for which nature
had cast him.

Little is known as to his attitude towards religion,
and one cannot tell whether he entertained any of the
atheistic doctrines which were then so widely preached,
nor does the fact that he allowed himself to be worshipped as Bacchus help us to form an opinion in this
regard. It is probable, however, that his faith was of
a simple kind in conformity with his character; and it
is known that he was superstitious and aware of the
presence of the supernatural. A certain Egyptian
diviner made a profound impression upon him by fore-
shadowing the future events of his life and warning him
against the power of Octavian. And again, when he
set out upon his Parthian campaign, he carried with
him a vessel containing the water of the Clepsydra,
an oracle having urged him to do so, while, at the
same time, he took with him a wreath made of the
leaves of the sacred olive-tree. He believed implicitly
in the divine nature of dreams, and we are told of one
occasion upon which he dreamed that his right hand
was thunderstruck, and thereupon discovered a plot
against his life. Such superstitions, however, were very
general, even amongst educated people; and Antony's
belief in omens has only to be noted here because it
played some part in his career. Until the last year of
his life he was attended with good luck, and a friendly
fortune helped him out of many difficult situations into
which his impetuosity had led him. It seemed to many
that Bacchus had really identified himself with Antony,
bringing to his aid the powers of his godhead; and
when at the end his downfall was complete, several

persons declared that they actually heard the clatter
and the processional music which marked the departure
of the deity from the destinies of the fallen giant.   The
historian cannot but find extenuating circumstances in
the majority of the culpable acts of the "colossal child";
and amongst these excuses there is none so urgent as
this continuous presence of a smiling fortune.   "Antony
in misfortune," says Plutarch, "was most nearly a virtuous man"; and if we wish to form a true estimate
of his character we must give prominence to his hardy
and noble attitude in the days of his flight from Rome
or of his retreat from Media.   It was then that he had
done with his boyish inconsequence and played the man.
At all other times he was the spoilt child of fortune,
rollicking on his triumphant way; jesting, drinking,
loving, and fighting; careless of public opinion; and,
like a god, sporting at will with the ball of the world.

When Dellius came to bring Cleopatra to him he was
at the height of his power.   Absolute master of the East,
he was courted by kings and princes, who saw in him
the future ruler of the entire Roman Empire.   Cæsar
must have often told the Queen of his faults and abilities, and she herself must have noticed the frank simplicity
of his character.   She set out, therefore, prepared to meet
not with a complex genius, but with an ordinary man,
representative, in a monstrous manner, of the victories
and the blunders of common human nature, and, incidentally, a man somewhat plagued by an emancipated
wife.

CHAPTER XII.

THE ALLIANCE BETWEEN CLEOPATRA AND ANTONY.

DETERMINED to win the fickle Antony back to her cause
and that of her son, Cleopatra set sail from Alexandria,
and, passing between Cyprus and the coast of Syria,
at length one morning entered the mouth of the Cydnus
in Cilicia, and made her way up to the city of Tarsus
which was situated on the banks of the river in the
shadow of the wooded slopes of the Taurus mountains.
The city was famous both for its maritime commerce and
for its school of oratory. The ships of Tarshish (*i.e.*,
Tarsus) had been renowned since ancient days, and
upon these vessels the rhetoricians travelled far and
wide, carrying the methods of their *alma mater* throughout the known world. Julius Cæsar and Cato may be
named as two of the pupils of this school who have
played their parts in the foregoing pages ;[1] and now
Antony, the foremost Roman of this period, was honouring Tarsus itself with his presence. The city stood some
miles back from the sea, and it was late afternoon before
its buildings and busy docks were observed by the
Egyptians, sheltering against the slopes of the mountains. As the fleet sailed up the Cydnus, the people of

---

[1] St Paul was also trained in this school.

the neighbourhood swarmed down to the water's edge to watch its stately progress; and the excitement was intense when it was seen that the Queen's vessel was fitted and decked out in the most extravagant manner. Near the city the river widens into a quiet lake, and here in the roads, where lay the world-renowned merchant vessels, Cleopatra's ships probably came to anchor, while the quays and embankments were crowded with the townsfolk who had gathered to witness the Queen's arrival.

On hearing of her approach Antony had seated himself upon the public tribunal in the market-place, expecting that she would land at once and come to pay her respects to him in official manner. But Cleopatra had no intention of playing a part which might in any way be interpreted as that of a vassal or suppliant; and she therefore seems to have remained on board her ship at a distance from the shore, as though in no haste to meet Antony.

Meanwhile reports began to spread of the magnificence of the Queen's vessels, and it was said that preparations were being made on board for the reception of the Triumvir. The crowds surrounding the tribunal thereupon hurried from the market-place to join those upon the quays, and soon Antony was left alone with his retinue. There he sat waiting for some time, till, losing patience, he sent a message to the Queen inviting her to dine with him. To this she replied by asking him to bring the Roman and local magnates to dine with her instead; and Antony, not wishing to stand upon ceremony with his old friend, at once accepted the invitation. At dusk, therefore, Cleopatra appears to have ordered her vessel to be brought across the lake to the city, and to be

P

moored at the crowded quay, where already Antony was waiting to come on board; and the burly Roman, always a lover of theatrical display, must then have been entertained by a spectacle more stirring than any he had known before.

Across the water, in which the last light of the sunset was reflected, the royal galley was rowed by banks of silver-mounted oars, the great purple sails hanging idly in the still air of evening. The vessel was steered by two oar-like rudders, controlled by helmsmen who stood in the stern of the ship under a shelter constructed in the form of an enormous elephant's head of shining gold, the trunk raised aloft.[1] Around the helmsmen a number of beautiful slave-women were grouped in the guise of sea-nymphs and graces; and near them a company of musicians played a melody upon their flutes, pipes, and harps, for which the slow-moving oars seemed to beat the time. Cleopatra herself, decked in the loose, shimmering robes of the goddess Venus, lay under an awning bespangled with gold, while boys dressed as Cupids stood on either side of her couch, fanning her with the coloured ostrich plumes of the Egyptian court. Before the royal canopy brazen censers stood upon delicate pedestals, sending forth fragrant clouds of exquisitely prepared Egyptian incense, the marvellous odour of which was wafted to the shore ere yet the vessel had come to its moorings.[2]

At last, as the light of day began to fade, the royal galley was moored to the crowded quay, and Antony

---

[1] The elephant's head I describe from that seen upon the Queen's vessel shown upon the coins.

[2] The recipe for the preparation of incense of about this period is inscribed upon a wall of the temple of Philæ, and shows a vast number of ingredients.

stepped on board, followed by the chief officers of his staff and by the local celebrities of Tarsus. His meeting with the Queen appears to have been of the most cordial nature, for the manner of her approach must have made it impossible for him at that moment to censure her conduct. Moreover, the splendid allurements of the scene in which they met, the enchantment of the twilight, the enticement of her beauty, the delicacy of the music blending with the ripple of the water, the intoxication of the incense and the priceless perfumes, must have stirred his imagination and driven from his mind all thought of reproach. Nor could he have found much opportunity for serious conversation with her, for presently the company was led down to the banqueting-saloon where a dinner of the utmost magnificence was served. Twelve triple couches, covered with embroideries and furnished with cushions, were set around the room, before each of which stood a table whereon rested golden dishes inlaid with precious stones, and drinking goblets of exquisite workmanship. The walls of the saloon were hung with embroideries worked in purple and gold, and the floor was strewn with flowers. Antony could not refrain from exclaiming at the splendour of the entertainment, whereupon Cleopatra declared that it was not worthy of comment; and, there and then, she made him a present of everything used at the banquet — dishes, drinking-vessels, couches, embroideries, and all else in the saloon. Returning once more to the deck, the elated guests, now made more impressionable by the effects of Egyptian wine, were amazed to find themselves standing beneath a marvellous kaleidoscope of lanterns, hung in squares and circles from a forest of branches interlaced above their heads, and in these almost magical surroundings they enjoyed the enlivening company of the fascinating young Queen until the wine-jars were emptied and the lamps had burnt low.

From the shore the figures of the revellers, moving to and fro amidst this galaxy of lights to the happy strains of the music, must have appeared to be actors in some divine masque; and it was freely stated, as though it had been fact, that Venus had come down to earth to feast with Dionysos (Antony) for the common good of Asia. Cleopatra, as we have already seen, had been identified with Venus during the time when she lived in Rome; and in Egypt she was always deified. And thus the character in which she presented herself at Tarsus was not assumed, as is generally supposed, simply for the purpose of creating a charming picture, but it was her wish actually to be received as a goddess, that Antony might behold in her the divine Queen of Egypt whom the great Cæsar himself had accepted and honoured as an incarnation of Venus. It must be remembered that at this period men were very prone to identify prominent persons with popular divinities. Julia, the daughter of Octavian, was in like manner identified with Venus Genetrix by the inhabitants of certain cities. We have seen how Cæsar seems to have been named Lupercus, and how Antony was called Dionysos (Bacchus); and it will be remembered how, at Lystra, Paul and Barnabas were saluted as Hermes and Zeus. In the many known cases, such as these, the people actually credited the identification; and though a little thought probably checked a continuance of such a belief, at the time there seemed to be no cause for doubt that these divinities had made themselves manifest on earth. The crowds who stood on the banks of the Cydnus that

night must therefore have really believed themselves to
be peeping at an entertainment provided by a manifestation of a popular goddess for the amusement of an
incarnation of a favourite god.

It would appear that Antony invited Cleopatra to sup
with him on the following evening, but the Queen seems
to have urged him and his suite again to feast with her.
This second banquet was so far more splendid than the
first that, according to Plutarch, the entertainment already described seemed by comparison to be contemp-
tible. When the guests departed, not only did she give
to each one the couch upon which he had lain, and the
goblets which had been set before him, but she also
presented the chief guests with litters, and with slaves
to carry them, and Ethiopian boys to bear torches in
front of them; while for the lesser guests she provided
horses adorned with golden trappings, which they were
bidden to keep as mementos of the banquet.

On the next night Cleopatra at last deigned to dine
with Antony, who had exhausted the resources of Tarsus
in his desire to provide a feast which should equal in
magnificence those given by the Queen; but in this he
failed, and he was the first to make a jest of his unsuc-
cess and of the poverty of his wits. The Queen's entertainments had been marked by that brilliancy of conversation and atmosphere of refinement which in past
years had so appealed to the intelligence of the great
Dictator; but Antony's banquet, on the contrary, was
notable for the coarseness of the wit and for what
Plutarch describes as a sort of rustic awkwardness.
Cleopatra, however, was equal to the occasion, and
speedily adjusted her conduct to suit that of her burly
host. "Perceiving that his raillery was broad and

gross, and that it savoured more of the soldier than of the courtier, she rejoined in the same taste, and fell at once into that manner, without any sort of reluctance or reserve."[1] Thus she soon succeeded in captivating this powerful Roman, and in making him her most devoted friend and ally. There was something irresistible in the excitement of her presence: for the daintiness of her person, the vivacity of her character, and the enchantment of her voice, were, so to speak, enhanced by the audacity of her treatment of the broad subjects introduced in conversation. Antony had sent for her to censure her for a supposed negligence of his interests; but speedily he was led to realise that he himself, and not the Queen, had deviated from the course upon which they had agreed in Rome. It was he who, by his association with Octavian, had appeared to desert what Cleopatra believed to be the genuine Cæsarian cause; whereas, on the other hand, the Queen was able to show that she had refrained from sending aid to the Triumvirate simply because she could not decide in what manner the welfare of her son, the little Cæsar, was to be promoted by such an action. Under the spell of her attraction Antony, who in the Dictator's lifetime had never been permitted to receive in his heart the full force of her charming attack, now fell an easy victim to her strategy, and declared himself ready to carry out her wishes in all things.

On the fourth night of her visit to Tarsus, Cleopatra entertained the Roman officers at another banquet; and on this occasion she caused the floor of the saloon to be strewn with roses to the depth of nearly two feet, the flowers being held in a solid formation by nets which

[1] Plutarch : Antony.

were tightly spread over them and fastened to the surrounding walls, the guests thus walking to their couches
upon a perfumed mattress of blooms, the cost of which,
for the one room, was some £250.

In this prodigious manner the next few days were
spent. The Queen made every possible effort to display to Antony her wealth and power, in order that
she might obtain his consent to some form of alliance
between them which should be directed against Octavian.
Her one desire now was to effect a break between these
two leaders, to set them at one another's throats, and
then, by lending Antony her support, to secure the
overthrow of Octavian, Cæsar's nephew, and the
triumph of Cæsarion, Cæsar's son. For this purpose
it was absolutely necessary to reveal the extent of her
wealth, and to exhibit the limitless stream of her resources. She therefore seems to have shown a mild
disdain for the Roman general's efforts to entertain
her, and at his banquets she seems to have conveyed
to him the disquieting impression that she was smiling
at his attempted magnificence, and was even puzzled by
his inability to give to his feasts that fairy aspect which
characterised her own.

Her attitude caused Antony some uneasiness, and at
length it seems that he asked the Queen directly what
more could be done to add to the splendour of his table.
During the course of the conversation which ensued he
appears to have told her how much an entertainment
of the kind cost him; whereupon she replied that she
herself could with ease expend the equivalent of a hundred and fifty thousand pounds sterling upon a single
meal. Antony promptly denied it, declaring that such
a thing was impossible; and the Queen thereupon offered

him a wager that she would do so on the next day. This was accepted, and a certain Plancus was invited to decide it. Antony does not appear to have recollected that in time past Clodius, the son of the comedian Æsop, was wont to mingle melted pearls with his food, that the cost of his meals might be interestingly enormous;[1] for he would then have realised that Cleopatra intended to employ some such device to win her wager, and he would perhaps have restrained her.

To the next day's banquet the Roman looked forward with some excitement; and he must have been at once elated and disappointed when he found the display to be not much above the ordinary. At the end of the meal he calculated with Plancus the expenses of the various dishes, and estimated the value of the golden plates and goblets. He then turned to the Queen, telling her that the total amount did not nearly reach the figure named in the wager.

"Wait," said Cleopatra. "This is only a beginning. I shall now try whether I cannot spend the stipulated sum upon myself."

A signal was given to the attendant slaves, who brought a table to her, upon which a single cup containing a little vinegar was set. She was wearing in her ears at the time two enormous pearls, the value of each of which was more than half the amount named in the wager; and one of these she rapidly detached, throwing it into the vinegar, wherein it soon disintegrated. The vinegar and some seventy-five thousand pounds having then trickled down her royal throat, she prepared to destroy the second pearl in like manner; but Plancus intervened, and declared the wager won,

[1] Hor. 1. ii. Sat. 3.

while Antony, no doubt, pondered not without gloom
upon the ways of women.

It has generally been thought that the Queen's extravagance was to be attributed to her vain desire to
impress Antony with the fact of her personal wealth.
But, as we have seen, there was certainly a strong
political reason for her actions; and there is no need
to suppose that she was actuated by vanity. Indeed,
the display of her wealth does not appear to have been
on any occasion as ostentatious as one might gather
from the Greek authors, whose writings suggest that
they attributed to her a boastful profligacy in financial
matters which could only be described as bad form. It
would seem rather that the instances of her prodigality
recorded here were all characterised in appearance by
a subtle show of unaffected simplicity and ingenuousness, a sort of breath-taking audacity, while in quality
they were largely political and speculative.

It is very important for the reader to understand the
attitude of Cleopatra at this time, and to divest his mind
of the views usually accepted in regard to the Queen's
alliance with Antony; and therefore I must repeat that
it was Cleopatra's desire at Tarsus to arouse the interest
of Antony in the possibilities of Egypt as the basis of
an attempt upon Rome. She wished to lead him, as
I have said, to put faith in the limitless wealth that
might flow down the Nile to fill the coffers which
should be his, were he to lead an army to claim the
throne for herself as Cæsar's wife, and for her son
as Cæsar's flesh and blood. Here was the man who
could conquer for her the empire which she had lost
by the premature death of the great Dictator. It was
necessary to make him understand the advantages of

partnership with her, and hence it became needful for her to display to him the untold wealth that she could command. There was no particular vanity in her actions, nor real wastefulness: she was playing a great game, and the stakes were high. A few golden goblets, a melted pearl or two, were not an excessive price to pay for the partisanship of Antony. Her son Cæsarion was too young to fight his own battles, and she herself could not lead an army. Antony's championship therefore had to be obtained, and there was no way of enlisting his sympathies so sure as that of revealing to him the boundless riches which she could bring to his aid. Let him have practical demonstration of the wealth of hidden Africa and mysterious Asia at her command, and he would surely not shun an enterprise which should make Cæsar's friend, Cæsar's wife, and Cæsar's son the three sovereigns of the world. She would show him the gold of Ethiopia and of Nubia; she would turn his attention to the great trade-routes to India; and she would remind him of the advantageous possibilities which the great Dictator had seen in an alliance with her. In this manner she would again win his support, as she believed she had already done in Rome; and thus through him the ambitious schemes of Julius Cæsar might at last be put into execution.

There were, however, one or two outstanding matters which required immediate attention. The Princess Arsinoe, who had walked the streets of Rome in Cæsar's Triumph and had been released after that event, was now residing either at Miletus or Ephesus,[1] where she had received sanctuary amongst the priests and priestesses attached to the temple of Artemis. The High Priest

---

[1] Josephus says Ephesus, Appian Miletus.

treated her kindly, and even honoured her as a queen, a fact which suggests that he had definitely placed himself upon her side in her feud with Cleopatra. She seems to have been a daring and ambitious woman, who, throughout her short life, struggled vainly to obtain the throne of Egypt for herself; and now it would appear that she was once more scheming to oust her sister, just as she had schemed in the Alexandrian Palace in the days when Ganymedes was her chamberlain.

It will be remembered that the Dictator had given the throne of Cyprus to Arsinoe and her brother, but it does not seem that this gift had ever been ratified, though no doubt the Princess attempted to style herself Queen of that island. It may be that she had come to some terms with Cassius and Brutus by offering them aid in their war with Antony if they would assist her in her endeavours to obtain the Egyptian throne; and it is possible that the Egyptian Viceroy of Cyprus, Serapion, was involved in this arrangement when he handed over his fleet to Cassius, as has been recorded in the last chapter. At all events, Cleopatra was now able to obtain Antony's consent to the execution both of Arsinoe and of Serapion. A number of men were despatched, therefore, with orders to put her to death, and these entering the temple while Arsinoe was serving in the sanctuary, killed her at the steps of the altar. The High Priest was indicted apparently on the charge of conspiracy, and it was only with great difficulty that the priesthood managed to obtain his pardon. Serapion, however, could not claim indulgence on account of his calling, and he was speedily arrested and slain.

Having thus rid herself of one serious menace to her

throne, Cleopatra persuaded Antony to assist her to remove from her mind another cause for deep anxiety. It will be remembered that when Cæsar defeated the Egyptian army in the south of the Delta in March B.C. 47, the young King Ptolemy XIV. was drowned in the rout, his body being said to have been recognised by his golden corselet. Now, however, a man who claimed to be none other than this unfortunate monarch was trying to obtain a following, and possibly had put himself in correspondence with his supposed sister Arsinoe. The pretender was residing at this time in Phœnicia, a fact which suggests that he had also been in communication with Serapion, who at the time of his arrest was likewise travelling in that country. Antony therefore consented to the arrest and execution of this pseudo-monarch, and in a few weeks' time he was quietly despatched.

Historians are inclined to see in the deaths of these three conspirators an instance of Cleopatra's cruelty and vindictiveness; and one finds them described as victims of her insatiable ambition, the killing of Arsinoe being named as the darkest stain upon the Queen's black reputation. I cannot see, however, in what manner a menace to her throne of this kind could have been removed, save by the ejection of the makers of the trouble from the earthly sphere of their activities. The death of Arsinoe, like that of Thomas à Beckett, is rendered ugly by the fact that it took place at the steps of a sacred altar; but, remembering the period in which these events occurred, the executions are not to be censured too severely, for what goodly king or queen of former days has not thus removed by death all pretenders to the throne?

Cleopatra's visit to Tarsus does not seem to have been

prolonged beyond a few weeks, but when at length she returned to Alexandria, she must have felt that her short residence with Antony had raised her prestige once more to the loftiest heights.   Not only had she used his dicta-torial power to sweep her two rivals and their presumed accomplice from the face of the earth, not only had she struck the terror of her power into the heart of the powerful High Priest of Artemis who, in the distant Ægean, had merely harboured a pretender to Egypt's throne, but she had actually won the full support of Antony once more, and had extracted from him a promise to pay her a visit at Alexandria in order that he might see with his own eyes the wealth which Egypt could offer.   For the first time, therefore, since the death of Cæsar, her prospects seemed once more to be brilliant; and it must have been with a light heart that she sailed across the Mediterranean once more towards her own splendid city.

CHAPTER XIII.

CLEOPATRA AND ANTONY IN ALEXANDRIA.

THERE can be little doubt that Antony was extremely anxious to form a solid alliance with Cleopatra at this juncture, for he needed just such an ally for the schemes which he had in view. His relations with Octavian were strained, and the insignificant part played by the latter in the operations which culminated at Philippi had led him to feel some contempt for the young man's abilities. The Triumvirate was, at best, a compromise; and Antony had no expectation that it would for one day outlive the acquisition either by Octavian or himself of preponderant power. At the back of his mind he hoped for the fall of Cæsar's nephew; and he saw in the alliance with Cleopatra the means whereby he could obtain a numerical advantage over his rival.

After the battle of Philippi Octavian had returned to Rome, and Antony now received news that the troops under their joint command were highly dissatisfied with the rewards which they had received for their labours. There was considerable friction between those who were loyal to Octavian and those who thought that Antony would treat them more generously; and the latter's agents in Rome, notably his wife Fulvia, were endeavouring to widen the breach, more probably of their own accord than with their leader's direct consent. Antony had no wish to break with Octavian until he could feel confident of success ; and, moreover, his attention was directed at this time more keenly to the question of the conquest of Parthia than to that of the destruction of Octavian. The great Dictator had stirred his imagination in regard to the Parthians, and possibly the project of the invasion of India was already exercising his mind, as it certainly did in later years.[1] His plans therefore, in broad outline, now seem to have been grouped into three movements : firstly, the formation of an offensive and defensive alliance with Cleopatra, in order that her money, men, and ships might be placed at his disposal ; secondly, the invasion of Parthia, so that the glory of his victories and the loot of the conquered country might raise his prestige to the highest point ; and thirdly, the picking of a quarrel with Octavian, in order that he might sweep him from the face of the earth, thereby leaving himself ruler of the world. Then, like Cæsar, he would probably proclaim himself King, would marry Cleopatra, and would establish a royal dynasty, his successor being either his stepson, the Dictator's child, or the future son of his marriage with the Queen of Egypt should their union be fruitful.

Filled with these hopes, which corresponded so close-ly to those of Cleopatra, Antony prepared to go to Alexandria in the autumn of the year B.C. 41, intent on sealing the alliance with the Queen of Egypt. He arranged for a certain Decidius Saxa, one of the late Dictator's chosen generals, to be placed in command of the forces in Syria ; and it was this officer's duty to keep

[1] Page 275.

him informed of the movements of the Parthians, and to prepare for the coming campaign against them. The King of Parthia, Orodes by name, had engaged the services of a Roman renegade named Quintus Labienus, a former colleague of Cassius and Brutus; and this man was now working in conjunction with Pacorus, the King's son, in organising the Parthian armies and preparing them for an offensive movement against the neighbouring Roman provinces. There seemed thus to be no doubt that war would speedily break out, and Antony was therefore very anxious to put himself in possession of the Egyptian military and naval resources as quickly as possible.

He was about to set sail for Alexandria when news seems to have reached him that the troubles in Rome were coming to a head, and that his brother Lucius Antonius, and his wife Fulvia, were preparing to attack Octavian. He must therefore have hesitated in deciding whether he should return to Rome or not. He must have been considerably annoyed at the turn which events had taken, for he knew well enough that he was not then in a position to wage a successful war against Octavian; and he was much afraid of being involved in a contest which would probably lead to his own downfall. If he returned to Italy it was possible that he might be able to patch up the quarrel, and to effect a reconciliation which should keep the world at peace until the time when he himself desired war. But if he failed in his pacific efforts, a conflict would ensue for which he was not prepared. It seems to me, therefore, that he thought it more desirable that he should keep clear of the quarrel, and should show himself to be absorbed in eastern questions. By going over to Egypt for a few weeks, not

OCTAVIAN.

only would he detach himself from the embarrassing tactics of his party in Rome, but he would also raise forces and money, nominally for his Parthian campaign, which would be of immense service to him should Octavian press the quarrel to a conclusive issue. Moreover, there can be little question that to Antony the thought of meeting his stern wife again and of being obliged to live once more under her powerful scrutiny was very distasteful; whereas, on the other hand, he looked forward with youthful enthusiasm to a repetition of the charming entertainment provided by Cleopatra. Antony was no great statesman or diplomatist; and jolly overgrown boy that he was, his effective actions were at all times largely dictated by his pleasurable desires. The Queen of Egypt had made a most disconcerting appeal to that spontaneous nature, which, in matters of this kind, required little encouragement from without; and now the fact that it seemed wise at the time to keep away from Rome served as full warrant for the manœuvre which his ambition and his heart jointly urged upon him.

Early in the winter of B.C. 41, therefore, he made his way to Alexandria, and was received by Cleopatra into the beautiful Lochias Palace as a most profoundly honoured guest. All the resources of that sumptuous establishment were concerted for his amusement, and it was not long before the affairs of the Roman world were relegated to the back of his genial mind. In the case of Cleopatra, however, there was no such laxity. The Queen's ambitions, fired by Cæsar, had been stirred into renewed flame by her success at Tarsus; and she was determined to make Antony the champion of her cause. From the moment when she had realised his pliability and his susceptibility to her overtures, she had made up her mind

Q

to join forces with him in an attempt upon the throne of
the Roman Empire; and it was now her business both to
fascinate him by her personal charms and, by the nature
of her entertainments, to demonstrate to him her wealth
and power.

"It would be trifling without end," says Plutarch, "to
give a particular account of Antony's follies at Alexandria."
For several weeks he gave himself up to amusements of
the most frivolous character, and to the enjoyment of a
life more luxurious than any he had ever known. His
own family had been simple in their style of living, and
although he had taught himself much in this regard, and
had expended a great deal of money on lavish entertainments, there were no means of obtaining in Rome a
splendour which could compare with the magnificence of
these Alexandrian festivities. His friends, too, many of
whom were common actresses and comedians, had not
been brilliant tutors in the arts of entertainment; nor
had they encouraged him to provide them so much with
refined luxury as with good strong drink and jovial
company. Now, however, in Cleopatra's palace, Antony
found himself surrounded on all sides by the devices and
appliances of the most advanced culture of the age; and
an appeal was made to his senses which would have put
the efforts even of the extravagant Lucullus to shame.
Alexandria has been called "the Paris of the ancient
world,"[1] and it is not difficult to understand the glamour
which it cast upon the imagination of the lusty Roman,
who, for the first time in his life, found himself surrounded
by a group of cultured men and women highly practised
in the art of living sumptuously. Moreover, he was
received by Cleopatra as prospective lord of all he sur-

[1] Ferrero.

veyed, for the Queen seems to have shown him quite clearly that all these things would be his if he would but cast in his lot with her.

Antony quickly adapted his manners to those of the Alexandrians. He set aside his Roman dress and clothed himself in the square-cut Greek costume, putting upon his feet the white Attic shoes known as *phœcasium*. He seems to have spoken the Greek language well; and he now made himself diplomatically agreeable to the Grecian nobles who frequented the court. He constantly visited the meeting-places of learned men, spending much time in the temples and in the Museum; and thereby he won for himself an assured position in the brilliant society of the Queen's Alexandrian court, which, in spite of its devotion to the pleasant follies of civilisation, prided itself upon its culture and learning.

Meanwhile he did not hesitate to endear himself by every means in his power to Cleopatra. He knew that she desired him, for dynastic reasons, to become her legal husband, and that there was no other man in the world, from her point of view, so suitable for the position of her consort. He knew, also, that as a young "widow," whose first union had been so short-lived, Cleopatra was eagerly desirous of a satisfactory marriage which should give her the comfort of a strong companion upon whom to lean in her many hours of anxiety, and an ardent lover to whom she could turn in her loneliness. He knew that she was attracted by his herculean strength and brave appearance; and it must have been apparent to him from the first that he could without much exertion win her devotion almost as easily as the great Cæsar had done. The Queen was young, passionate, and exceedingly lonely; and it did not require any keen perception on his

part to show him how great was her need, both for
political and for personal reasons, of a reliable marriage.
He therefore paid court to his hostess with confidence;
and it was not long before she surrendered herself to him
with all the eagerness and whole-hearted interest of her
warm, impulsive nature.

The union was at once sanctioned by the court and the
priesthood, and was converted in Egypt into as legal a
marriage as that with Cæsar had been. There can be
little doubt that Cleopatra obtained from him some sort
of promise that he would not desert her; and at this time
she must have felt herself able to trust him as implicitly
as she had trusted the great Dictator. Cæsar had not
played her false; he had taken her to Rome and had
made no secret of his intention to raise her to the throne
by his side. In like manner she believed that Antony,
virtually Cæsar's successor, would create an empire over
which they should jointly rule; and she must have
rejoiced in her successful capture of his heart, whereby
she had obtained both a good-natured, handsome lover
and a bold political champion.

In the union between these two powerful personages
the historian may thus see both a diplomatic and a
romantic amalgamation. Neither Cleopatra nor Antony
seem to me yet to have been very deeply in love, but I
fancy each was stirred by the attractions of the other,
and each believed for the moment that the gods had
provided the mate so long awaited. Cleopatra with her
dainty beauty, and Antony with his magnificent physique,
must have appeared to be admirably matched by Nature;
while their royal and famous destinies could not, in the
eyes of the material world, have been more closely allied.

We have seen how Antony allowed his more refined

instincts full play in Alexandria, and how, in order to win
the Queen's admiration, he showed himself devoted to
the society of learned men.   In like manner Cleopatra
gave full vent to the more frivolous side of her nature, in
order to render herself attractive to her Roman comrade,
whose boyish love of tomfoolery was so pronounced.
Sometimes in the darkness of the night, as we have
already seen, she would dress herself in the clothes of a
peasant woman, and disguising Antony in the garments
of a slave, she would lead him through the streets of the
city in search of adventure.   They would knock ominously
at the doors or windows of unknown houses, and disappear like ghosts when they were opened.   Occasionally,
of course, they were caught by the doorkeepers or servants,
and, as Plutarch says, " were very scurvily answered and
sometimes even beaten severely, though most people
guessed who they were."

Cleopatra provided all manner of amusements for her
companion.   She would ride and hunt with him in the
desert beyond the city walls, boat and fish with him on
the sea or the Mareotic Lake, romp with him through
the halls of the Palace, watch him wrestle, fence, and
exercise himself in arms, play dice with him, drink with
him, and fascinate him by the arts of love.   The following story presents a characteristic picture of the
jovial life led by them in Alexandria during this memor-
able winter.   Antony had been fishing from one of the
vessels in the harbour; but, failing to make any catches,
he employed a diver to descend into the water and to
attach newly-caught fishes to his hook, which he then
landed amidst the applause of Cleopatra and her friends.
The Queen, however, soon guessed what was happening,
and at once invited a number of persons to come on

the next day to witness Antony's dexterity. She then procured some preserved fish which had come from the Black Sea, and instructed a slave to dive under the vessel and to attach one to the hook as soon as it should strike the water. This having been done, Antony drew to the surface the salted fish, the appearance of which was greeted with hearty laughter; whereupon Cleopatra, turning to the discomfited angler, tactfully said, "Leave the fishing-rod, general, to us poor sovereigns of Pharos and Canopus: *your* game is cities, provinces, and kingdoms."

During this winter Antony and the Queen together founded a kind of society or club which they named the *Amimetobioi*, or Inimitable Livers, the members of which entertained one another in turn each day in the most extravagant manner. Antony, it would seem probable, was the president of this society; and two inscriptions have been found in which he is named "The Inimitable," perhaps not without reference to this office. A story told by a certain Philotas, a medical student at that time residing in Alexandria, will best illustrate the prodigality of the feasts provided by the members of this club. Philotas was one day visiting the kitchens of Cleopatra's palace, and was surprised to see no less than eight wild boars roasting whole. "You evidently have a great number of guests to-day," he said to the cook; to which the latter replied, "No, there are not above twelve to dine, but the meat has to be served up just roasted to a turn: and maybe Antony will wish to dine now, maybe not for an hour; yet if anything is even one minute ill-timed it will be spoilt, so that not one but many meals must be in readiness, as it is impossible to guess at his dining-hour."

As an example of the food served at these Alexandrian banquets, I may be permitted to give a list of the dishes provided some years previously at a dinner given in Rome by Mucius Lentulus Niger, at which Julius Cæsar had been one of the guests; but it is to be remembered that Cleopatra's feasts are thought to have been far more prodigious than any known in Rome. The *menu* is as follows: Sea-hedgehogs; oysters; mussels; sphondyli; fieldfares with asparagus; fattened fowls; oyster and mussel pasties; black and white sea-acorns; sphondyli again; glycimarides; sea-nettles; becaficoes; roe-ribs; boar's ribs; fowls dressed with flour; becaficoes again; purple shell-fish of two kinds; sow's udder; boar's head; fish pasties; ducks; boiled teals; hares; roasted fowls; starch-pastry; and Pontic pastry. Varro, in one of his satires, mentions some of the most noted foreign delicacies which were to be found upon the tables of the rich. These include peacocks from Samos; grouse from Phrygia; cranes from Melos; kids from Ambracia; tunny-fish from Chalcedon; muraenas from the Straits of Gades; ass-fish from Pessinus; oysters and scallops from Tarentum; sturgeons from Rhodes; scarus-fish from Cilicia; nuts from Thasos; and acorns from Spain. The vegetables then known included most of those now eaten, with the notable exception, of course, of potatoes.[1] The main meal of the day, the *cœna*, was often prolonged into a drinking party, known as *commissatio*, at which an *Arbiter bibendi*, or Master of Revels, was appointed by the throwing of dice, whose duty it was to mix the wine in a large bowl. The diners lay upon couches usually arranged round three sides of the table, and they ate their food with their fingers. Chap-

---

[1] Marquardt: Privatleben, p. 409.

lets of flowers were placed upon their heads, cinnamon
was sprinkled upon the hair, and sweet perfumes were
thrown upon their bodies, and sometimes even mixed
with the wines. During the meals the guests were entertained by the performances of dancing-girls, musicians,
actors, acrobats, clowns, dwarfs, or even gladiators; and
afterwards dice - throwing and other games of chance
were indulged in. The decoration of the rooms and the
splendour of the furniture and plate were always very
carefully considered, Cleopatra's banquets being specially
noteworthy for the magnificence of the table services.
These dishes and drinking-vessels, which the Queen was
wont modestly to describe as her *Kerama* or "earthenware," were usually made of gold and silver encrusted
with precious stones; and so famous were they for their
beauty of workmanship that three centuries later they
formed still a standard of perfection, Queen Zenobia of
Palmyra being related to have collected them eagerly
for her own use.

Thus, with feasting, merry-making, and amusements
of all kinds, the winter slipped by. To a large extent
Plutarch is justified in stating that in Alexandria Antony
"squandered that most costly of all valuables, time";
but the months were not altogether wasted. He and
Cleopatra had cemented their alliance by living together
in the most intimate relations; and both now thought
it probable that when the time came for the attempted
overthrow of Octavian they would fight their battle side
by side. By becoming Cleopatra's lover, and by appealing to the purely instinctive side of her nature, Antony
had obtained from her the whole-hearted promise of
Egypt's support in all his undertakings; and these happy
winter months in Alexandria could not have seemed to

him to be wasted when each day the powerful young Queen come to be more completely at his beck and call. The course of Cleopatra's love for Antony seems to have followed almost precisely the same lines as had her love for Julius Cæsar. Inspired at first by a political motive, she had come to feel a genuine and romantic affection for her Roman consort; and the intimacies which ensued, though largely due to the weaknesses of the flesh, seemed to find full justification in the fact that her dynastic ambitions were furthered by this means. Cleopatra thought of Antony as her husband, and she wished to be regarded as his wife. The fact that no public marriage had taken place was of little consequence; for she, as goddess and Queen, must have felt herself exempt from the common law, and at perfect liberty to contract whatever union seemed desirable to her for the good of her country and dynasty, and for the satisfaction of her own womanly instincts. Early in the year B.C. 40 she and Antony became aware that their union was to be fruitful; and this fact must have made Cleopatra more than ever anxious to keep Antony in Alexandria with her, and to bind him to her by causing him to be recognised as her consort. He was not willing, however, to assume the rank and status of King of Egypt; for such a move would inevitably precipitate the quarrel with Octavian, and he would then be obliged to stake all on an immediate war with the faction which would assuredly come to be recognised as the legitimate Roman party. This unwillingness on his part to bind himself to her must have caused her some misgiving; and, as the winter drew to a close, I think that the Queen must have felt somewhat apprehensive in regard to Antony's sincerity.

Setting aside all sentimental factors in the situation, and leaving out of consideration for the moment all physical causes of the alliance, it will be seen that Antony's position was now more satisfactory than was that of the often sorely perplexed Queen. By spending the winter at Alexandria the Roman Triumvir had kept himself aloof from the political troubles in Italy at a time when his presence at home might have complicated matters to his own disadvantage; he had obtained the full support of Egyptian wealth and Egyptian arms should he require them; and he had prepared the way for a definite marriage with Cleopatra at the moment when he should desire her partnership in the foundation of a great monarchy such as that for which Julius Cæsar had striven. He had not yet irrevocably compromised himself, and he was free to return to his Roman order of life with superficially clean hands. Nobody in Rome would think the less of him for having combined a certain amount of pleasure with the obvious business which had called him to Egypt; and his friends would certainly be as easily persuaded to accept the political excuses which he would advance for his lengthy residence in Alexandria as the Cæsarian party had been to admit those put forward by the great Dictator under very similar circumstances. Like Julius Cæsar and like Pompey, Antony was certainly justified in making himself the patron of the wealthy Egyptian court; and all Roman statesmen were aware how desirable it was at this juncture for a party leader to cement an alliance with the powerful Queen of that country.

On the part of Cleopatra, however, the circumstances were far less happy. She had staked all on the alliance with Antony—her personal honour and prestige as well as her dynasty's future; and in return for her great gifts she must have been beginning to feel that she had received nothing save vague promises and unsatisfactory assurances. Without Antony's help not only would she lose all hope of an Egypto - Roman throne for herself and her son Cæsarion, but she would inevitably fail to keep Egypt from absorption into the Roman dominions. There were only two mighty leaders at that time in the Roman world—Octavian and Antony; and Octavian was her relentless enemy, for the reason that her son Cæsarion was his rival in the claim on the Dictator's worldly and political estate. Failing the support of Antony there were no means of retaining her country's liberty, except perhaps by the desperate eventuality of some sort of alliance with Parthia. It must have occurred to her that Egypt, with its growing trade with southern India, might join forces with Parthia, whose influence in northern India must have been great, and might thus effect an amalgamation of nations hostile to Rome, which in a vast semicircle should include Egypt, Ethiopia, Arabia, Persia, India, Scythia, Parthia, Armenia, Syria, and perhaps Asia Minor. Such a combination might be expected to sweep Rome from the face of the earth; but the difficulties in the way of the huge union were almost insuperable, and the alliance with Antony was infinitely more tangible. Yet, towards the end of the winter, she must constantly have asked herself whether she could trust Antony, to whom she had given so much. She loved him, she had given herself to him; but she must have known him to be unreliable, inconsequent, and, in certain aspects, merely an overgrown boy. The stakes for which she was fighting were so absolutely essential to herself and to her country: the champion whose services she had enlisted was so light-hearted, so reluctant to pledge himself. And now that she was about to bear him a son, and thus to bring before his wayward notice the grave responsibilities which she felt he had so flippantly undertaken, would he stand by her as Cæsar had done, or would he desert her?

Her feelings may be imagined, therefore, when in February B.C. 40, Antony told her that he had received disconcerting news from Rome and from Syria, and that he must leave her at once. The news from Rome does not appear to have been very definite, but it gave him to understand that his wife and his brother had come to actual blows with Octavian, and, being worsted, had fled from Italy. From Syria, however, came a very urgent despatch, in regard to which there could be no doubts. Some of the Syrian princes whom he had deposed in the previous autumn, together with Antigonus, whose claims to the throne of Palestine he had rejected, had made an alliance with the Parthians and were marching down from the north-east against Decimus Saxa, the governor of Syria. The Roman forces in that country were few in number, consisting for the most part of the remnants of the army of Brutus and Cassius; and they could hardly be expected to put up a good fight against the invaders. Antony's own trusted legions were now stationed in Italy, Gaul, and Macedonia; and there were many grave reasons for their retention in their present quarters. The situation, therefore, was very serious, and Antony was obliged to bring his pleasant visit to Alexandria to an abrupt end. Plutarch describes him as "rousing himself with difficulty from sleep, and shaking off the fumes of wine" in preparation for his departure; but I do not think that his winter had been so debauched as these words suggest. He had combined business and pleasure, as the saying is, and at times had lost sight of the one in his eager prosecution of the other; but, looking at the matter purely from a hygienic point of view, it seems probable that the hunting, riding, and military exercises of which Plutarch speaks, had kept him in a fairly healthy condition in spite of the stupendous character of the meals set before him.

The parting of Antony and Cleopatra early in March must have contained in it an element of real tragedy. He could not tell what difficulties were in store for him, and at the moment he had not asked the Queen for any military help. He must have bade her lie low until he was able to tell her in what manner she could best help their cause; and thereby he consigned her to a period of deep anxiety and sustained worry. In loneliness she would have to face her coming confinement, and, like a deserted courtesan, would have to nurse a fatherless child. She would have to hold her throne without the comfort of a husband's advice; and in all things she would once more be obliged to live the dreary life of a solitary unmated Queen. It was a miserable prospect, but, as will be seen in the following chapter, the actual event proved to be far more distressing than she had expected; for, as Antony sailed out of the harbour of Alexandria, and was shut out from sight behind the mighty tower of Pharos, Cleopatra did not know that she would not see his face again for four long years.

CHAPTER XIV.

THE ALLIANCE RENEWED BETWEEN CLEOPATRA AND ANTONY.

In the autumn of the year B.C. 40, some six months after the departure of Antony, Cleopatra gave birth to twins, a boy and a girl, whom she named Alexander Helios and Cleopatra Selene, the Sun and the Moon. With this event she passes almost entirely from the pages of history for more than three years, and we hear hardly anything of her doings until the beginning of B.C. 36. During this time she must have been considerably occupied in governing her own kingdom and in watching, with a kind of despair, the complicated events [in the Roman world. Despatches from Europe must have come to her from time to time telling of the progress of affairs, but almost all the news which she thus received was disappointing and disconcerting to her; and one must suppose that she passed these years in very deep sadness and depression. I do not think that any historian has attempted to point out to his readers the painful condition of disillusionment in which the little Queen now found herself. When Antony left her she must have expected him either to return soon to her, or presently to send his lieutenants to bring her to him; but the weeks passed and no such event took place. While she suffered all the misery of lonely child-birth, her consort was engaged in absorbing affairs in which she played no immediate part; and it seems certain that in the stress of his desperate circumstances the inconsequent Antony had put her almost entirely from his thoughts.

When he left her in the spring of B.C. 40 he sailed straight across the Mediterranean to Tyre, where he learnt to his dismay that practically all Syria and Phœnicia had fallen into the hands of the Parthians, and that there was no chance of resisting their advance successfully with the troops now holding the few remaining seaport towns. He therefore hastened with 200 ships by Cyprus and Rhodes to Greece, abandoning Syria for the time being to the enemy. Arriving at Ephesus, he heard details of the troubles in Italy; how his supporters had been besieged by Octavian in Perugia, which had at length been captured; and how all his friends and relatives had fled from Italy. His wife Fulvia, he was told, escorted by 3000 cavalry, had sailed from Brundisium for Greece, and would soon join him there; and his mother, Julia, had fled to the popular hero, Sextus Pompeius, the outlawed son of the great Pompey, who had received her very kindly. Thus, not only was Italy shut to Antony, since Octavian was now sole master of the country, but he seemed likely also to be turned out of his eastern provinces by the advance of the Parthians. His position was a desperate one; and he must now have both reproached himself very deeply for his waste of time in Alexandria and blamed his relations for their impetuosity in making war against Octavian.

Towards the end of June Antony arrived in Athens,

and there he was obliged to go through the ordeal of
meeting the domineering Fulvia, of whom he was not
a little afraid, more especially in view of his notorious
intrigue with the Queen of Egypt. The ensuing interviews between them must have been of a very painful
character. Fulvia probably bitterly reproved her errant
husband for deserting her and for remaining so long with
Cleopatra, while Antony must have abused her roundly
for making so disastrous a mess of his affairs in Italy.
Ultimately the unfortunate woman seems to have been
crushed and dispirited by Antony's continued anger; and
having fallen ill while staying at Sicyon, some sixty miles
west of Athens, and lacking the desire to live, she there
died in the month of August. Meanwhile Antony, having
made an alliance with Sextus Pompeius, was ravaging
the coasts of Italy in a rather futile attempt to regain
some of his lost prestige; but no sooner was the death
of Fulvia announced than he shifted the entire blame for
the war on to his late wife's shoulders, and speedily made
his peace with Octavian. The two rivals met at Brundisium in September B.C. 40, and a treaty was made
between them by which the peace of the Roman world
was expected to be assured for some years to come. It
was arranged that Octavian should remain autocrat in
Italy, and should hold all the European provinces, including Dalmatia and Illyria; and that Antony should
be master of the East, his dominions comprising Macedonia, Greece, Bithynia, Asia, Syria, and Cyrene. The
remaining provinces of North Africa, west of Cyrene,
fell to the lot of the third Triumvir, the insignificant
Lepidus. This treaty was sealed by the marriage of
Antony with Octavia, the sister of Octavian, a young
woman who had been left a widow some months pre-

viously, and the wedding was celebrated in Rome in October B.C. 40, the populace showing peculiar pleasure at seeing the two rivals, whose quarrels had caused such bloodshed and misery, thus fraternising in the streets of the capital.

The consternation of Cleopatra, when the news of Antony's marriage reached her, must have been sad to witness. The twins whom she had borne to him were but a few weeks old at the time when their father's perfidy was thus made known to her; and bitterly must she have chided herself for ever putting her trust in so unstable a man. It now seemed to her that he had come to Alexandria as it were to fleece her of her wealth, and she, falling a victim to his false protestations of love, had given her all to him, only to be deserted when most she needed him. With the news of his marriage, her hopes of obtaining a vast kingdom for herself and for Cæsar's son were driven from her mind, and her plans for the future had to be diverted into other directions. She must have determined at once to give no more assistance to Antony, either in money or in materials of war; and we have no evidence of any such help being offered to him in the military operations which ensued during the next two years. Cleopatra had perhaps known Antony's new wife in Rome, and certainly she must have heard much of her charms and her goodness. Plutarch tells us that Octavia was younger and more beautiful than the Queen, and one may therefore understand how greatly Cleopatra must have suffered at this time. Not only was her heart heavy with the thought of the miscarriage of all her schemes, but her mind it would seem was aflame with womanly jealousy.

In the following year, B.C. 39, by the force of public

opinion, Sextus Pompeius was admitted to the general peace, the daughter of the sea-rover marrying Marcellus, the son of Octavian. The agreement was made at Misenum (not far from Naples), and was celebrated by a banquet which was given by Sextus Pompeius on board his flag-ship, a galley of six banks of oars, "the only house," as the host declared, "that Pompey is heir to of his father's." During the feast the guests drank heavily, and presently many irresponsible jests began to be made in regard to Antony and Cleopatra. Antony very naturally was annoyed at the remarks which were passed, and there seems to have been some danger of a fracas. Observing this, a pirate-chief named Menas, who was one of the guests, whispered to Sextus: "Shall I cut the cables and make you master of the whole Roman Empire?" "Menas," replied he, after a moment's thought, "this might have been done without telling me, but now we must rest content. I cannot break my word." Thus Antony was saved from assassination, and incidentally it may be remarked that had he been done to death at this time, history would probably have had to record an alliance between Sextus and Cleopatra directed against Octavian, which might have been as fruitful of romantic incident as was the story which has here to be related. We hear vaguely of some sort of negotiations between Sextus and the Queen, and it is very probable that with his rise to a position of importance Cleopatra would have attempted to make an alliance with this son of Egypt's former patron.

In September B.C. 39, Octavia presented Antony with a daughter who was called Antonia, and who subsequently became the grandmother of the Emperor Nero. Shortly after this he took up his quarters at Athens, where he threw himself as keenly into the life of the Athenians as he had into that of the Alexandrians. He dressed himself in the Greek manner, with certain Oriental touches, and it was noticed that he ceased to take any interest in Roman affairs. He feasted sumptuously, drank heavily, spent a very great deal of money, and wasted any amount of time. The habits of the East appealed to him, and in his administration he adopted the methods sometimes practised by Greeks in the Orient. He abolished the Roman governorships in many of the provinces under his control, converting them into vassal kingdoms. Thus Herod was created King of Judea; Darius, son of Pharnaces, was made King of Pontus; Amyntas was raised to the throne of Pisidia; Polemo was given the crown of Lycaonia, and so on. His rule was mild and kindly, though despotic; and on all sides he was hailed as the jolly god Dionysos, or Bacchus, come to earth. Like Julius Cæsar, he was quite willing to accept divinity, and he even went so far as personally to take the place of the statue of Dionysos in the temple of that god, and to go through the mystical ceremony of marriage to Athene at Athens. His popularity was immense, and this assumption of a godhead was received quite favourably by the Athenians; but when one of his generals, Ventidius Bassus, who had been sent to check the advance of the Parthians, returned with the news that he had completely defeated them, public enthusiasm knew no bounds, and Antony was fêted and entertained in the most astonishing manner.

The contrast between Antony's benevolent government of his eastern provinces and Octavian's conduct in the west was striking. Octavian was a curious - tempered man, morose, quietly cruel, and secretly vicious. So many persons were tortured and crucified by him that he came to be known as the "Executioner." His manner was imperturbable and always controlled in public; but in private life at this time he indulged in the wildest debauches, gambled, and surrounded himself with the lowest companions. His rule in Italy in these days constituted a Reign of Terror; and large numbers of the populace hated the very sight of him. His appearance was unimposing, for he was somewhat short and was careless in his deportment; while, although his face was handsome, it had certain very marked defects. His complexion was very sallow and unhealthy, his skin being covered with spots, and his teeth were much decayed; but his eyes were large and remarkably brilliant, a fact of which he was peculiarly proud. He did not look well groomed or clean, and he was notably averse to taking a bath, though he did not object to an occasional steaming, or Turkish bath, as we should now call it. He was eccentric in his dress, though precise and correct in business affairs. He disliked the sunshine, and always wore a broad-brimmed hat to protect his head from its brilliancy; but at the same time he detested cold weather, and in winter he is said to have worn a thick toga, at least four tunics, a shirt, and a flannel stomacher, while his legs and thighs were swathed in yards of warm cloth. In spite of this he was constantly suffering from colds in his head, and was always sneezing and snuffling. His liver, too, was generally out of order, a fact to which perhaps his ill-temper may be attributed. His clothes were all made at home by his wife and sister, and fitted him badly; and his light-brown, curly hair always looked unbrushed. He was a poor general, but an able statesman; and his cold nature, which was lacking in all ardour as was his personality in all magnetism, caused him to be better fitted for the office than for the public platform. He was not what would now be called a gentleman: he was, indeed, very distinctly a parvenu. His grandfather had been a wealthy money-lender of bourgeois origin, and his father had raised himself by this ill-gotten wealth to a position in Roman society, and had married into Cæsar's family.

These facts were not calculated to give him much of a position in public esteem: and there was no question at this time that Antony was the popular hero, while Sextus Pompeius, the former outlaw, was fast rising in favour. In the spring of B.C. 38 Octavian decided to make war upon this roving son of the great Pompey, and he asked Antony to aid him in the undertaking. The latter made some attempt to prevent the war, but his efforts were not successful. In the following July, to the delight of a large number of Romans, Octavian was badly defeated by Sextus; and Cæsar's nephew thus lost a very considerable amount of prestige. At about the same time Antony's reputation made an equally extensive gain, for in June Ventidius Bassus, acting under Antony's directions, again defeated the Parthians, Pacorus, the King's son, being killed in the battle. The news stirred the Romans to wild enthusiasm. At last, after sixteen years, Crassus [1] had been avenged; and Antony appeared to have put into execution with the utmost ease the plans of the late Dictator in regard to the Parthians, while, on the other hand, Octavian, the Dictator's nephew, had failed even to suppress the sea-roving Pompeians. A Triumph was

[1] Page 59.

decreed both for Antony and for Ventidius, and before
the end of the year this took place.

In January B.C. 37 the Triumvirate, which had then
expired, was renewed for a period of five years, in spite
of a very considerable amount of friction between the
happy-go-lucky Antony and the morose Octavian. At
length these quarrels were patched up by means of an
agreement whereby Antony gave Octavian 130 ships with
which to fight Sextus Pompeius, and Octavian handed
over some 21,000 legionaries to Antony for his Parthian
war. In this agreement it will be observed that Antony,
in order to obtain troops, sacrificed the man who had
befriended his mother and who had assisted his cause
against Octavian at a time when his fortunes were at a
low ebb; and it must be presumed, therefore, that his
desire to conquer Parthia and to penetrate far into the
Orient was now of such absorbing importance to him
that all other considerations were abrogated by it.
Antony, in fact, enthusiastically contemplating an en-
larged eastern empire, desired to have no part in the
concerns of the west; and he cared not one jot what fate
awaited his late ally, Sextus, who, he felt, was certain in
any case ultimately to go down before Octavian. He
was beginning, indeed, to trouble himself very little in
regard to Octavian either; for he now seems to have
thought that, when the Orient had been conquered and
consolidated, he would probably be able to capture the
Occident also from the cruel hands of his unpopular rival
with little difficulty. Two years previously he had found
it necessary to keep himself on friendly terms with
Octavian at all costs, and for this reason he had abandoned Cleopatra with brutal callousness. Now, however,
his position was such that he was able to defy Cæsar's

nephew, and the presentation to him of the 130 ships was no more than a shrewd business deal, whereby he had obtained a new contingent of troops. One sees that his thoughts were turning once more towards the Queen of Egypt; and he seems at this time to have recalled to mind both the pleasure afforded him by her brilliant society and the importance to himself of the position which she held in eastern affairs. The Egyptian navy was large and well-equipped, and the deficiency in his own fleet due to his gift to Octavian might easily be made good by the Queen.

In the autumn of B.C. 37 these considerations bore their inevitable fruit. On his way to Corfu, in pursuit of his Parthian schemes, he came to the conclusion that he would once and for all cut himself off from Rome until that day when he should return to it as the earth's conqueror. He therefore sent his wife Octavia back to Italy, determined never to see her again; and at the same time he despached a certain Fonteius Capito to Alexandria to invite Cleopatra to meet him in Syria. Octavia was a woman of extreme sweetness, goodness, and domesticity. Her gentle influence always made for peace; and her invariable good behaviour and meekness must have almost driven Antony crazy. No doubt she wanted to make his clothes for him, as she had made those of her brother; and she seems always to have been anxious to bring before his notice, in her sweet way, the charms of old-fashioned, respectable, family life, a condition which absolutely nauseated Antony. She now accepted her marching orders with a wifely meekness which can hardly command one's respect; and in pathetic obedience she returned forthwith to Rome. I cannot help thinking that if only she had now shown

some spirit, and had been able to substitute energy for
sweetness in the movements of her mind, the history of
the period would have been entirely altered.

It must surely be clear to the impartial reader that
Antony's change of attitude was due more to political
than to romantic considerations.[1] We have heard so
much of the arts of seduction practised by Cleopatra that
it is not easy at first to rid the mind of the traditional
interpretation of this reunion; and we are, at the outset,
inclined to accept Plutarch's definition of the affair when
he tells us that " Antony's passion for Cleopatra, which
better thoughts had seemed to have lulled and charmed
into oblivion, now gathered strength again, and broke
into flame; and like Plato's restive and rebellious horse
of the human soul, flinging off all good and wholesome
counsel, and fairly breaking loose, he sent Fonteius
Capito to bring her into Syria." But it is to be remembered that this " passion " for the Queen had not
been strong enough to hold him from marrying Octavia
a few months after he had left the arms of Cleopatra;
and now three and a half years had passed since he
had seen the Queen,—a period which, to a memory so
short as Antony's, constituted a very complete hiatus
in this particular love-story. So slight, indeed, was his
affection for her at this time that, in speaking of the
twins with which she had presented him, he made the
famous remark already quoted, that he had no intention
of confining his hopes of progeny to any one woman,
but, like his ancestor Hercules, he hoped to let nature
take her will with him, the best way of circulating noble
blood through the world being thus personally to beget
in every country a new line of kings. Antony doubtless

[1] Prof. Ferrero and others have already pointed this out.

looked forward with youthful excitement to a renewal of his relations with the Queen, and, to some extent, it may be true that he now joyously broke loose from the gentle, and, for that reason, galling, bonds of domesticity; but actually he purposed, for political reasons, to make a definite alliance with Cleopatra, and it is unreasonable to suppose that any flames of ungoverned passion burnt within his jolly heart at this time.

On Cleopatra's side the case was somewhat different. The stress of bitter experience had knocked out of her all that harum-scarum attitude towards life which had been her marked characteristic in earlier years; and she was no longer able to play with her fortune nor to romp through her days as formerly she had done. Antony, whom in her way she had loved, had cruelly deserted her, and now was asking for a renewal of her favours. Could she believe (for no doubt such was his excuse) that his long absence from her and his marriage to another woman were purely political manœuvres which had in no way interfered with the continuity of his love for her? Could she put her trust in him this second time? Could she, on the other hand, manage her complicated affairs without him? Evidently he was now omnipotent in the East; Parthia was likely to go down before him; and Octavian's sombre figure was already almost entirely eclipsed by this new Dionysos, save only in little Italy itself. Would there be any hope of enlarging her dominions, or even of retaining those she already possessed, without his assistance? Such questions could only have one solution. She must come to an absolutely definite understanding with Antony, and must make a binding agreement with him. In a word, if there was to be any renewal of their relationship, he must marry her. There must be no

more diplomatic manœuvring, which, to her, meant
desertion, misery, and painful anxiety. He must become
the open enemy of Octavian, and, with her help, must aim
at the conquest both of the limitless East and of the
entire West. He must act in all things as the successor
of the divine Julius Cæsar, and the heir to their joint
power must be Cæsar's son, the little Cæsarion, now a
growing boy of over ten years of age.

With this determination fixed in her mind she accepted the invitation presented to her by Fonteius Capito,
and set sail for Syria. A few weeks later, towards the
end of the year B.C. 37, she met Antony in the city of
Antioch; and at once she set herself to the execution
of her decision. History does not tell us what passed
between them at their first interviews; but it may be
supposed that Antony excused his previous conduct on
political grounds, and made it clear to the Queen that
he now desired a definite and lasting alliance with her;
while Cleopatra, on her part, intimated her willingness
to unite herself with him, provided that the contract was
made legal and binding on both sides.

The fact that she obtained Antony's consent to an
agreement which was in every way to her advantage, not
only shows what a high value was set by Antony upon
Egypt's friendship at this time, but it also proves how
great were her powers of persuasion. It must be remembered that Cleopatra had been for over three years
a wronged woman, deserted by her lover, despairing of
ever obtaining the recognition of her son's claims upon
Rome, and almost hopeless even of retaining the independence of Egypt. Now she had the pluck to demand
from him all manner of increased rights and privileges
and the confirmation of all her dynastic hopes; and, to

her great joy, Antony was willing to accede to her wishes.
I have already shown that he did not really love her with
a passion so deep that his sober judgment was obscured
thereby, and the agreement is therefore to be attributed
more to the Queen's shrewd bargaining, and to her very
understandable anxiety not to be duped once more by her
fickle lover. She must have worked upon Antony's feelings by telling him of her genuine distress; and at the
same time she must warmly have confirmed his estimate
of Egypt's importance to him at this juncture.

The terms of the agreement appear to me to have
been as follows :—

Firstly, it seems to have been arranged that a legal
marriage should be contracted between them according
to Egyptian custom. We have already seen how, many
years previously, Julius Cæsar had countenanced a law
designed to legalise his proposed marriage with Cleopatra,
by the terms of which he would have been able to marry
more than one wife;[1] and Antony now seems to have
based his attitude upon a somewhat similar understanding. The marriage would not be announced to the
Senate in Rome, since he intended no longer to regard
himself as subject to the old Roman Law in these
matters; but in Egypt it would be accepted as a legal
and terrestrial confirmation of the so-called celestial
union of B.C. 40.

Secondly, it was agreed that Antony should not assume
the title of King of Egypt, but should call himself
Autocrator — *i.e.*, "absolute ruler," of the entire East.
The word αὐτοκράτωρ was a fair Greek equivalent of the
Roman *Imperator*, a title which, it will be remembered,
was made hereditary in Julius Cæsar's behalf, and which

---

[1] Page 160.

was probably intended by him to obtain its subsequent significance of " Emperor." Antony would not adopt the title of βασιλεύς or *rex*, which was always objectionable to Roman ears; nor was the word *Imperator* quite distinguished enough, since it was held by all commanders - in - chief of Roman armies. But the title *Autocrator* was significant of omnipotence; and it is to be noted that from this time onwards every " Pharaoh " of Egypt was called by that name, which in hieroglyphs reads *Aut'k'r'd'r*. Antony also retained for the time being his title of Triumvir.

Thirdly, Antony probably promised to regard Cæsarion, the son of Cleopatra and Julius Cæsar, as the rightful heir to the throne;[1] and he agreed to give his own children by the Queen the minor kingdoms within their empire.

Fourthly, Antony appears to have promised to increase the extent of Egyptian power to that which existed fourteen hundred years previously, in the days of the mighty Pharaohs of the Eighteenth dynasty. He therefore gave to the Queen Sinai; Arabia, including probably the rock-city of Petra; the east coast of the Dead Sea; part of the valley of the Jordan and the City of Jericho; perhaps a portion of Samaria and Galilee; the Phœnician coast, with the exception of the free cities of Tyre and Sidon; the Lebanon; probably the north coast of Syria; part of Cilicia, perhaps including Tarsus; the island of Cyprus; and a part of Crete. The Kingdom of Judea, ruled by Herod, was thus enclosed within Cleopatra's dominions; but the deduction of this valuable land from the Egyptian sphere was compensated for by the addition of the Cilician territory, which had always lain

---

[1] See pp. 196, 197, 291, 305.

beyond Egypt's frontiers, even in the days of the great Pharaohs.

Lastly, in return for these gifts Cleopatra must have undertaken to place all the financial and military resources of Egypt at Antony's disposal whenever he should need them.

As soon as this agreement was made I think there can be little doubt that Cleopatra and Antony were quietly married;[1] and in celebration of the event coins were struck, showing their two heads, and inscribed with both their names, she being called Queen and he Autocrator. In honour of the occasion, moreover, Cleopatra began a new dating of the years of her reign; and on a coin minted six years later, the heads of Antony and the Queen are shown with the inscription, "In the reign of Queen Cleopatra, in the 21st, which is also the 6th, year of the goddess." It will be remembered that Cleopatra came to the throne in the summer of B.C. 51, and therefore the 21st year of her reign would begin after the summer of B.C. 31, which period would also be the close of the 6th year dating from this alliance at Antioch at the end of B.C. 37. Thus these coins must have been struck in the autumn of B.C. 31, at which time the beginning of the 21st year of Cleopatra's reign as Queen of Egypt coincided with the end of the 6th year of her reign with Antony. There are, of course, many arguments to be advanced against the theory that she was now definitely married; but in view of the facts that their two heads now appear on the coins, that Antony now settled upon her this vast estate, that she began a new dating to her reign, that

[1] The suggestion that an actual marriage took place was first made by Letronne, was confirmed by Kromayer, and was accepted by Ferrero.

Antony henceforth lived with her, and that, as we know from his letter to Octavian,[1] he spoke of her afterwards as his *wife*, I do not think that there is any good reason for postponing the wedding until a later period.

The winter was spent quietly at Antioch, Antony being busily engaged in preparations for his new Parthian campaign which was to bring him, he hoped, such enormous prestige and popularity in the Roman world. The city was the metropolis of Syria, and at this time must already have been recognised as the third city of the world, ranking immediately below Rome and Alexandria. The residential quarter, called Daphnæ, was covered with thick groves of laurels and cypresses for ten miles around, and a thousand little streams ran down from the hills and passed under the shade of the trees where, even in the height of summer, it was always cool. The city was famous for its art and learning, and was a centre eminently suited to Cleopatra's tastes. The months passed by without much event. The Queen is said to have tried to persuade Antony to dethrone Herod and to add Judea to her new dominions, but this he would not do, and he begged her not to meddle with Herod's affairs, a correction which she at once accepted, thereafter acting with great cordiality to the Jewish King.

In March B.C. 26, Antony set out for the war, Cleopatra accompanying him as far as Zeugma, a town on the Euphrates, near the Armenian frontier, a march of about 150 miles from Antioch. It is probable that she wished to go through the whole campaign by his side, for, at a later date, we find her again attempting to remain by him under similar circumstances; but at Zeugma a dis-

[1] Page 298.

covery seems to have been made in regard to her condition which necessitated her going back to Egypt, there to await his triumphant return. In spite of the anxieties and disappointments of her life the Queen had retained her energy and pluck in a marked degree, and she was now no less hardy and daring than she had been in the days when Julius Cæsar had found her invading Egypt at the head of her Syrian army. She enjoyed the open life of a campaign, and she took pleasure in the dangers which had to be faced. An ancient writer, Florus, has described her, as we have already noticed, as being " free from all womanly fear," and this attempt to go to the wars with her husband is an indication that the audacity and dash so often notice-able in her actions had not been impaired by her misfortunes. She does not appear to have been altogether in favour of the expedition, for it seemed a risky undertaking, and one which would cost her a great deal of money, but the adventure of it appealed to her, and added that quality of excitement to her days which seems to have been so necessary to her existence. Antony, however, fond as he was of her, could not have appreciated the honour of her company at such a time; and he must have been not a little relieved when he saw her retreating cavalcade disappear along the road to Antioch.

From Antioch Cleopatra made her way up the valley of the Orontes to Apamea, whence she travelled past Arethusa and Emesa to the Anti-Lebanon, and so to Damascus. From here she seems to have crossed to the Sea of Galilee, and thence along the river Jordan to Jericho. Hereabouts she was met by the handsome and adventurous Herod, who came to her in order that

they might arrive at some agreement in regard to the
portions of Judea which Antony had given to her;
and, after some bargaining, it was finally decided that
Herod should rent these territories from her for a certain
sum of money.   Jericho's tropical climate produced
great abundance of palms, henna, sometimes known as
camphire, myrobalan or *zukkûm*, and balsam, the "balm
of Gilead," so much prized as perfume and for medicinal
purposes.   Josephus speaks of Jericho as a "divine
region," and strategically it was the key of Palestine.
It may be understood, therefore, how annoying it must
have been to Herod to be dispossessed of this jewel of
his crown; and it is said that, after he had rented it
from Cleopatra, it became his favourite place of residence.   The transaction being settled, the Queen seems
to have continued her journey to Egypt, at the Jewish
King's invitation, by way of Jerusalem and Gaza—that
is to say, across the Kingdom of Judea; but no sooner
had she set her foot on Jewish territory than Herod
conceived the plan of seizing her and putting her to
death.   The road from Jericho to Jerusalem ascends
the steep, wild mountain-side, and zigzags upwards
through rugged and bare scenery.   It would have been
a simple matter to ambush the Queen in one of the
desolate ravines through which she had to pass, and
the blame might be placed with the brigands who infested
these regions.   He pointed out to his advisers, as Josephus
tells us, that Cleopatra by reason of her enormous influence upon the affairs of Rome had become a menace to
all minor sovereigns; and now that he had her in his
power he could, with the greatest ease, rid the world
of a woman who had become irksome to them all, and
thereby deliver them from a very multitude of evils and

misfortunes. He told them that Cleopatra was actually turning her beautiful eyes upon himself, and he doubted not but that she would make an attempt upon his virtue before he had got her across his southern frontier. He argued that Antony would in the long-run come to thank him for her murder; for it was apparent that she would never be a faithful friend to him, but would desert him at the moment when he should most stand in need of her fidelity. The councillors, however, were appalled at the King's proposal, and implored him not to put it into execution. "They laid hard at him," says the *naïf* Josephus, "and begged him to undertake nothing rashly; for that Antony would never bear it, no, not though any one should lay evidently before his eyes that it was for his own advantage. This woman was of the supremest dignity of any of her sex at that time in the world; and such an undertaking would appear to deserve condemnation on account of the insolence Herod must take upon himself in doing it."

The Jewish King, therefore, giving up his treacherous scheme, politely escorted Cleopatra to the frontier fortress of Pelusium, and thus she came unscathed to Alexandria, where she settled down to await the birth of her fourth child. It is perhaps worth noting that she is said to have brought back to Egypt from Jericho many cuttings of the balsam shrubs, and planted them at Heliopolis, near the modern Cairo.[1] The Queen's mind must now have been full of optimism. Antony had collected an enormous army, and already, she supposed, he must have penetrated far into Parthia. In spite of her previous fears, she now expected that he would return to her covered with glory, having opened the road through

[1] Brocardus : Descriptio Terræ Sanctæ, xiii.

S

Persia to India and the fabulous East. Rome would hail him as their hero and idol, and the unpopular Octavian would sink into insignificance. Then he would claim for himself and for her the throne of the West as well as that of the Orient, and at last her little son Cæsarion, as their heir, would come into his own.

With such hopes as these to support her, Cleopatra passed through her time of waiting; and in the late autumn she gave birth to a boy, whom she named Ptolemy, according to the custom of her house. But ere she had yet fully recovered her strength she received despatches from Antony, breaking to her the appalling news that his campaign had been a disastrous failure, and that he had reached northern Syria with only a remnant of his grand army, clad in rags, emaciated by hunger and illness, and totally lacking in funds. He implored her to come to his aid, and to bring him money wherewith to pay his disheartened soldiers, and he told her that he would await her coming upon the Syrian coast somewhere between Sidon and Berytus.

Once more the unfortunate Queen's hopes were dashed to the ground; but pluckily rising to the occasion, she collected money, clothes, and munitions of war, and set out with all possible speed to her husband's relief.

The history of the disaster is soon told. From Zeugma Antony had marched to the plateau of Erzeroum, where he had reviewed his enormous army, consisting of 60,000 Roman foot (including Spaniards and Gauls), 10,000 Roman horse, and some 30,000 troops of other nationalities, including 13,000 horse and foot supplied by Artavasdes, King of Armenia, and a strong force provided by King Polemo of Pontus. An immense number of heavy engines of war had been collected; and these were despatched towards Media along the valley of the Araxes, together with the contingents from Armenia and Pontus and two Roman legions. Antony himself, with the main army, marched by a more direct route across northern Assyria into Media, being impatient to attack the enemy. The news of his approach in such force, says Plutarch, not only alarmed the Parthians but filled North India with fear, and, indeed, made all Asia shake. It was generally supposed that he would march in triumph through Persia; and there must have been considerable talk as to whether he would carry his arms, like Alexander the Great, into India, where Cleopatra's ships, coming across the high sea trade-route from Egypt, would meet him with money and supplies. Towards the end of August, Antony reached the city of Phraaspa, the capital of Media-Atropatene, and there he awaited the arrival of his siege-train and its accompanying contingent. He had expected that the city would speedily surrender, but in this he was mistaken; and, ere he had settled down to the business of a protracted siege, he received the news that his second army had been attacked and defeated, that his entire siege-train had been captured, that the King of Armenia had fled with the remnant of his forces back to his own country, and that the King of Pontus had been taken prisoner. In spite of this crushing loss, however, Antony bravely determined to continue the siege; but soon the arrival of the Parthian army, fresh from its victory, began to cause him great discomfort, and his lines were constantly harassed from the outside by bodies of the famous Parthian cavalry, though not once did the enemy allow a general battle to take place. At last, in October, he was obliged to open negotiations with the enemy; for, in view of the general lack of pro-

visions, and the deep despondency of the troops, the
approach of winter could not be contemplated without
the utmost dread. He therefore sent a message to the
Parthian King stating that if the prisoners captured from
Crassus were handed over, together with the lost eagles,
he would raise the siege and depart. The enemy refused
these terms, but declared that if Antony would retire, his
retreat would not be molested; and to this the Romans
agreed. The Parthians, however, did not keep their
word; and as the weary legionaries crossed the snow-
covered mountains they were attacked again and again
by the fierce tribesmen, who ambushed them at every pass,
and followed in their rear to cut off stragglers. The
intense cold, the lack of food, and the extreme weariness
of the troops, caused the number of these stragglers to be
very great; and besides the thousands of men who were
thus cut off or killed in the daily fighting, a great number
perished from exposure and want of food. At one period
so great was the scarcity of provisions that a loaf of bread
was worth its weight in silver; and it was at this time
that large numbers of men, having devoured a certain
root which seemed to be edible, went mad and died.
" He that had eaten of this root," says Plutarch, "remembered nothing in the world, and employed himself only in
moving great stones from one place to another, which he
did with as much earnestness and industry as if it had
been a business of the greatest consequence; and thus
through all the camp there was nothing to be seen but
men grubbing upon the ground at stones, which they
carried from place to place, until in the end they vomited
and died." This account, though of course exaggerated
and confused, gives a vivid picture of the distressed
legionaries, some dying of this poison, some going mad,

some perishing from exposure and vainly endeavouring to build themselves a shelter from the biting wind.

All through the long and terrible march Antony behaved with consummate bravery and endurance. He shared every hardship with his men, and when the camp was pitched at night he went from tent to tent, talking to the legionaries, and cheering them with encouraging words. His sympathy and concern for the wounded was that of the tenderest woman; and he would throw himself down beside sufferers and burst into uncontrolled tears. The men adored him; and even those who were at the point of death, arousing themselves in his presence, called him by every respectful and endearing name. "They seized his hands," says Plutarch, "with joyful faces, bidding him go and see to himself and not be concerned about them; calling him their Emperor and their General, and saying that if only he were well they were safe." Many times Antony was heard to exclaim, "O, the ten thousand!" as though in admiration for Xenophon's famous retreat, which was even more arduous than his own. On one occasion so serious was the situation that he made one of his slaves, named Rhamnus, take an oath that in the event of a general massacre he would run his sword through his body, and cut off his head, in order that he might neither be captured alive nor be recognised when dead.

At last, after twenty-seven terrible days, during which they had beaten off the Parthians no less than eighteen times, they crossed the Araxes and brought the eagles safely into Armenia. Here, making a review of the army, Antony found that he had lost 20,000 foot and 4000 horse, the majority of which had died of exposure and illness. Their troubles, however, were by no means at an end;

for although the enemy had now been left behind, the snows of winter had still to be faced, and the march through Armenia into Syria was fraught with difficulties. By the time that the coast was reached eight thousand more men had perished; and the army which finally went into winter quarters at a place known as the White Village, between Sidon and Berytus, was but the tattered remnant of the great host which had set out so bravely in the previous spring. Yet it may be said that had not Antony proved himself so dauntless a leader, not one man would have escaped from those terrible mountains, but all would have shared the doom of Crassus and his ill-fated expedition.

At the White Village Antony eagerly awaited the coming of Cleopatra; yet so ashamed was he at his failure, and so unhappy at the thought of her reproaches for his ill-success, that he turned in despair to the false comfort of the wine-jar, and daily drank himself into a state of oblivious intoxication. When not in a condition of coma he was nervous and restless. He could not endure the tediousness of a long meal, but would start up from table and run down to the sea-shore to scan the horizon for a sight of her sails. Both he and his officers were haggard and unkempt, his men being clad in rags; and it was in this condition that Cleopatra found them when at last her fleet sailed into the bay, bringing clothing, provisions, and money.

CHAPTER XV.

THE PREPARATIONS OF CLEOPATRA AND ANTONY FOR
THE OVERTHROW OF OCTAVIAN.

WHEN Cleopatra carried Antony back to Alexandria to recuperate after his exertions, it seems to me that she spoke to him very directly in regard to his future plans. She seems to have pointed out to him that Roman attempts to conquer Parthia always ended in failure, and that it was a sheer waste of money, men, and time to endeavour to obtain possession of a country so vast and having such limitless resources. Wars of this kind exhausted their funds and gave them nothing in return. Would it not be much better, therefore, at once to concentrate all their energies upon the overthrow of Octavian and the capture of Rome? Antony had proved his popularity with his men and their confidence in him and his powers as a leader, for he had performed with ultimate success that most difficult feat of generalship—an orderly retreat. Surely, therefore, it would be wise to expend no further portion of their not unlimited means upon their eastern schemes, but to concentrate their full attention first upon Italy. The Parthians, after all, had been turned out of Armenia and Syria, and they might now be left severely alone within their own country until that day when Antony would march against them, in accordance with the prophecies of the Sibylline Books, as King of Rome. Cleopatra had never favoured the Parthian expedition, though she had helped to finance it as being part of Julius Cæsar's original design; and she had accepted as reasonable the argument put forward by Antony, that if successful it would enhance enormously his prestige and ensure his acceptance as a popular hero in Rome. The war, however, had been disastrous, and it would be better now to abandon the whole scheme than to risk a further catastrophe. Antony, fagged out and suffering from the effects of his severe drinking-bout, appears to have acquiesced in these arguments; and it seems that he arrived in Alexandria with the intention of recuperating his resources for a year or two in view of his coming quarrel with Octavian. In Syria he had received news of the events which had occurred in Rome during his absence at the wars. Octavian had at last defeated Sextus Pompeius, who had fled to Mytilene; and Lepidus, the third Triumvir, had retired into private life, leaving his province of Africa in Octavian's hands. His rival, therefore, now held the West in complete subjection, and it was not unlikely that he himself would presently pick a quarrel with Antony.

The comforts of the Alexandrian Palace, and the pleasures of Cleopatra's brilliant society, must have come to Antony as an entrancing change after the rigours of his campaign; and the remainder of the winter, no doubt, slipped by in happy ease. The stern affairs of life, however, seem to have checked any repetition of the frivolities of his earlier stay in the Egyptian capital; and we now hear nothing of the Inimitable Livers or of their prodigious entertainments. Antony wrote a long letter to Rome, giving a more or less glowing account of the war, and stating that in many respects it had been very successful. Early in the new year, B.C. 35, Sextus Pompeius attempted to open negotiations with the Egyptian court; but the envoys whom he sent to Alexandria failed to secure any favourable response. Antony, on the other hand, learnt from them that Sextus was engaged in a secret correspondence with the Parthians, and was attempting to corrupt Domitius Ahenobarbus, his lieutenant in Asia. Thereupon he and Cleopatra determined to capture this buccaneering son of the great Pompey and to put him to death. The order was carried out by a certain Titius, who effected the arrest in Phrygia; and Sextus was executed in Miletus shortly afterwards. This action was likely to be extremely ill received in Rome, for the outlaw, in the manner of a Robin Hood, had always been immensely popular; and for this reason Antony never seems to have admitted his responsibility for it, the order being generally said to have been signed by his lieutenant, Plancus.

Shortly after this the whole course of events was suddenly altered by the arrival in Alexandria of no less a personage than the King of Pontus, who, it will be remembered, had been captured by the Parthians[1] at the outset of Antony's late campaign, and had been held prisoner by the King of Media. The latter now sent him to Egypt with the news that the lately allied kingdoms of Media and Parthia had come to blows; and the King of Media proposed that Antony should help him to overthrow his rival. This announcement caused the greatest upheaval in Cleopatra's palace. Here was an unexpected

[1] Page 275.

opportunity to conquer the terrible Parthians with comparative ease; for Media had always been their powerful ally, and the Roman arms had come to grief on former occasions in Median territory. Cleopatra, however, fearing the duplicity of these eastern monarchs, and having set her heart on the immediate overthrow of Octavian, whose power was now so distinctly on the increase, tried to dissuade her husband from this second campaign, and begged him to take no further risks in that direction. As a tentative measure Antony sent a despatch to Artavasdes, the King of Armenia, who had deserted him after his defeat in Media, ordering him to come to Alexandria without delay, presumably to discuss the situation. Artavasdes, however, showed no desire to place himself in the hands of his overlord whom he had thus betrayed, and preferred to seek safety, if necessary, in his own hills or to throw in his lot with the Parthians.

Antony was deaf to Cleopatra's advice; and at length accepting the proposal conveyed by the King of Pontus, he prepared to set out at once for the north-east. Thereupon Cleopatra made up her mind to accompany him; and in the late spring they set out together for Syria. No sooner had they arrived in that country, however, than Antony received the disconcerting news that his Roman wife Octavia was on her way to join him once more, and proposed to meet him in Greece. It appears that her brother Octavian had chosen this means of bringing his quarrel with Antony to an issue; for if she were not well received he would have just cause for denouncing her errant husband as a deserter; and in order to show how justly he himself was dealing he despatched with Octavia two thousand legionaries and some munitions of war. As a matter of fact the legionaries served actually as

a bodyguard for Octavia,[1] while their ultimate presenta-
tion to Antony was to be regarded partly as a payment
for the number of his ships which had been destroyed in
Octavian's war against Sextus, and partly as a sort of
formal present from one autocrat to another. Antony
at once sent a letter to Octavia telling her to remain at
Athens, as he was going to Media; and in reply to this
Octavia despatched a family friend, named Niger, to ask
Antony what she should do with the troops and supplies.
Niger had the hardihood to speak openly in regard to
Octavia's treatment, and to praise her very highly for
her noble and quiet bearing in her great distress; but
Antony was in no mood to listen to him, and sent him
about his business with no satisfactory reply. At the
same time he appears to have been very sorry for
Octavia, and there can be little doubt that, had such a
thing been possible, he would have liked to see her for
a short time, if only to save her from the added insult of
his present attitude. He was an irresponsible boy in
these matters, and so long as everybody was happy he
really did not care very deeply which woman he lived
with, though he was now, it would seem, extremely
devoted to Cleopatra, and very dependent upon her lively
society.

The Queen, of course, was considerably alarmed by
this new development, for she could not be sure whether
Antony would stand by the solemn compact he had made
with her at Antioch, or whether he would once more
prove a fickle friend. She realised very clearly that the
insult offered to Octavia would precipitate the war between East and West, and she seems to have felt even

[1] Fulvia, it will be remembered (page 255), employed 3000 cavalry as a
bodyguard under similar circumstances.

more strongly than before that Antony would be ill
advised at this critical juncture to enter into any further
Parthian complication.   To her mind it was absolutely
essential that she should carry him safely back to Alexandria, where he would be, on the one hand, well out of
reach of Octavia, and, on the other, far removed from the
temptation of pursuing his Oriental schemes.   Antony,
however, was as eager to be at his old enemy once more
as a beaten boy might have been to revenge himself upon
his rival; and the thought of giving up this opportunity
for vengeance in order to prepare for an immediate
fight with Octavian was extremely distasteful to him.
Everything now seemed to be favourable for a successful
invasion of Parthia.   Not only had he the support of the
King of Media, but the fickle King of Armenia had
thought it wise at the last moment to make his peace
with Antony, and the new agreement was to be sealed
by the betrothal of his daughter to Antony's little son
Alexander Helios.   Cleopatra, however, did not care so
much about the conquest of Parthia as she did for the
overthrow of her son's rival, who seemed to have usurped
the estate which ought to have passed from the great
Cæsar to Cæsarion and herself; and she endeavoured
now, with every art at her disposal, to prevent Antony
taking any further risk in the East, and to urge his return
to Alexandria.   " She feigned to be dying of love for
Antony," says Plutarch, " bringing her body down by
slender diet.   When he entered the room she fixed her
eyes upon him in adoration, and when he left she seemed
to languish and half faint away.   She took great pains
that he should see her in tears, and, as soon as he
noticed it, she hastily dried them and turned away, as

if it were her wish that he should know nòthing of it. Meanwhile Cleopatra's agents were not slow to forward her design, upbraiding Antony with his unfeeling hard-hearted nature for thus letting a woman perish whose soul depended upon him and him alone. Octavia, it was true, was his wife; but Cleopatra, the sovereign queen of many nations, had been contented with the name of his mistress,[1] and if she were bereaved of him she would not survive the loss."

In this manner she prevailed upon him at last to give up the proposed war; nor must we censure her too severely for her piece of acting. She was playing a desperate game at this time. She had persuaded Antony to turn his back upon Octavia in a manner which could but be final; and yet immediately after this, as though oblivous to the consequences of his action, he was eager to go off to Pérsia at a time when Octavian would prob-ably attempt to declare him an enemy of the Roman people. Of course, in reality the Queen was no more deeply in love with Antony than he with her; but he was absolutely essential to the realisation of her hopes, and the necessity of a speedy trial of strength with Octavian became daily more urgent. For this he must prepare by a quiet collecting of funds and munitions, and all other projects must be given up.

Very reluctantly, therefore, Antony returned to Alex-andria, and there he spent the winter of B.C. 35-34 in soberly governing his vast possessions. In the following spring, however, he determined to secure Armenia and

---

[1] This passage is sometimes quoted to show that no definite marriage had taken place at Antioch; but it only indicates that the marriage to Cleopatra was not accepted as legal in Rome.

Media for his own ends; and when he transferred his
headquarters to Syria for the summer season[1] he again
sent word to King Artavasdes to meet him in order to
discuss the affairs of Parthia. The Armenian king, however, seems to have been intriguing against Antony
during the winter; and now he declined to place himself
in Roman hands lest he might suffer the consequence of
his duplicity. Thereupon Antony advanced rapidly into
Armenia, took the King prisoner, seized his treasure,
pillaged his lands, and declared the country to be henceforth a Roman province. The loot obtained in this rapid
campaign was very great. The legionaries seized upon
every object of value which they observed: and they even
plundered the ancient temple of Anaitis in Acilisene, laying hands on the statue of the goddess which was made
of pure gold, and pounding it into pieces for purposes of
division.

On his return to Syria Antony entered into negotiations
with the King of Media, the result of which was that the
Median Princess Iotapa was married to the little Alexander
Helios, whose betrothal to the King of Armenia's daughter
had, of course, terminated with the late war. As we shall
presently see, it is probable that the King of Media had
consented to make the youthful couple his heirs to the
throne of Media, for it would seem that he had no son;
and thus Antony is seen to have once more put into
practice his jesting scheme of founding royal dynasties of

---

[1] For the governing of his Eastern Empire Antony found it convenient to
make his headquarters at Alexandria during the winter and Syria during the
summer, and his movements to and fro were not due to pressing circumstances.
The whole Court moved with him, just as, for example, at the present day the
Viceregal Court of India moves from Calcutta to Simla. Thutmosis III. and
other great Pharaohs of Egypt had gone over to Syria in the summer in this
manner.

his own flesh and blood in many lands. Antony then
returned to Alexandria, well satisfied with his summer's
work, but "with his thoughts," as Plutarch says, "now
taken up with the coming civil war." Octavia had returned to Rome, and had made no secret of her ill-
treatment. Her brother, therefore, told her to leave
Antony's house, thus to show her resentment against
him; but she would not do this, nor did she permit
Octavian to make war upon her husband on her account,
for, she declared, it would be intolerable to have it said
that two women, herself and Cleopatra, had been the
cause of such a terrific contest. Nevertheless, there was
little chance of the quarrel being patched up; and
Antony must have realised now the wisdom of Cleopatra's objection to an expensive and exhausting campaign in Parthia.

On his return to Alexandria in the autumn of B.C. 34,
Antony set the Roman world agog by celebrating his
triumph over Armenia in the Egyptian capital. Never
before had a Roman General held a formal Triumph outside Rome; and Antony's action appeared to be a definite
proclamation that Alexandria had become the rival, if not
the successor, of Rome as the capital of the world. It
will be remembered that Julius Cæsar had talked of
removing the seat of government from Rome to Alexandria; and now it seemed that Antony had transferred the capital, at any rate of the Eastern Empire,
to that city, and was regarding it as his home. Alexandria was certainly far more conveniently situated than
Rome for the government of the world. It must be remembered that the barbaric western countries—the
unexplored Germania, the newly conquered Gallia, the
insignificant Britannia, the wild Hispania, and others—

were not of nearly such value as were the civilised eastern provinces; and thus Rome stood on the far western outskirts of the important dominions she governed. From Alexandria a march of 600 or 800 miles brought one to Antioch or to Tarsus; whereas Rome was nearly three times as far from these great centres. The southern Peloponnesus was, by way of Crete, considerably nearer to Alexandria than it was to Rome by way of Brundisium. Ephesus and other cities of Asia Minor could be reached more quickly by land or sea from Egypt than they could from Rome. Rhodes, Lycia, Bithynia, Galatia, Pamphylia, Cilicia, Cappadocia, Pontus, Armenia, Commagene, Crete, Cyprus, and many other great and important lands, were all closer to Alexandria than to Rome; while Thrace and Byzantium, by the land or sea route, were about equidistant from either capital. As a city, too, Alexandria was far more magnificent, more cultivated, more healthy, more wealthy in trade, and more "go-ahead" than Rome. Thus there was really very good ground for supposing that Antony, by holding his Triumph here, was proclaiming a definite transference of his home and of the seat of government; and one may imagine the anxiety which it caused in Italy.

The Triumph was a particularly gorgeous ceremony. At the head of the procession there seems to have marched a body of Roman legionaries, whose shields were inscribed with the large C which is said to have stood for "Cleopatra," but which, with equal probability, may have stood for "Cæsar," that is to say, for the legitimate Cæsarian cause. Antony rode in the customary chariot drawn by four white horses, and before him walked the unfortunate King Artavasdes loaded with golden chains, together with his queen and their sons. Behind the chariot walked a long procession of Armenian captives, and after these came the usual cars loaded with the spoils of war. Then followed a number of municipal deputations drawn from vassal cities, each carrying a golden crown or chaplet which had been voted to Antony in commemoration of his conquest. Roman legionaries, Egyptian troops, and several eastern contingents, brought up the rear.

The procession seems to have set out in the sunshine of the morning from the Royal Palace on the Lochias Promontory, and to have skirted the harbour as far as the temple of Neptune. It then travelled probably through the Forum, past the stately buildings and luxuriant gardens of the Regia, and so out into the Street of Canopus at about the point where the great mound of the Paneum rose up against the blue sky, its ascending pathway packed with spectators. Turning now to the west, the procession moved slowly along this broad paved street, the colonnades on either side being massed with sightseers. On the right-hand side the walls of the Sema, or Royal Mausoleum, were passed, where lay the bones of Alexander the Great; and on the left the long porticos of the Gymnasium and the Law Courts formed a shaded stand for hundreds of people of the upper classes. On the other side of the road the colonnades and windows of the Museum were crowded, I suppose, with the professors and students who had come with their families to witness the spectacle. Some distance farther along, the procession turned to the south, and proceeded along the broad Street of Serapis, at the end of which, on high ground, stood the splendid building of the Serapeum. Here Cleopatra and her court,

T

together with the high functionaries of Alexandria, were
gathered, while the priests and priestesses of Serapis
were massed on either side of the street and upon the
broad steps which led up to the porticos of the temple.
At this point Antony dismounted from his chariot; and
probably amidst the shouts of the spectators and the
shaking of hundreds of systra, he ascended to the temple
to offer the prescribed sacrifice to Serapis, as in Rome he
would have done to Jupiter Capitolinus. This accomplished he returned to the court in front of the sacred
building, where a platform had been erected, the sides of
which were plated with silver. On this platform, upon a
throne of gold, sat Cleopatra, clad in the robes of Isis or
Venus; and to her feet Antony now led the royal captives of Armenia, all hot and dusty from their long walk,
and dejected by the continuous booing and jeering of
the crowds through which they had passed. Artavasdes
was no barbarian : he was a refined and cultured man, to
whose sensitive nature the ordeal must have been most
terrible. He was something of a poet, and in his time
had written plays and tragedies not without merit. He
was now told to abase himself before Cleopatra, and to
salute her as a goddess; but this he totally refused to do,
and, in spite of some rough handling by his guards, he
persisted in standing upright before her and in addressing
her simply by her name. In Rome it was customary at
the conclusion of a Triumph to put to death the royal
captives who had been exhibited in the procession; and
now that he had openly insulted the Queen of Egypt he
could not have expected to see another sun rise. Antony
and Cleopatra, however, appear to have been touched at
his dignified attitude; and neither he nor his family were

ANTONIA, THE DAUGHTER OF ANTONY.

harmed. Instead, they were treated with some show of honour,[1] and thereafter were held as state prisoners in the Egyptian capital.

The Triumph ended, a vast banquet was given to all the inhabitants of Alexandria; and late in the afternoon a second ceremony was held in the grounds of the Gymnasium. Here again a silver-covered platform had been erected, upon which two large and four smaller thrones of gold had been set up; and, when the company was assembled, Antony, Cleopatra, and her children took their seats upon them. Certain formalities having been observed, Antony arose to address the crowd; and, after referring no doubt to his victories, he proceeded to confer upon the Queen and her offspring a series of startling honours. He appears to have proclaimed Cleopatra sovereign of Egypt, and of the dominions which he had bestowed upon her at Antioch nearly three years previously. He named Cæsarion, the son of Julius Cæsar, co-regent with his mother, and gave him the mighty title of King of Kings.[2] Cæsarion was now thirteen and a half years of age; and since, as Suetonius remarks, he resembled his father, the great Dictator, in a remarkable manner, Antony's feelings must have been strangely complicated as he now conferred upon him these vast honours. To Alexander Helios, his own child, Antony next gave the kingdom of Armenia; the kingdom of Media, presumably after the death of the reigning monarch, whose daughter had just been married to him; and ultimately the kingdom of Parthia, provided that it had been conquered. This seems to have been

---

[1] Velleius Paterculus.

[2] I here adopt the statement of Dion, and not that of Plutarch.

arranged by treaty with the King of Media in the previous summer,[1] the agreement probably being that, on the death of that monarch, Alexander Helios and the Median heiress, Iotapa, should ascend the amalgamated thrones of Armenia, Media, and Parthia, Antony promising in return to assist in the conquest of the last-named country. The boy was now six years of age, and his chubby little figure had been dressed for the occasion in Median or Armenian costume. Upon his head he wore the high, stiff tiara of these countries, from the back of which depended a flap of cloth covering his neck; his body was clothed in a sleeved tunic, over which was worn a flowing cloak, thrown over one shoulder and hanging in graceful folds at the back; and his legs were covered by the long, loosely-fitting trousers worn very generally throughout Persia. To Cleopatra Selene, Alexander's twin-sister, Antony gave Cyrenaica, Libya, and as much of the north-African coast as was in his gift; and finally he proclaimed the small Ptolemy King of Phœnicia, northern Syria, and Cilicia. This little boy, only two years of age, had been dressed up for the occasion in Macedonian costume, and wore the national mantle, the boots, and the cap encircled with the diadem, in the manner made customary by the successors of Alexander. At the end of this surprising ceremony the children, having saluted their parents, were each surrounded by a bodyguard composed of men belonging to the nations over whom they were to rule; and at last all returned in state to the Palace as the sun set behind the Harbour of the Happy Return.

In celebration of the occasion coins were struck bearing the inscription *Cleopatræ reginæ regum filiorum regum* —"Of Cleopatra the Queen, and of the Kings the chil-

[1] Page 286.

dren of Kings." Antony perhaps also caused a bronze statue to be made, representing his son Alexander Helios dressed in the royal costume of his new kingdom, for a figure has recently been discovered which appears to represent the boy in this manner. He then wrote an account of the whole affair to the Senate in Rome, together with a report on his Armenian war; and in a covering letter he told his agents to obtain a formal ratification of the changes which he had made in the distribution of the thrones in his dominions. The news was received in Italy with astonishment, and in official circles the greatest exasperation was felt. Antony's agents very wisely decided not to read the despatches to the Senate; but Octavian insisted, and after much wrangling their contents were at last publicly declared. Stories at once began to circulate in which Antony figured as a kind of Oriental Sultan, living at Alexandria a life of voluptuous degeneracy. He was declared to be constantly drunken; and, since no such charge could be brought against Cleopatra, the Queen was said to keep sober by means of a magical ring of amethyst, which had the virtue of dispelling the fumes of wine from the head of the wearer.

There can, indeed, be little doubt that Antony was very intemperate at this period. He was worried to distraction by the approach of the great war with Octavian; and he must have felt that his popularity in Rome was now very much at stake. While waiting for events to shape themselves, therefore, he attempted to free his mind from its anxieties by heavy drinking; but in so doing, it would seem from subsequent events, he began to lose the place in Cleopatra's esteem which he had formerly held. She herself did not ever drink much wine, if we may judge from the fact, just now quoted, that she was at all times notably sober; and she must have watched with increasing uneasiness the dissolute habits of the man upon whom she was obliged to rely for the fulfilment of her ambitions.

The fact that he was ceasing to be a Roman, and was daily becoming more like an Oriental potentate, did not trouble her so much. It differentiated him, of course, from the great Dictator, whose memory became more dear to her as she contrasted his activities with Antony's growing laziness; but all her life she had been accustomed to the ways of Eastern monarchs, and she could not have been much shocked at her husband's new method of life, except in so far as it modified his abilities as an active leader of men. Now that the quarrel with Octavian was coming to a head, her throne and her very existence depended on Antony's ability to inspire and to command; and I dare say a limited adoption of the manners of the East made him more agreeable to the people with whom he had to deal. "Cleopatra," says the violently partisan Florus, "asked of the drunken general as the price of her love the Roman Empire, and Antony promised it to her, as though Romans were easier to conquer than Parthians. . . . Forgetting his country, his name, his toga, and the insignia of his office, he had degenerated wholly, in thought, feeling, and dress, into that monster of whom we know. In his hand was a golden sceptre, at his side a scimitar; his purple robes were clasped with great jewels; and he wore a diadem upon his head so that he might be a King to match the Queen he loved."

The Palace at Alexandria had been much embellished and decorated during recent years; and it was now a

fitting setting for the ponderous movements of this burly
monarch of the East. Lucan tells us how sumptuous
a place the royal home had come to be. The ceilings
were fretted and inlaid, and gold-foil hid the rafters.
The walls and pillars were mainly made of fine marble,
but a considerable amount of purple porphyry[1] and
agate were used in the decoration. The flooring of some
of the halls was of onyx or alabaster; ebony was used
as freely as common wood; and ivory was to be seen
on all sides. The doors were ornamented with tortoise-
shells brought from India and studded with emeralds.
The couches and chairs were encrusted with gems; much
of the furniture was shining with jasper and carnelian;
and there were many priceless tables of carved ivory.
The coverings were bright with Tyrian dye, shining with
spangled gold, or fiery with cochineal. About the halls
walked slaves, chosen for their good looks. Some were
dark-skinned, others were white; some had the crisp
black hair of the Ethiopians; others the golden or flaxen
locks of Gaul and Germania. Pliny tells us that Antony
bought two boys for £800 each, and that they were supposed to be twins, but that actually they came from
different countries. Of Cleopatra, Lucan writes: "She
breathes heavily beneath the weight of her ornaments;
and her white breasts shine through the Sidonian fabric
which, wrought in close texture by the sley of the
Chinese, the needle of the workmen of the Nile has
separated, loosening the warp by stretching out the
web." The newly-developed trade with India had filled

---

[1] I suppose the "purple stone" referred to by Lucan was the famous
imperial porphyry from the quarries of Gebel Dukhan, though I am not
certain that the stone was used as early as this. Cf. my expedition to these
quarries described in my 'Travels in the Upper Egyptian Deserts.'

the Palace with the luxurious fabrics of the Orient; and the Greek, or even Egyptian, character of the materials and objects in daily use was beginning to be lost in the medley of heterogenous articles drawn from all parts of the world.

Amidst these theatrical surroundings Antony acted, with a kind of childish extravagance, the part of the half-divine Autocrator of the East. When he was sober his mind must have been full of cares and anxieties; but on the many occasions when he was somewhat intoxicated he behaved himself in the manner of an over-grown boy. He delighted in the general recognition of his identity with Bacchus or Dionysos; and he loved to hear himself spoken of as the new "Liber Pater." In the festivals of that deity he was driven through the streets of Alexandria in a car constructed like that traditionally used by the bibulous god; a golden crown upon his head, often poised, it would seem, at a peculiar angle, garlands of ivy tossed about his shoulders, buskins on his feet, and the thyrsus in his hand. In this manner he was trundled along the stately Street of Canopus, surrounded by leaping women and prancing men, the crowds on either side of the road shouting and yelling their merry salutations to him. A temple in his honour was begun in the Regia at Alexandria, just to the west of the Forum; but this was not completed until some years afterwards, when it was converted into a shrine in honour of Octavian, and was known as the Cæsareum. On one occasion he assigned the part of the sea-god Glaucus to his friend Plancus, who forthwith danced about at a banquet, naked and painted blue, a chaplet of sea-weed upon his head and a fish-tail tied from his waist.

Antony had never troubled himself much in regard
to his dignity; and now, in the character of the jolly
ruler of the East, he was quite unmindful of his appearance in the eyes of serious men. Often he was to be
seen walking on foot by the side of Cleopatra's chariot,
talking to the eunuchs and servants who followed in her
train. He caused the Queen to give him the post of
Superintendent of the Games, — a position which was
not considered to be particularly honourable. It is apparent that her company had become very essential to
him, and much notice was taken of the fact that he
now accompanied her wherever she went. He rode
through the streets at her side, conducted the official
and religious ceremonies for her, or sat by her when
she was trying cases in the public tribunal. Sometimes
when he himself was alone upon the judicial bench, looking out of the window in the midst of some intricate
judgment and by chance seeing Cleopatra's chariot passing by across the square, he would without explanation
start up from his seat, run over to her, and walk back
to the Palace at her side, leaving the magistrate, police,
and prisoners in open-mouthed astonishment.

We hear nothing in regard to Antony's relations with
his children, and it is difficult to picture him as he
appeared in the family circle. His stepson Cæsarion,
his two sons Alexander and Ptolemy, and his daughter
Cleopatra, were all at this time residing in the Palace;
and moreover his son by Fulvia, Antyllus, a boy somewhat younger than Cæsarion, had now come to live
with him in Alexandria. It is probable that he was
an affectionate and indulgent father; and there must
have been many happy scenes enacted in the royal
nurseries, which, could they have been recorded, would

have gone far to correct the popular estimate of the
nature of Antony's home - life with Cleopatra.   The
Queen was his legal wife;[1] and in contemplating the
extravagances and eccentricities of his behaviour at
Alexandria, we must not lose sight of the obvious fact
that his life at this period had also its domestic aspect.
He did not admit to himself that his union with
Cleopatra was in any way scandalous; and writing to
Octavian in the following year he seems to be quite
surprised that his family life should be regarded as
infamous.   " Is it because I live in intimate relations
with a Queen ? " he asks.   " *She is my wife.* Is this a
new thing with me ?   Have I not acted so for these nine
years ? "   Indeed, as compared with Octavian's private
life, the family circle at Alexandria, in spite of Antony's
buffoonery and heavy drinking, was by no means wholly
shameful.   In Rome Octavian was at this time employing his friends to search the town for women to amuse
him, and these agents, acting on his orders, are related
to have kidnapped respectable girls, and to have torn
their clothes from them, as did the common slave-
dealers, in order to ascertain whether they were fit
presents for their vile master.   We hear no such stories
in regard to the jovial Antony.

A characteristic tale is told by Plutarch which illus-
trates the open - handed opulence of the Alexandrian
court at this time.   A certain Philotas, while dining
with Antony's son Antyllus, shut the mouth of a rather
noisy comrade by a very absurd syllogism, which made

---

[1] Even Athenæus refers to Antony as being *married* to Cleopatra ; and
the reader must remember that, not the fact of the marriage, but only the
date at which it occurred, is at all open to question.   I do not think this is
generally recognised.

everybody laugh. Antyllus was so delighted that he promptly made a present of a sideboard covered with valuable plate to the embarrassed Philotas, who, of course, refused it, not imagining that a youth of that age could dispose in this light manner of such costly objects. Having returned to his house, however, a friend presently arrived, bringing the plate to him; and on his still objecting to receive it, "What ails the man?" said the bearer of the gift. "Don't you know that he who gives you this is Antony's son, who is free to give it even if it were all gold?"

Thus the winter of B.C. 34-33 passed, and in the spring of 33 Antony set out for his summer quarters in Syria. He desired to cement the agreement with the King of Media, in order to guard himself against a Parthian attack while engaged in the coming war with Octavian; and for this purpose he determined to proceed at once to the borders of that country. Cleopatra, therefore, did not accompany him; and in this fact we may perhaps see an indication of some loss of interest on her part, due to her growing disrespect for him. Passing through Syria he went north-eastwards into Armenia, and there he seems to have effected a meeting with the King of Media. To him he now gave a large portion of Greater Armenia, and to the King of Pontus he handed over the territory known as Lesser Armenia. The little Median princess, Iotapa, who had been married to the young Alexander Helios, was placed in the care of Antony with the idea that she should be educated at Alexandria. With her the King sent Antony a present of the eagles captured from his army at the time when the siege-train was lost in B.C. 36; and he also presented him with a regiment of the famous mounted archers who had wrought so much havoc on the Roman lines in the late campaign, while in return for these men Antony sent a detachment of legionaries to the Median capital.

The Parthian danger being thus circumvented by this extremely important and far-reaching compact with Media, Antony set out for Egypt with the idea of spending the winter there once more.[1] He took with him the little Princess Iotapa, and in the early autumn he reached Alexandria. His news in regard to Media must have been very satisfactory to Cleopatra, and Iotapa thenceforth became the companion of the royal children in the Palace. But the news which he had to relate in connection with Octavian was of the worst, and Cleopatra must have asked him in astonishment how he could think of spending the winter quietly in Alexandria in view of the imminence of war. In the first place, the Triumvirate[2] came to an end at the close of the year, and it seemed likely that Octavian would bring matters to an issue on that date. Then Octavian had attacked him violently in the Senate, and excited the public mind against his rival; and Antony, hearing of this while in Armenia, wrote to him an obscene letter, much too disgusting to quote here. To this Octavian replied in like manner. Antony then charged him with acting unfairly, firstly, by not dividing the spoils captured from Sextus Pompeius; secondly, by not returning the ships which had been lent to him for the Pompeian war; thirdly, by not sharing the province of Africa taken over after the retirement of Lepidus; and lastly, that he had parcelled out almost all the free land in Italy amongst

[1] Ferrero thinks he went direct to Ephesus, but Bouche-Leclerq and others are of opinion that he went first to Alexandria, and with this I agree.
[2] Page 262.

his own soldiers, thus leaving none for Antony's legionaries. Octavian had replied that he would divide all the spoils of war as soon as Antony gave him a share in Armenia and Egypt, while in regard to the lands given as rewards to his legionaries, Antony's troops could hardly want them, since, no doubt, by now they had all Media and Parthia to share amongst themselves. This reference to Egypt, as though it were a province of Rome instead of an independent kingdom, must have been deeply annoying to Cleopatra; but, on the other hand, it was pleasant to hear that Octavian had abused Antony for living immorally with the Queen, and that Antony had replied by stating emphatically that she was his legal wife.

The war, thus, was now on the eve of breaking out, and Cleopatra must have been in a fever of excitement. Antony's vague and casual behaviour seems, therefore, to have annoyed her very considerably; and it was not until he had decided to take up his winter quarters at Ephesus instead of in Egypt that harmony was restored. Once aroused, he acted with energy. He sent messengers in all directions to gather in his forces; and he eagerly helped Cleopatra to make her warlike preparations in her own country. In a few weeks the arrangements were complete, and Antony and Cleopatra set out for Ephesus early in the winter of B.C. 33, at the head of a huge assemblage of naval and military armaments and munitions. The people of Alexandria must have realised that their Queen was going forth upon the most marvellous adventure. Only a few years ago they had lain prone under the heel of Italy, expecting at any moment to be deprived of their independent existence. Now, thanks to the skill, the tact, and the charm of their divine

Queen, their incarnate Isis-Aphrodite, they were privileged to witness the departure of the ships, the hosts, and the captains of Egypt for the conquest of mighty Rome. They had heard Cleopatra swear to seat herself and her son Cæsarion in the Capitol; and there could have been few in the cheering crowds whose hearts did not swell with pride at the thought of the glorious future which awaited their country and their royal house.

CHAPTER XVI.

THE DECLINE OF ANTONY'S POWER.

THE city of Ephesus was situated near the mouth of the river Caystrus in the shadow of the Messogis mountains, not far south of Smyrna, and overlooking the island of Samos. Standing on the coast of Asia Minor, near the frontier which divided Lydia from Caria, it looked directly across the sea to Athens, and was sheltered from the menacing coasts of Italy by the intervening Greek peninsula. Ephesus, I need hardly remind the reader, was famous for its temple, dedicated to Diana of the Ephesians. The building was constructed of white marble and cypress- and cedar-wood, and was richly ornamented with gold. Many statues adorned its colonnades, and there were many celebrated paintings upon its walls, including a fine picture of Alexander the Great. Diana was here worshipped under the name Artemis, and was often identified with Venus, with whom Cleopatra claimed identity. Here Antony and Cleopatra collected their forces, and soon the ancient city came to be the largest military and naval centre in the world. Cleopatra had brought with her from Egypt a powerful fleet of two hundred ships of war, and a host of soldiers, sailors, workmen, and slaves.

She had drawn 20,000 talents (*i.e.*, £4,000,000) from her treasury; and, besides this, she had brought a vast amount of corn, foodstuffs, clothing, arms, and munitions of war. From Syria, Armenia, and Pontus, vessels were arriving daily with further supplies; and Antony's own fleet of many hundred battleships and vessels of burden was rapidly mobilising at the mouth of the river. All day and all night the roads to the city thundered with the tread of armed men, as the kings and rulers of the East marched their armies to the rendezvous. Bocchus, King of Mauritania; Tarcondimotus, ruler of Upper Cilicia; Archelaus, King of Cappadocia; Philadelphus, King of Paphlagonia; Mithridates, King of Commagene; Sadalas and Rhœmetalces, Kings of Thrace; Amyntas, King of Galatia, and many other great rulers, responded to the call to arms, and hastened to place their services at the disposal of Antony and his Queen.

One cannot help wondering whether these mighty men realised for what they were about to fight. They were flocking to the standard of a man who had held supreme power over their countries for many years, and whose rule had been kindly and easy. They owed a great deal to him,—in some cases their very thrones; and, were he now to be defeated by his rival, they would probably fall with him. Success, however, seemed certain in view of Antony's enormous forces; and they therefore felt that the assistance which they gave would undoubtedly bear abundant fruit, and that their reward would be great. Antony, of course, told them, perhaps with his tongue in his cheek, that he was fighting to some extent on behalf of the Roman Republic, in order to free the country from the oppression of an autocratic rule, and to restore the old constitution. He was not such a fool

CLEOPATRA AND HER SON CÆSARION.

REPRESENTED CONVENTIONALLY UPON A WALL OF THE TEMPLE OF DENDERA.

as to admit that he was aiming at a throne: Julius Cæsar had been assassinated on that very account, and a declaration of this kind would likewise alienate a large number of his supporters in Rome. He still had numerous friends in the capital, men who disliked the forbidding personality of Octavian, and who admired his own frank and open manners. Moreover, a considerable body supported him in memory of the great Dictator, regarding Antony as the guardian of young Cæsarion, whose rights they had at heart. A story, of which we have already heard, had been circulated in regard to Julius Cæsar's will. It was said that the document which decreed Octavian the heir was not the Dictator's last testament, but that he had made a later will in favour of Cleopatra's son, Cæsarion, which had been suppressed, probably by Calpurnia. Thus, to many of his Roman friends, Antony was fighting to carry out the Dictator's wishes, and to overthrow the usurping Octavian. Was this, one asks, the justification which he placed before the consideration of the vassal kings? At any rate Dion Cassius states definitely that Antony's recognition of Cæsarion's right to this great inheritance was the real cause of the war.

It does not seem to me that this point is fully recognised by historians; but it is very apparent that Antony's position at Ephesus would have been almost untenable without a justification such as that of the championing of Cæsarion. It was plain to every eastern eye that he was acting in conjunction with Egypt and with Cleopatra; and all men now knew that the Queen was his legal wife. It was obvious that, if successful, he would enter Rome with the Queen of Egypt by his side. Yet, at the same time, he was denying that he intended to establish a monarchy in Rome on the lines proposed

U

by the Dictator, and he was talking a great deal of
rubbish about reviving the Republic. There is, surely,
only one way in which these divergent interests could
be made to fit into a scheme capable of satisfying both
his Roman and his Oriental supporters, and would serve
as a professed justification for the war: he was going to
establish the Dictator's son, Cæsarion, in his father's
seat, and to turn out the wrongful heir, Octavian. He
himself would be the boy's guardian, and would act,
at any rate in Italy, on republican lines. Cleopatra, as
his wife, would doff her crown while in Italy, but would
assume it once more within her own dominions, just as
Julius Cæsar had proposed to do in the last year of his
life.[1] Of course it must have been recognised that the
throne of Rome would ultimately be offered to him, and
that he would hand it on to Cæsarion in due course,
thus founding a dynasty of the blood of the divine Julius;
but this fact was kept severely in the background. If
Cæsarion and his cause had not formed part of the *casus
belli*, it is unlikely that Antony would have been at all
widely supported in Rome; and what man would have
tolerated the armed presence of Cleopatra and her
Egyptians, save in her capacity as mother of the
claimant and wife of the claimant's guardian? Without Cæsarion, what was Antony's justification for the
war? I can find very little. He would have been
fighting to turn out Octavian, who, in that case, would
have been the rightful and only heir; he would have
been introducing Cleopatra into Roman politics with
the obvious intention of creating a throne for her, the
very step which had been Cæsar's undoing; and he
would have been offering her royal view of life in

[1] Page 162.

exchange for Octavian's republican sentiments, not as something of which the best had to be made under the circumstances, but as a habit of mind desirable in itself. His apparent deference to Cleopatra, and the manner in which she shared his supremacy, must have been liable to cause much offence in Rome and in Ephesus, and would never have been tolerated had she not been put forward as Julius Cæsar's widow and the mother of his son.

The armies marching into the city comprised soldiers of almost every nation. There were nineteen Roman legions; troops of Gauls and Germans; contingents of Moorish, Egyptian, Sudanese, Arab, and Bedouin warriors; the wild tribesmen from Media; hardy Armenians; barbaric fighting men from the coast of the Black Sea; Greeks, Jews, and Syrians. The streets of the city were packed with men in every kind of costume, bearing all manner of arms, and talking a hundred languages. Never, probably, in the world's history had so many nationalities been gathered together; and Cleopatra's heart must have been nigh bursting with feminine pride and gratification at the knowledge that in reality she had been the cause of the great mobilisation. They had come together at Antony's bidding, it is true; but they had come to fight her battles. They were here to vindicate her honour, to place her upon the throne of the World. With their forests of swords and spears they were about to justify those nights, nearly sixteen years ago, when, as the wild little queen of little Egypt, she lay in the arms of Rome's mighty old reprobate. In those far-off days she was fighting to retain the independence of her small country and her dynasty: now she was Queen of dominions more extensive than any governed by the proudest of the Pharaohs, and she would soon see her royal house raised to a height never before attained by man. It was her custom at this time to use as an oath the words, "As surely as I shall one day administer justice on the Capitol"; and, proudly acting the part of hostess in Ephesus, she must have felt that the great day was very near. Already the Ephesians were hailing her as their Queen, and the deference paid to her by the vassal-kings was very marked.

In the spring of B.C. 32 some four hundred Roman senators arrived at Antony's headquarters. These men stated that Octavian, after denouncing his rival in the Senate, had advised all who were on the enemy's side to quit the city, whereupon they had set sail for Ephesus, leaving behind them some seven or eight hundred senators who either held with Octavian or pursued a non-committal policy. War had not yet been declared, but no declaration seemed now to be necessary.

With the arrival of the senators trouble began to brew in the camp. Cleopatra's power and authority were much resented by the new-comers, to whom the existing situation was something of a revelation. They had not realised that the Queen of Egypt was playing an active part in the preparations, and many of them speedily recognised the fact that Antony, as Autocrat of the East and husband of Cleopatra, was hardly the man to restore a republican government to Rome. It was not long before some of them began to show their dislike of the Queen and to hint that she ought to retire into the background, at any rate for the time being. There was one old soldier, Cnæus Domitius Ahenobarbus, the representative of an ancient republican family, who would never acknowledge Cleopatra's right to the supremacy which she had attained, nor, on any occasion, would he address her by her title, but always called her simply by her name. This man at length told Antony in the most direct manner that he ought to send Cleopatra back to Egypt, there to await the conclusion of the war.   He seems to have pointed out that her presence with the army gave a false impression, and would be liable to alienate the sympathies of many of his Roman friends.   He suggested, perhaps, that the Queen should vacate her place in favour of Cæsarion, whose rights few denied.   Antony, seeing the wisdom of this advice, told Cleopatra to return to Alexandria; but she, in great alarm, is said to have bribed Publius Canidius, one of Antony's most trusted councillors, to plead with him on her behalf—the result being that the proposal of Domitius Ahenobarbus was discarded, and the Queen remained with the army. Publius Canidius had pointed out to Antony that the Egyptian fleet would fight much more willingly if their Queen were with them, and Egyptian money would be more readily obtained if she herself were felt to be in need of it.   "And, besides," said he, " I do not see to which of the kings who have joined this expedition Cleopatra is inferior in wisdom; for she has for a long time governed by herself a vast kingdom, and has learnt in your company the handling of great affairs." [1]

The Queen's continuance at Ephesus and her connection with the war was the cause of great dissensions, and the Roman senators began to range themselves into two distinct parties: those who fell in with Antony's schemes, and those who now favoured a reconciliation with Octavian as a means of ridding Roman politics of Cleopatra's disturbing influence.   When the efforts of the

[1] Plutarch.

peacemakers came to her ears her annoyance must have been intense. Were all her hopes to be dashed to the ground just because a few stiff-backed senators disliked the idea of a foreign sovereign concerning herself with republican politics? She no longer trusted Antony, for it seemed apparent to her that he was, at heart, striving only for his own aggrandisement, and was prepared to push her into the background at the moment when her interests threatened to injure his own. It was she who had incited him into warfare, who had kept him up to the mark, aroused him to his duties, and financed to a large extent his present operations; and yet he was, even at this eleventh hour, half-minded to listen to those who urged him to make peace. Only recently he had made some sort of offer to Octavian to lay down his arms if the latter would do likewise. At the time Cleopatra had probably thought this simply a diplomatic move designed to gain popularity; but now she seems to have questioned seriously Antony's desire for war, and to have asked herself whether he would not much prefer peace, quietness, and leisure wherein to drink and feast to his jovial heart's content. Yet war was essential to her ambitions, and to the realisation of the rights of her son. If Octavian were not overthrown, she would never have any sense of security; and with all her heart she desired to come to a safe harbour after these years of storm and stress.

It will be seen, then, that to her the need of preventing peace was paramount. She therefore made one last effort in this direction; and, bringing all her arts and devices to bear upon her husband, she began to persuade him to issue a writ casting off Octavia and thereby insulting Octavian beyond the limits of apology.

As soon as the scheme came to the ears of the peace
party pressure was brought to bear on Antony to effect
a reconciliation with Octavia; and the unfortunate man
appears to have been badgered and pestered by both
factions until he must have been heartily sick of the
subject. Cleopatra's councils, however, at last prevailed
to this extent, that Antony decided to make a forward
movement and to cross the sea to Greece, thus bringing
hostilities a step nearer. At the end of April he sailed
over from Ephesus to the island of Samos, leaving a
part of the army behind him. Here he remained for
two or three weeks, during which time, in reaction after
his worries, he indulged in a round of dissipations. He
had told his various vassals to bring with them to the
rendezvous their leading actors and comedians, so that
the great gathering should not lack amusement; and
now these players were shipped across to Samos, there
to perform before this audience of kings and rulers.
These sovereigns competed with one another in the
giving of superb banquets, but we do not now hear of
any such extravagances on the part of Cleopatra, who
was probably far too anxious, and too sobered, to give
any extraordinary attention to her duties as hostess.
Splendid sacrifices were offered to the gods in the island
temples, each city contributing an ox for this purpose;
and the sacred buildings must have resounded with
invocations to almost every popular deity of the east and
west. The contrast was striking between the brilliancy
and festivity at Samos and the anxiety and dejection of
the cities of the rest of the world, which had been bereft
of their soldiers and their money, and were about to
be plunged into all the horrors of internecine warfare.
" While pretty nearly the whole world," says Plutarch,

"was filled with groans and lamentations, this one island for some days resounded with piping and harping, theatres filling, and choruses playing; so that men began to ask themselves what would be done to celebrate victory when they went to such an expense of festivity at the opening of the war."

Towards the end of May the great assemblage crossed over the sea to Athens, and here Antony and Cleopatra held their court. The Queen's mind was now, I fancy, in a very disturbed condition, owing to the ominous dissensions arising from her presence with the army, and to the lack of confidence which she was feeling in her husband's sincerity. I think it very probable that they were not on the best of terms with one another at this time, and, although Antony was perhaps a good deal more devoted to the Queen than he had been before, there may have been some bickering and actual quarrelling. Cleopatra desired the divorce of Octavia and immediate war, but Antony on his part was seemingly disinclined to take any decisive steps. He was, in fact, in a very great dilemma. He had, apparently, promised the Queen that if he were victorious he would at once aim for the monarchy proposed by Julius Cæsar, and would arrange for Cæsarion to succeed in due course to the throne; but now it had been pointed out to him by the majority of the senators who were with him that he was earnestly expected to restore the republic, and to celebrate his victory by becoming once more an ordinary citizen. In early life he would have faced these difficulties with a light heart, and devised some means of turning the situation to his own advantage. Now, however, the power of his will had been undermined by excessive drinking; and, moreover, he had come to be extremely dependent upon Cleopatra in all things. He was very fond of her, and was becoming daily more maudlin in his affections. He was now nearly fifty years old; and, with the decrease of his vitality, he had ceased to be so promiscuous in affairs of the heart, centering his interest more wholly upon the Queen, though she herself was no longer very youthful, being at this time some thirty-eight years of age. His quarrels with her seemed to have distressed him very much, and in his weakened condition, her growing disrespect for him caused him to be more devotedly her slave. He seems to have watched with a sort of bibulous admiration her masterly and energetic handling of affairs, and he was anxious to do his best to retain her affection for him, which he could see, was on the wane. To the dauntless heart of a woman like Cleopatra, however, no appeal could be made save by manly strength and powerful determination; and one seems to observe the growth in the Queen's mind of a kind of horror at the rapid degeneration of the man whom she had loved and trusted.

To make matters worse, there arrived at Athens Antony's fourteen-year-old son, Antyllus, whom we have already met at Alexandria. He had recently been in Rome, where he had been kindly treated by the dutiful Octavia, whose attitude to all her husband's children was invariably generous and noble. Antony regarded this boy, it would seem, with great affection, and had caused him to be proclaimed an hereditary prince. The lad became something of a rival to Cæsarion, to whom Cleopatra was devotedly attached; and one may perhaps see in his presence at Athens a further cause for dissension.

At length, however, early in June the Queen persuaded Antony to take the final step, and to divorce Octavia. Having placed the matter before his senators, by whom the question was angrily discussed, he sent messengers to Rome to serve Octavia with the order of ejection from his house; and at the same time he issued a command to the troops still at Ephesus to cross at once to Greece. This was tantamount to a declaration of war, and Cleopatra's mind must have been extremely relieved thereby. No sooner, however, had this step been taken than many of Antony's Roman friends appear to have come to him in the greatest alarm, pointing out that the brutal treatment of Octavia, who had won all men's sympathy by her quiet and dutiful behaviour, would turn from him a great number of his supporters in Italy, and would be received as a clear indication of his subserviency to Cleopatra. They implored him to correct this impression; and Antony, harrassed and confused, thereupon made a speech to his Roman legions promising them that within two months of their final victory he would re-establish the republic.

The announcement must have come as a shock to Cleopatra, and must have shown her clearly that Antony was playing a double game. She realised, no doubt, that the promise did not necessitate the abandonment of their designs in regard to the monarchy; for, after establishing the old constitution, Antony would have plenty of time in which to build the foundations of a throne. Yet the declaration unnerved her, and caused her to recognise with more clarity the great divergence between her autocratic sentiments and the democratic principles of the country she was attempting to bring under her

sway.   She saw that, little by little, the basis upon which
the project of the war was founded was being changed.
At first the great justification for hostilities had been the
ousting of Octavian from the estate belonging by right
to her son, Cæsarion.   Now the talk was all of liberty,
of democracy, and of the restoration of republican insti-
tutions.

Her overwrought feelings, however, were somewhat
soothed by Antony's personal behaviour, which at this
time was anything but democratic.   He was allowing
himself to be recognised as a divine personage by the
Athenians, and he insisted on the payment of the most
royal and celestial honours to Cleopatra, of whom he
was at this time inordinately proud.   The Queen was,
indeed, in these days supreme, and the early authors
are all agreed that Antony was to a large extent under
her thumb.   The Athenians, recognising her as their
fellow-Greek, were eager to admit her omnipotence.
They caused her statue to be set up in the Acropolis
near that already erected to Antony; they hailed her
as Aphrodite; they voted her all manner of municipal
honours, and, to announce the fact, sent a deputation
to her which was headed by Antony in his *rôle* as a
freeman of the city.   Octavia, it will be remembered,
had resided at Athens some years previously, and had
been much liked by the citizens; but the memory of
her quiet and pathetic figure was quickly obliterated
by the presence of the splendid little Queen of Egypt
who sat by Antony's side at the head of a gathering
of kings and princes.   Already she seemed to be Queen
of the Earth; for, acting as hostess to all these
monarchs, speaking to each in his own language, and
entertaining them with her brilliant wit, she appeared

to be the leading spirit both in their festivities and in their councils.

Antony, meanwhile, having quieted the dissensions amongst his supporters, gave himself up to merry-making in his habitual manner; and presently he caused the Athenians to recognise him formally as Dionysos, or Bacchus, come down to earth. In anticipation of a certain Bacchic day of festival he set all the carpenters in the city to make a huge skeleton roof over the big theatre, this being then covered with green branches and vines, as in the caves sacred to this god; and from these branches hundreds of drums, faun-skins, and other Bacchic toys and symbols were suspended. On the festal day Antony sat himself, with his friends around him, in the middle of the theatre, the afternoon sun splashing down upon them through the interlaced greenery; and thus, in the guise of Bacchus, he presided at a wild drinking-bout, hundreds of astonished Athenians watching him from around the theatre. When darkness had fallen the city was illuminated, and, in the light of a thousand torches and lanterns, Antony rollicked up to the Acropolis, where he was proclaimed as the god himself.

Many were the banquets given at this time both by Antony and Cleopatra, and the behaviour of the former was often uproarious and undignified. On one state occasion he caused much excitement by going across to Cleopatra in the middle of the meal and rubbing her feet, a ministration always performed by a slave, and now undertaken by him, it is said, to fulfil a wager. He was always heedless of public opinion, and at this period of his life the habit of indifference to comment had grown upon him to a startling extent. Frequently he would rudely interrupt an audience which he was giving to one of the vassal kings by receiving and openly reading some message from Cleopatra written upon a tablet of onyx or crystal; and once when Furnius, a famous orator, was pleading a case before him, he brought the eloquent speech to an abrupt end by hurrying off to join the Queen outside, having entirely forgotten, it would seem, that the orator's arguments were being addressed to himself.

An event now occurred which threw the whole of the Antonian party into a state of the utmost anxiety. Two of the leading men at that time in Athens deserted and went over to Octavian. One of these, Titius, has already been noticed in connection with the arrest and execution of Sextus Pompeius; the other, Plancus, was the man who made so great a fool of himself at Alexandria when he painted himself blue and danced naked about the room, as has been described already.[1] Velleius speaks of him as "the meanest flatterer of the Queen, a man more obsequious than any slave"; and one need not be surprised, therefore, that Cleopatra was rude to him, which was the cause, so he said, of his desertion. These two men had both been witnesses to Antony's will, a copy of which had been deposited with the Vestal Virgins; and as soon as they were come to Rome they informed Octavian of its contents, who promptly went to the temple of Vesta, seized the document, and, a few days later, read it out to the Senate. Many senators were scandalised at the proceedings; but they were, nevertheless, curious to hear what the will set forth, and therefore did not oppose the reading. The only clause, however, out of which Octavian was able to make much

[1] Page 296.

capital was that wherein Antony stated that if he were to die in Rome he desired his body, after being carried in state through the Forum, to be sent to Alexandria, there to be buried beside Cleopatra.

The two deserters now began to spread throughout Italy all manner of stories derogatory to Antony, and to heap abuse upon the Queen, whom they described as having complete ascendancy over her husband, due, they were sure, to the magical love-potions which she secretly administered to him. When we consider that the accusations made by disreputable tattlers, such as Plancus, were all concerned with Antony's devotion to her, we may realise how little there really was to be brought against her. Antony, they said, was under her magical spell; he had allowed the Ephesians to hail her as Queen; she had forced him to present to her the library of Pergamum (a city not far from Ephesus), consisting of 200,000 volumes; he was wont to become drunken while she, of course by magic, remained sober; he had become her slave and even rubbed her feet always for her, and so on. Such rubbishy tales as these were the basis upon which the fabulous story of Cleopatra's terrible wickedness was founded, and presently we hear her spoken of as "the harlot queen of incestuous Canopus, who aspired to set up against Jupiter the barking Anubis, and to drown the Roman trumpet with her jangling systrum." [1]

The friends of Antony in Rome, alarmed by the hostile attitude of the majority of the public, sent a certain Geminius to Athens to warn their leader that

---

[1] Propertius. Canopus was an Egyptian port with a reputation much like that once held by the modern Port Said. Anubis was the Egyptian jackal-god, connected with the ritual of the dead.

he would soon be proclaimed an enemy of the State. On his arrival at the headquarters, he was thought to be an agent of Octavia, and both Cleopatra and Antony treated him with considerable coldness, assigning to him the least important place at their banquets, and making him a continual butt for their most biting remarks. For some time he bore this treatment patiently; but at length one night, when both he and Antony were somewhat intoxicated, the latter asked him point-blank what was his business at Athens, and Geminius, springing to his feet, replied that he would keep that until a soberer hour, but one thing he would say here and now, drunk or sober, that if only the Queen would go back to Egypt all would be well with their cause. At this Antony was furious, but Cleopatra, keeping her temper, said in her most scathing manner: "You have done well, Geminius, to tell your secret without being put to torture." A day or two later he slipped away from Athens and hurried back to Rome.

The next man to desert was Marcus Silanus, formerly an officer of Julius Cæsar in Gaul, who also carried to Rome stories of Cleopatra's power and Antony's weakness. ¦Shortly after this Octavian issued a formal declaration of war, not, however, against Antony but against Cleopatra. The decree deprived Antony of his offices and his authority, because, it declared, he had allowed a woman to exercise it in his place. Octavian added that Antony had evidently drunk potions which had bereft him of his senses, and that the generals against whom the Romans would fight would be the Egyptian court-eunuchs, Mardion and Potheinos;[1]

---

[1] An earlier eunuch of the same name, it will be remembered, played an important part in Cleopatra's youth.

Cleopatra's hair-dressing girl, Iras, and her attendant, Charmion; for these nowadays were Antony's chief state-councillors. The Queen was thus made to realise that her husband's cause in Rome was suffering very seriously from her presence with the army; but, at the same time, were she now to return to Egypt she knew that Antony might play her false, and the fact that war had not been declared upon him but upon her would give him an easy loophole for escape. To counteract the prevailing impression in Italy Antony despatched a large number of agents who were to attempt to turn popular opinion in his favour, and meanwhile he disposed his army for the final struggle. He had decided to wait for Octavian to attack him, partly because he felt confident in the ability of his great fleet to destroy the enemy before ever it could land on the shores of Greece, and partly because he believed that Octavian's forces would become disaffected long before they could be brought across the sea. The state of war would be felt in Italy very soon, whereas in Greece and Asia Minor it would hardly make any difference to the price of provisions. Egypt alone would supply enough corn to feed the whole army, while Italy would soon starve; and Egypt would provide money for the regular payment of the troops, while Octavian did not know where to turn for cash. Indeed, so great was the distress in Italy, and so great the likelihood of mutinies in the enemy's army, that Antony did not expect to have to fight a big battle on land. For this reason he had felt it safe to leave four of his legions at Cyrene, four in Egypt, and three in Syria; and he linked up the whole of the sea coast around the eastern Mediterranean with small garrisons. The army which he kept with him in Greece consisted of some 100,000 foot and 12,000 horse, a force which must certainly have seemed adequate, since it was greater than that of the enemy. Octavian had at least 250 ships of war, 80,000 foot, and 12,000 horse.

When winter approached Cleopatra and Antony advanced with the whole army from Athens to Patrae, and there went into winter quarters. Patrae stood near the mouth of the Gulf of Corinth, on the Achaian side, not much more than 200 miles from the Italian coast. The fleet, meanwhile, was sent farther north to the Gulf of Ambracia, which formed a huge natural harbour with a narrow entrance; and outposts were placed at Corcyra, the modern Corfu, some 70 miles from the Italian coast. In the period of waiting which followed, when the storms of winter made warfare almost out of the question, Antony and Octavian exchanged several pugnacious messages. Octavian, constrained by the restlessness of his men and the difficulty of providing for them during the winter, is said to have written to Antony asking him not to protract the war, but to come over to Italy and fight him at once. He even promised not to oppose his disembarkation, but to offer him battle only when he was quite prepared to meet him with his full forces. Antony replied by challenging Octavian to a single combat, although, as he stated, he was already an elderly man. This challenge Octavian refused to accept, and thereupon Antony invited him to bring his army over to the plains to Pharsalia and to fight him there, where Julius Cæsar and Pompey had fought nearly seventeen years before. This offer was likewise refused; and thereafter the two huge armies settled down once more to glare at one another across the Ionian Sea.

Octavian now sent a message to Greece inviting the

x

Roman senators who were still with Antony to return to Rome where they would be well received; and this offer must have found many ready ears, though none yet dared to act upon it. Several of these senators felt disgust at their leader's intemperate habits, and were deeply jealous of the power of Cleopatra, whose influence did not seem likely to serve the cause of the Republic. The declaring of war against the Queen and not against themselves had touched them sharply, and to add to their discomfort in this regard news now came across the sea that Octavian, in making his official sacrifices to the gods at the opening of hostilities, had employed the ritual observed before a campaign against a *foreign* enemy. He had stood, as the ancient rites of Rome prescribed, before the temple of Bellona in the Campus Martius, and, clad in the robes of a Fetial priest, had thrown the javelin, as a declaration that war was undertaken against an alien enemy.

Now came disconcerting rumours from the Gulf of Ambracia which could not be kept secret. During the winter the supplies had run out, and all manner of diseases had attacked the rowing-slaves and sailors, the result being that nearly a third of their number had perished. To fill their places Antony had ordered his officers to press into service every man on whom they could lay their hands. Peasants, farm hands, harvesters, ploughboys, donkey-drivers, and even common travellers had been seized upon and thrust into the ships, but still their complements were incomplete, and many of them were unfit for action. The news caused the greatest anxiety in the camp, and when, in March B.C. 31, the cessation of the storms of winter brought the opening of actual hostilities close at hand, there was many a man at Patrae who wished with all his heart that he were safe in his own country.

The first blow was struck by Octavian, who sent a flying squadron across the open sea to the south coast of Greece, under the command of his great friend Marcus Vipsanius Agrippa. This force seized Methone, and appeared to be seeking a landing-place for the main army; and Antony at once prepared to march down and hold the coast against the expected attack. But while his eyes were turned in this direction Octavian slipped across with his army from Brindisi and Tarentum to Corcyra, and thence to the mainland, marching down through Epirus towards the Gulf of Ambracia, thus menacing the ill-manned fleet lying in those waters. Antony thereupon hastened northwards with all possible speed, and arrived at the promontory of Actium, which formed the southern side of the mouth of the Gulf, almost at the same moment at which Octavian reached the opposite, or northern, promontory. Realising that an attack was about to be made upon the fleet, Antony drew his ships up in battle array, manning them where necessary with legionaries; and thereupon Octavian gave up the project of immediate battle. Antony then settled himself down on his southern promontory where he formed an enormous camp, and a few days later he was joined there by Cleopatra.

CHAPTER XVII.

THE BATTLE OF ACTIUM AND THE FLIGHT TO EGYPT.

THE story of the battle of Actium has troubled historians of all periods, and no one has been able to offer a satisfactory explanation of the startling incidents which occurred in it or of the events which led up to them. I am not able to accept the ingenious theory set forward by Ferrero, nor is it easy to agree wholly with the explanations given by classical authors. In the following chapter I relate the events as I think they occurred, but of course my interpretation is open to question. The reader, however, may refer to the early authors to check my statements; and there he will find, as no doubt he has already observed in other parts of this volume, that while the incidents and facts all have the authority of these early writers, the theories which explain them, representing my own opinion, are frankly open to discussion.

For the time being Octavian did not care to be at too close quarters to Antony, and he therefore fortified himself in a position a few miles back from the actual entrance to the Gulf of Ambracia. Antony at once shipped a part of his army across from Actium to the north side of the great harbour's mouth, and thus placed himself in command of the passage into the inland water.

Octavian soon threw up impregnable earthworks around
his camp, and built a wall down to the shore of the
Ionian Sea, so that the enemy could not interfere with
the landing of his supplies, all of which had to come from
across the water.   He stationed his ships in such a position that they could command the entrance to the Gulf
of Ambracia; and, these vessels proving to be extremely
well manned and handled, Antony soon found that his
own fleet was actually bottled up in the Gulf, and could
not pass into the open sea without fighting every inch of
the passage out through the narrow fairway.   Octavian
was thus in command of the Ionian Sea, and was free to
receive provisions or munitions of war day by day from
Italy.   He could not, however, leave his fortified camp,
for Antony commanded all the country around him.
Thus, while Octavian blockaded Antony's fleet in the
Gulf, Antony besieged Octavian's army in their camp;
and while Octavian commanded the open sea and obtained
his supplies freely from Italy, Antony commanded the
land and received his provisions without interruption
from Greece.   A deadlock therefore ensued, and neither
side was able to make a hostile move.   It seems clear to
me that a decisive battle could only be brought on by
one of two manœuvres: either Antony must retire from
Actium and induce Octavian to come after him into
Greece, or else his fleet must fight its way out of the
Gulf and cut off Octavian's supplies, thus starving him into
surrender.   Many of Antony's generals were of opinion
that the former movement should be undertaken, and
they pressed him to retire and thus draw Octavian from
his stronghold.   Cleopatra, however, appears to have
been in favour of breaking the blockade and regaining
possession of the sea.   She may have considered Antony's

army to be composed of too many nationalities to make success on land absolutely assured, and any retreat at this moment might easily be misinterpreted and might lead to desertions. On the other hand, she had confidence in her Egyptian fleet and in Antony's own ships, if, by cutting down their number, their crews could be brought up to the full complement; and she believed that with, say, 300 vessels Octavian's blockade could be forced, and his own position subjected to the same treatment. I gather that this plan, however, was hotly opposed by Domitius Ahenobarbus and others; and, since a loss of time was not likely to alter the situation to their disadvantage, no movement was yet made.

Some time in June Antony sent a squadron of cavalry round the shores of the Gulf to try to cut off Octavian's water-supply, but the move was not attended with much success and was abandoned. Shortly after this the deserter Titius defeated a small body of Antony's cavalry, and Agrippa captured a few of his ships which had been cruising from stations outside the Gulf; whereupon Octovian sent despatches to Rome announcing these successes as important victories, and stating that he had trapped Antony's fleet within the Gulf. He also sent agents into Greece to try to shake the confidence of the inhabitants in his enemy, and these men appear to have been partially successful in their endeavours.

These small victories of Octavian seem to have unnerved Antony, and to have had a dispiriting effect upon the army. Cleopatra, too, must have been particularly depressed by them, for they seemed to be a confirmation of the several ominous and inauspicious occurrences which had recently taken place. An Egyptian soothsayer had once told Antony that his genius would go down before that of Octavian; and Cleopatra, having watched her husband's rapid deterioration in the last two years, now feared that the man's words were indeed true. News had lately come from Athens that a violent hurricane had torn down the statue of Bacchus, the god whom Antony impersonated, from a group representing the Battle of the Giants; and two colossal statues of Fumenes and Attalus, each of which was inscribed with Antony's name, had also been knocked over during the same cyclone. This news recalled the fact that a few months previously at Patrae the temple of Hercules, the ancestor of Antony, had been struck by lightning; and at about the same time a small township founded by him at Pisaurum, on the east coast of Italy, north of Ancona, had been destroyed by an earthquake. These and other ill-omened accidents had a very depressing effect on Cleopatra's spirits, and her constant quarrels with Antony and his generals seem to have caused her to be in a state of great nervous tension. Towards the end of July or early in August, when the low-lying ground on which their camp was pitched became infested with mosquitos, and when the damp heat of summer had set the tempers of everybody on edge, the quarrels in regard to the conduct of the campaign broke out with renewed fury. Domitius Ahenobarbus, Dellius, Amyntas, and others, again urged Antony to retire inland and to fight a pitched battle with Octavian as soon as he should come after them. Cleopatra, however, still appears to have considered that the forcing of the blockade was the most important operation to be undertaken, and this she urged upon her undecided husband. It was of course a risky undertaking, but by reason of the very danger it made a strong appeal to Cleopatra's mind. If their fleet could

destroy that of Octavian, they would have him caught in
his stronghold as in a trap. They would not even have
to wait for the surrender; but, leaving eighty or a hundred
thousand men to prevent his escape, they might sail over
to Italy with twenty or thirty thousand legionaries and
take possession of empty Rome. There was not a senator
nor a military force in the capital, for Octavian had lately
made the entire senate in Rome come over to his camp, in
order to give tone to his proceedings; and, when once
Octavian's sea-power had been destroyed, Antony and
Cleopatra would be free to ride unchecked into Rome
while the enemy was starved into surrender in Greece.
A single naval battle, and Rome would be theirs! This,
surely, was better than a slow and ponderous retreat into
the interior.

Antony, however, could not persuade his generals to
agree to this. The risk was great, they seem to have
argued; and even if they were victorious, was he going
to march into Rome with Cleopatra by his side? The
citizens would never stand it, after the stories they had
heard in regard to the Queen's magical power over him.
Let her go back to Egypt, nor any longer remain to
undermine Antony's popularity. How could he appear
to the world as a good republican with royal Cleopatra's
arm linked in his? By abandoning the idea of a naval
battle the Egyptian fleet could be dispensed with, and
could be allowed to depart to Egypt if it succeeded in
running the blockade. Cleopatra had supplied ships but
hardly any soldiers, and a land battle could be fought
without her aid, and therefore without cause for criticism;
nor would Octavian any longer be able to say that he was
waging war against Cleopatra and not against Antony.
The money which she had supplied for the campaign was

almost exhausted, and thus she was of no further use to the cause. Let Antony then give up the projected naval battle, and order the Queen to go back quickly with her ships to her own country: for thus, and thus only, could the disaffected republican element in their army be brought into line. Cleopatra, they said, had been the moving spirit in the war; Cleopatra had supplied the money; it was against Cleopatra that Octavian had declared war; it was Cleopatra's name, and the false stories regarding her, which had aroused Rome to Octavian's support; it was Cleopatra who was now said on all sides to be supreme in command of the whole army; and it was of Cleopatra that every senator, every vassal king, and every general, was furiously jealous. Unless she were made to go, the whole cause was lost.

Antony seems to have realised the justice of these arguments, and to have promised to try to persuade his wife to retire to Egypt to await the outcome of the war; and he was further strengthened in this resolve when even Canidius, who had all along favoured the keeping of Cleopatra with the army, now urged him to ask her to leave them to fight their own battle. He therefore told the Queen, it would seem, that he desired her to go, pointing out that in this way alone could victory be secured.

Cleopatra, I take it, was furious. She did not trust Antony, and she appears to have been very doubtful whether he would still champion her cause after victory. She even doubted that he would be victorious. He was now but the wreck of the man he had once been, for a too lifelike impersonation of the god Bacchus had played havoc with his nerves and with his character. He had no longer the strength and the determination necessary

for the founding of an imperial throne in Rome; and
she felt that, even if he were successful in arms against
Octavian, he would make but a poor regent for her son
Cæsarion. Having used her money and her ships for
his war, he might abandon her cause; and the fact that
they were fighting for Cæsar's son and heir, which had
already been placed in the background, might be for
ever banished. It must have seemed madness for her
to leave her husband at this critical juncture. In order
to prevent further desertions he would probably proclaim
his republican principles as soon as her back was turned;
and, in his drunken weakness, he might commit himself
so deeply that he would never be able to go back upon
his democratic promises. Since she was unpopular with
his generals, he would perhaps at once tell them that
she was nothing to him; and for the sake of assuring
victory he might even divorce her. Of course, it was
obvious that he was devoted to her, and relied on her
in all matters, seeming to be utterly lost without her;
but, for all she knew, his ambition might be stronger
than his love. She therefore refused absolutely to go;
and Antony was too kind-hearted, and perhaps too much
afraid of her anger, to press the matter.

His talk with her, however, seems to have decided him
to break the blockade as soon as possible, and at the
same time to invest Octavian's lines so that he could
not escape from the stronghold which would become his
death-trap. Once master of the sea, he would, at any
rate, have opened a path for Cleopatra's departure, and
she could retire unmolested with her fleet to her own
country. He therefore hurried on the manning of his
ships, and at the same time sent Dellius and Amyntas
into Thrace to recruit a force of cavalry to supplement

those at his disposal. Cleopatra pointed out to him that the ground upon which their camp was pitched at Actium was extremely unhealthy, and if they remained there much longer the troops would be decimated by malaria; and she seems perhaps to have urged him to move round to the north of the Gulf of Ambracia, in order both to obtain more healthy conditions for the army and to invest more closely the camp of Octavian in preparation for the naval fight.   Domitius Ahenobarbus was still hotly opposed to this fight; and now, finding that not only was Cleopatra to be allowed to remain with the army, but also that her plan of breaking the blockade was to be adopted, instead of that of the retreat inland, he was deeply incensed, and could no longer bear to remain in the same camp with the Queen.   Going on board a vessel, therefore, as he said, for the sake of his health, he slipped over to Octavian's lines and offered his services to the enemy.   He did not live, however, to enjoy the favourable consequences of his change, for, having contracted a fever while at Actium, he died before the battle of that name was fought.

This desertion, which occurred probably early in August, came as a terrible shock to Antony, and he seems to have accused his wife of being the cause of it, which undoubtedly she was.   This time he insisted more vehemently on her leaving the army and retiring to Egypt; and thereupon a violent quarrel ensued, which lasted, I think, without cessation during the remainder of their stay in Greece.   At first, it seems to me, the Queen positively refused to leave him, and she probably accused him of wishing to abandon her cause.   With a sneer, she may have reminded him that his compact with her, and his arrangements for an Egypto-Roman monarchy, were made at a time when he had, to a great extent, cut himself off from Rome and when he required financial aid; but now he had four hundred respectable republican senators to influence him, and, no doubt, their support at this juncture was far more valuable to him than her own. He had deserted her once before, and she was quite prepared for him to do so again.

Her anger, mistrust, and unhappiness must have distressed Antony deeply, and he would, perhaps, have given way once again had not three more desertions from his camp taken place. The King of Paphlagonia, jealous, apparently, of Cleopatra's power, slipped across to Octavian's lines, carrying thither an account of the dissensions in Antony's camp. The two others, a Roman senator named Quintus Postumius, and an Arab chieftain from Emesa, named Iamblichus, were both caught; and, to terrify those who might intend to go over to the enemy, both were put to death, the one being torn to pieces and the other tortured. Every day Octavian's cause was growing in popularity, and Antony was being subjected to greater ridicule for his subserviency to the little Queen of Egypt, who appeared to direct all his councils and who now seemed to frighten him by her anger. Octavian's men were becoming self-confident and even audacious. On one occasion while Antony, accompanied by an officer, was walking at night down to the harbour between the two ramparts which he had thrown up to guard the road, some of the enemy's men crept over the wall and laid in wait for him. As they sprang up from their ambush, however, they seized Antony's attendant officer in mistake for himself, and, by a rapid flight down the road, he was able to escape.

Thoroughly unnerved by the course events were taking, he again ordered the Queen to retire to Egypt; and at last, stung by Antony's reproaches, Cleopatra made up her mind to go and to take her fleet with her. Having formed this decision, she appears to have treated Antony with the utmost hostility; and he, being in a highly nervous condition, began to fear that she might kill him. Her great eyes seemed to blaze with anger when she looked upon him, and the contempt which she now felt for him was shown in the expression of her face. He appears to have cowered before her in the manner of a naughty boy, and to have told his friends that he believed she would murder him in her wrath. On hearing this, Cleopatra decided to teach him a lesson which he should not forget. One night at supper, she caused her goblet to be filled from the same wine-jar from which all had been drinking, and having herself drunk some of the wine, she handed the cup to Antony as though in token of reconciliation; and he, eagerly raising it to his mouth, was about to place his lips where those of the Queen had rested a moment before, when, as though to add grace to her act, she took the wreath of flowers from her hair and dipped it into the wine. Antony again lifted the cup, but suddenly Cleopatra dashed it from his hand, telling him that the wine was poisoned. Antony appears to have protested that she was mistaken, since she herself had just drunk from the same cup; but Cleopatra calmly explained that the wreath which she had dipped into the wine as she handed it to him was poisoned, and that she had chosen this means of showing him how baseless were his fears for his life, for that, did she wish to rid herself of him, she could do so at any moment by some such subtle means. "I could have killed you at any time," she said, "if I could have done without you."

The Queen, I imagine, now carried herself very proudly and disdainfully, regarding Antony's insistence on her departure as a breach of faith. In her own mind she must have feared lest he would actually abandon her, and the anxiety in regard to the future of her country and dynasty must have gnawed at her heart all day and all night; but to him she seems only to have shown coldness and contempt, thus driving him to a condition of complete wretchedness. He did not dare, however, to alter his decision in regard to her departure, for he seems to have admitted some of his senators and generals into the secret of this coming event, and it had much quieted the volcanic atmosphere so long prevalent in the camp. I am of opinion that the plan upon which he and his wife had agreed was as follows: Having invested Octavian's lines more closely, and having taken all steps to prevent him issuing from his stronghold, the pick of Antony's legionaries would be embarked upon as many of the vessels in the Gulf of Ambracia as were seaworthy, and these warships would force their way out and destroy Octavian's fleet. As soon as this was done an assault would be made on the enemy's position by sea and land; and Cleopatra, taking with her the Egyptian fleet, could then sail away to Alexandria, leaving Antony to enter Rome alone.

This scheme, in my opinion, presented the only possible means by which the Antonian army could rid itself of Egyptian influence. If Cleopatra was made to retire overland by way of Asia Minor and Syria, not only would her passage through these countries be regarded by the inhabitants as a flight, thus causing instant panic and

revolt, but also the Egyptian fleet would still remain
in the Gulf of Ambracia to show by its presence that
Cleopatra and her Kingdom of Egypt were yet the main
factors in the war.   On the other hand, if the Queen
retired by sea with her ships, a naval battle designed to
force the blockade would have to be fought in order
to permit her to escape by that route.   Thus, the republican demand that the Queen should go to her own
country, and Cleopatra's own reiterated proposal that
the war should be decided by a sea-fight, here concurred
in determining Antony to stake all upon a naval engagement.

This being settled, Antony announced to the army
that the fleet should break the blockade on August 29,
but the fact that the Egyptian ships were to depart immediately after the battle was not made known, save to a
few.   A great many of the vessels were ill furnished for
the fight, and were much under-manned; and Antony
now ordered these to be burnt, for, though they were
useless to him, they might be of value to the enemy,
and might be seized by them while the fleet was away
scouring the Ionian Sea.   Sixty of the best Egyptian
vessels, and at least three hundred[1] other ships, were
made ready for the contest; and during these preparations it was no easy matter to keep the secret of the
Egyptian departure from leaking out.   In order to cross
to Egypt Cleopatra's sixty ships required their large sails,
but these sails would not under ordinary circumstances
be taken into battle; and in order that the Egyptian
vessels should not be made conspicuous by alone preparing for a long voyage, thereby causing suspicions to

---

[1] The numbers given by the early authors are very contradictory, but
Plutarch states that Octavian reported the capture of three hundred ships.

arise, all the fleet was ordered to ship its big sails;
Antony, therefore, having to explain that they would
be required in the pursuit of the enemy. Another difficulty arose from the fact that Cleopatra had to ship
her baggage, including her plate and jewels; but this
was ultimately done under cover of darkness without
arousing suspicion.

Many of the generals, not realising that the naval
battle was largely forced upon Antony by those who
desired to rid his party of the Egyptians, were much
opposed to the scheme; and one infantry officer, pointing
to the many scars and marks of wounds which his body
bore, implored Antony to fight upon land. "O General," he said, "what have our wounds and our swords
done to displease you, that you should give your confidence to rotten timbers? Let Egyptians and Phœnicians fight on the sea; but give us the land, where we
well know how to die where we stand or else gain the
victory." Antony, however, gave him no reply, but
made a motion with his hand as though to bid him
be of good courage.

On August 28 twenty thousand legionaries and two
thousand archers were embarked upon the ships of
war[1] in preparation for the morrow's battle. The vessels
were much larger than those of Octavian, some of them
having as many as ten banks of oars; and it seemed
likely that victory would be on their side. On the next
day, however, the sea was extremely rough, and the
battle had to be postponed. The storm proved to be
of great violence, and all question of breaking the blockade had to be abandoned for the next four days. The

---

[1] Not upon the sixty Egyptian ships, as Plutarch states: that is an evident
mistake, as the proportion of numbers per ship will at once show.

delay was found to be a very heavy strain upon the nerves of all concerned, and so great was the anxiety of the two important generals, Dellius[1] and Amyntas, that they both deserted to Octavian's lines, the latter taking with him two thousand Galatian cavalry. Dellius had probably heard rumours about the proposed departure of Cleopatra, and he was able to tell Octavian something of the plans for the battle. In after years he stated that his desertion was partly due to his fear of the Queen, for he believed her to be angry with him for having once remarked that Antony's friends were served with sour wine, whereas even Sarmentus, Octavian's *delicia*, or page, drank Falernian. One may understand Cleopatra's annoyance at this hint that money and supplies were running short, more especially since this must actually have been the fact.

On September 1st the storm abated, and in the evening Antony went from ship to ship encouraging his men. Octavian, informed by Dellius, also prepared for battle, embarking eight legions and five pretorian cohorts upon his ships of war, which seem to have been more numerous, but much smaller, than those of Antony.

The morning of September 2nd was calm, and at an early hour Octavian's workmanlike ships stationed themselves about three-quarters of a mile from the mouth of the Gulf of Ambracia, where they were watched by the eyes of both armies. They were formed into three divisions, the left wing being commanded by Agrippa, the centre by Lucius Arruntius, and the right wing by Octavian. At about noon Antony's huge men-o'-war began to pass out from the harbour, under cover of the

---

[1] The fact that Dellius knew something of the plans for the battle fixes the date of his desertion to this period, as Ferrero has pointed out.

troops and engines of war stationed upon the two promontories.   Octavian seems to have thought that it
would be difficult to attack them in the straits, and
therefore he retired out to sea, giving his enemies the
opportunity of forming up for battle.   This was speedily
done, the fleet being divided, like Octavian's, into three
squadrons, C. Sossius moving against Octavian, Marcus
Insteius opposing Arruntius, and Antony facing Agrippa.
The sixty Egyptian ships, under Cleopatra's command,
were the last to leave the Gulf, and formed up behind
the central division.

Antony appears to have arranged with Cleopatra that
her ships should give him full assistance in the fight, and
should sail for Egypt as soon as the victory was won.
He intended, no doubt, to board her flagship at the
close of the battle and to bid her farewell.   They had
separated that morning, it would seem from subsequent
events, with anger and bitterness.   Cleopatra, I imagine,
had once more told him how distasteful was her coming
departure to her, and had shown him how little she
trusted him.   She had bewailed the misery of her life
and the bitterness of her disillusionment.   She had
accused him of wishing to abandon her cause, and she
had, no doubt, called him coward and traitor.   Very
possibly in her anger she had told him that she was
leaving him with delight, having found him wholly
degenerate, and that she hoped never to see his face
again.   Her accusations, I fancy, had stung Antony to
bitter retorts; and they had departed, each to their own
flagship, with cruel words upon their lips and fury in
their minds.   Antony's nature, however, always boyish,
impulsive, and quickly repentant, could not bear with
equanimity so painful a scene with the woman to whom

he was really devoted, and as he passed out to battle
he must have been consumed by the desire to ask her
forgiveness.   The thought, if I understand him aright,
was awful to him that they should thus separate in
anger ; and being probably a little intoxicated, the con-
templation of his coming loneliness reduced him almost
to tears.   He was perhaps a little cheered by the thought
that when next he saw her the battle would probably
be won, and he would appear to her in the *rôle* of conqueror — a theatrical situation which made an appeal
to his dramatic instincts; yet, in the meantime, I think
he was as miserable as any young lover who had
quarrelled with his sweetheart.

The battle was opened by the advance of Antony's
left wing, and Agrippa's attempt to outflank it with his
right.   Antony's other divisions then moved forward,
and the fight became general.   " When they engaged,"
writes Plutarch, " there was no ramming or charging
of one ship into another, because Antony's vessels, by
reason of their great bulk, were incapable of the speed
to make the stroke effectual, and, on the other side,
Octavian's ships dared not charge, prow to prow, into
Antony's, which were all armed with solid masses and
spikes of brass, nor did they care even to run in on their
sides, which were so strongly built with great squared
pieces of timber, fastened together with iron bolts, that
their own vessels' bows would certainly have been
shattered upon them.   Thus the engagement resembled
a land fight, or, to speak more properly, the assault and
defence of a fortified place; for there were always three
or four of Octavian's vessels around each one of Antony's,
pressing upon them with spears, javelins, poles, and
several inventions of fire which they flung into them,

Antony's men using catapults also to hurl down missiles from their wooden towers."

The fight raged for three or four hours, but gradually the awful truth was borne in upon Antony and Cleopatra, that Octavian's little ships were winning the day. Antony's flagship was so closely hemmed in on all sides that he himself was kept busily occupied, and he had no time to think clearly. But as, one by one, his ships were fired, sunk, or captured, his desperation seems to have become more acute. If his fleet were defeated and destroyed, would his army stand firm? That was the question which must have drummed in his head, as in an agony of apprehension he watched the confused battle and listened to the clash of arms and the cries and shouts of the combatants. Cleopatra, meanwhile, after being subjected to much battering by the enemy, had perhaps freed her flagship for a moment from the attentions of Octavian's little warships, and, in manœuvring for a better position, she was able to obtain a full view of the situation. With growing horror she observed the struggle around Antony's flagship, and heard the cheers of the enemy as some huge vessel struck or was set on fire. Her Egyptian fleet had probably suffered heavily, though her sailors would hardly have fought with the same audacity as had those under Antony's command. As she surveyed the appalling scene no doubt remained in her mind that Octavian had beaten them, and she must even have feared that Antony would be killed or captured. The anxieties which had harassed her overwrought brain during the last few weeks as to her husband's intentions in regard to her position and that of her son Cæsarion, were now displaced by the more frightful thought that the opportunity would never be given to him of proving his constancy; for, here and now, he would meet his end. Her anger against him for his vacillation, her contempt for the increasing weakness of his character, and her misgivings in regard to his ability to direct his forces in view of the growing intemperance of his habits, were now combined in the one staggering certainty that defeat and ruin awaited him. He had told her to go back to Egypt, he had ordered her to take herself off with her fleet at the end of the battle. That end seemed to her already in sight. It was not from a riotous scene of victory, however, that she was to retire, nor was she to carry over to Alexandria the tidings of her triumph with which to cover the shame of her banishment from her husband's side; but now she would have to sail away from the spectacle of the wreck of their cause, and free herself by flight from a man who, no longer a champion of her rights, had become an encumbrance to the movement of her ambitions.

In the late afternoon, while yet the victory was actually undecided, although there could have been no hope for the Antonian party left in Cleopatra's weary mind, a strong wind from the north sprang up, blowing straight from unconquered Rome towards distant Egypt. The sea grew rough, and the waves beat against the sides of the Queen's flagship, causing an increase of confusion in the battle. As the wind blew in her face, suddenly, it seems to me, the thought came to her that the moment had arrived for her departure. Antony had told her with furious words to go: why, then, should she wait? In another hour, probably, he would be captured or killed, and she, too, would be taken prisoner, to be marched in degradation to the Capitol whereon she had hoped to sit enthroned. She would pay her husband back in his own coin: she would desert him as he had deserted her. She would not stand by him to await an immediate downfall. Though he was sodden with wine, she herself was still full of life. She would rise above her troubles, as she had always risen before. She would cast him off, and begin her life once more. Her throne should not be taken from her at one blow. She would, at this moment, obey Antony's command and go; and in distant Egypt she would endeavour to start again in the pursuit of that dynastic security which had proved so intangible a vision.

Having arrived at this decision she ordered the signal to be given to her scattered ships, and hoisting sail she passed right through the combatants, and made off down the wind, followed by her damaged fleet. At that moment, it seems, Antony had freed his flagship from the surrounding galleys, and thus obtained an uninterrupted view of the Queen's departure. His feelings must have overwhelmed him,—anger, misery, remorse, and despair flooding his confused mind. Cleopatra was leaving him to his fate: she was obeying the order which he ought never to have given her, and he would not see her face again. All the grace, the charm, the beauty which had so enslaved him, was being taken from him; and alone he would have to face the horrors of probable defeat. He had relied of late so entirely upon her that her receding ships struck a kind of terror into his degenerate mind. It was intolerable to him, moreover, that she should leave him without one word of farewell, and that the weight of his cruelty and anger should be the last impression received by her. He could not let her depart unreconciled and unforgiving; he must go after her, if only to see her for a moment. Yet what did it matter if he did not return to the battle? There was little hope of victory. His fevered and exhausted mind saw no favourable incident in the fight which raged around him. Disgrace and ruin stared him in the face; and the sooner he fled from the horror of defeat the better would be his chance of retaining his reason.

"Here it was," says Plutarch, "that Antony showed to all the world that he was no longer actuated by the thoughts and motives of a commander or a man, or indeed by his own judgment at all; and what was once said in jest, that the soul of a lover lives in the loved one's body, he proved to be a serious truth. For, as if he had been born part of her, and must move with her wheresoever she went, as soon as he saw her ships sailing away he abandoned all that were fighting and laying down their lives for him, and followed after her." Hailing one of his fastest galleys, he quickly boarded her and told the captain to go after Cleopatra's flagship with all possible speed. He took with him only two persons, Alexander the Syrian, and a certain Scellias. It was not long before the galley, rowed by five banks of oars, overhauled the retreating Egyptians, and Cleopatra then learnt that Antony had followed her and had abandoned the fight. Her feelings may be imagined. Her leaving the battle had, then, terminated the struggle, and her retreat had removed the last hope of victory from the Antonians. Antony was a ruined and defeated man, and a speedy death was the best thing he could hope for; but not so easily was she to be rid of him. He was going to cling to her to the end: she would never be able to shake herself clear of him, but, drowning, he would drag her down with him. Yet he was her husband, and she could not abandon him in defeat as in victory he had wished to abandon her. She therefore signalled to him to come aboard; and having done this she retired to her cabin, refusing to see him or speak to him. Antony, having been helped on to the deck, was too dazed to ask to be taken to her, and too miserable to wish to be approached by her. He walked, as in a dream, to the prow of the ship, and there seating himself, buried his face in his hands, uttering not a word.

Thus some hours passed, but after it had grown dark the beat of the oars of several galleys was heard behind them, and presently the hull of the foremost vessel loomed out of the darkness. The commotion on board and the shouts across the water aroused Antony. For a moment he seems to have thought that the pursuing ships were bringing him some message from Actium—perhaps that the tide of battle had turned in his favour. He therefore ordered the captain to turn about to meet them, and to be ready to give battle if they belonged to the enemy; and, standing in the prow, he called across the black waters: "Who is this that follows Antony?" Through the darkness a voice responded: "I am Eurycles, the son of Lachares, come to revenge my father's death." Antony had caused Lachares to be beheaded for robbery, although he came of the noblest family in the Peloponnese; and his son had fitted out a galley at his own expense and had sworn to avenge his father. Eurycles could now be seen standing upon his deck, and handling a lance as though about to hurl it; but a moment later, by some mistake which must have been due to the darkness, he had charged with terrific force into another Egyptian vessel which was sailing close to the flagship. The blow turned her round, and in the darkness and confusion which followed, Cleopatra's

captain was able to get away. The other vessel, however, was captured, together with a great quantity of
gold plate and rich furniture which she was carrying
back to Egypt.

When the danger was passed Antony sat himself down
once more in the prow, nor did he move from that part
of the ship for three whole days.   Hour after hour he sat
staring out to sea, his hands idly folded before him, his
mind dazed by his utter despair. By his own folly he
had lost everything, and he had carried down with him
in his fall all the hope, all the ambition, and all the
fortune of Cleopatra. It is surprising that he did not
at once put an end to his life, for his misery was pitiable ;
yet, when at last the port of Tænarus was reached, at the
southern end of the Greek peninsula, he was still seated
at the prow, his eyes fixed before him. At length, however, Iras, Charmion, and other of Cleopatra's women
induced the Queen to invite him to her cabin ; and after
much persuasion they consented to speak to one another,
and, later, to sup and sleep together. Cleopatra could
not but pity her wretched husband, now so sobered and
terribly conscious of the full meaning of his position ;
and I imagine that she gave him what consolation she
could.[1]

---

[1] Dion Cassius states (though he afterwards contradicts himself by speaking
of the Queen's panic) that Antony had agreed to fly to Egypt with Cleopatra,
and this view is upheld by Ferrero, Bouché-Leclercq, and others ; but I do
not consider it probable.   One can understand Antony flying after the depart-
ing Queen in the agony and excitement of the moment ; but it is difficult to
believe that such a movement was the outcome of a carefully considered plan
of action, for all are agreed that previous to the battle of Actium his chances
of success had been very fair.   If the two had arranged to retire to Egypt
together, why was Cleopatra's treasure, but not his own, shipped ; and why
did they refuse to speak to one another for three whole days?   Ferrero thinks
that he had arranged amicably with Cleopatra to retire to Egypt with her, and

As their ship lay at anchor several vessels came into the harbour, bringing fugitives from Actium; and these reported to him that his fleet was entirely destroyed or captured, more than five thousand of his men having been killed, but that the army stood firm and had not at once surrendered. At this news Cleopatra, who had not been wholly crushed under the weight of her misfortunes, seems to have advised Antony to try to save some remnant of his forces, and to send messengers to Canidius to march his legions with all speed through Macedonia into Asia Minor. This he did; and then, sending for those of his friends who had come into the port, he begged them to leave him and Cleopatra to their fate, and to give their whole attention to their own safety. He and the Queen handed to the fugitives a large sum of money and numerous dishes and cups of gold and silver wherewith to purchase their security; and he wrote letters in their behalf to his steward at Corinth, that he should provide for them until they had made their peace with Octavian. In deep dejection these defeated officers attempted to refuse the gifts, but Antony, pressing them to accept, " cheered them," as Plutarch says, "with all the goodness and humanity imaginable," so that they could not refrain from tears. At length the fleet put out to sea once more, and set sail for the coast of Egypt, arriving many days later at Parætonium, a desolate spot some 160 miles west of Alexandria, where a small Roman garrison was stationed.[1] Here Antony decided to stay for a time in hiding, while the braver

---

that the naval battle had not gone much against him; but surely it is difficult to suppose that he would deliberately desert his huge army and his undefeated navy for strategic reasons.

[1] Scholz : Reise zwischen Alex. und Parætonium.

Cleopatra went on to the capital to face her people; and for the next few weeks he remained in the great solitude of this desert station. A few mud huts, a palm-tree or two, and a little fort constituted the dreary settlement, which in the damp heat of September must have presented a colourless scene of peculiarly depressing aspect. This part of the coast is absolutely barren, and only those who have visited these regions in the summer time can realise the strange melancholy, the complete loneliness, of this sun-scorched outpost. The slow, breaking waves beat upon the beach with the steady insistence of a tolling bell which counts out a man's life; the desert rolls back from the bleak sea-shore, carrying the eye to the leaden haze of the far horizon; and overhead the sun beats down from a sky which is, as it were, deadened by the heat. In surroundings such as these heart-broken Antony remained for several weeks, daily wandering along the beach accompanied only by two friends, one, a certain Aristocrates, a Greek rhetorician, and the other the Roman soldier Lucilius, who, fighting on the side of the enemy at Philippi, as we have read, had heroically prevented the capture of the defeated Brutus, and had been pardoned by Antony as a reward for his courage, remaining thereafter, and until the last, his devoted friend.

At length one of his ships, putting into the little port, seems to have brought him the news of events at Actium. After his flight the battered remnant of his fleet, having continued the fight until sunset, sailed back into the Gulf of Ambracia; and next day Octavian invited them and the army to surrender on easy terms. No one, however, would believe that Antony had fled, and the offer was refused. Next day, however, some of the vassal kings laid down their arms, and, after a week of suspense, Canidius fled. Part of the legions scattered into Macedonia, and on September 9th the remainder surrendered together with the fleet. Octavian then sailed round to Athens, and there received the submission of every city in Greece, with the exception of Corinth. He at once began a general massacre of Antony's adherents, and, to save their skins, the townspeople in every district heaped honours upon the conqueror, erecting statues to him and decreeing him all manner of civic distinctions. Shortly after this a messenger reached Antony from the west stating that the legions left in North Africa had also gone over to Octavian; and thereupon he attempted to commit suicide. He was, however, restrained by his two faithful friends; and in the deepest dejection he was at last persuaded by them to sail for Alexandria, once more to comfort himself with the presence of Cleopatra.

CHAPTER XVIII.

CLEOPATRA'S ATTEMPT TO BEGIN AGAIN.

CRUSHED and broken by her misfortunes, it might have been expected that Cleopatra would now give up the fight. She was not made, however, of ordinary stuff; and she could not yet bring herself to believe that her cause was hopeless. On her voyage across the Mediterranean she seems to have pulled herself together after the first shock of defeat; and, with that wonderful recuperative power, of which we have already seen many instances in her life, she appears, so to speak, to have regained her feet, standing up once more, eager and defiant, to face the world. The defeat of Antony, though it postponed for many years all chance of obtaining a footing in Rome, did not altogether preclude that possibility. He would now probably kill himself, and though the thought of his suicide must have been very distressing to her, she could but feel that she would be well rid of him. A drunken and discredited outlaw with a price upon his head was not a desirable consort for a Queen; and he had long since ceased to make an appeal to any quality in her, save to her pity. Octavian would hunt him down, and would not rest until he had driven him to the land of the shades; but she herself might possibly be spared and her throne be saved in recognition of the fact that she had been the great Dictator's "wife." Then, some chance occurrence, such as the death of Octavian, might give her son Cæsarion the opportunity of putting himself forward once more as Cæsar's heir.

Antony was now a terrible encumbrance. His presence with her endangered her own life, and, what was more important, imperilled the existence of her royal dynasty. Had he not the courage, like defeated Cato at Utica, like her uncle Ptolemy of Cyprus, like Brutus after Philippi, and like hundreds of others, to kill himself and so end his misfortunes? It is to be remembered that suicide after disaster was a doctrine emphatically preached throughout the civilised world at this time, and so frequently was it practised that it was felt to be far less terrible than we are now accustomed to think it. The popular spectacle of gladiatorial fights, the many wars conducted in recent years, and the numerous political murders and massacres, had made people very familiar with violent death. The case of Arria, the wife of Pætus, is an illustration of the light manner in which the termination of life was regarded. Her husband having been condemned to death, Arria determined to anticipate the executioner; and therefore, having driven a dagger into her breast, she coolly handed the weapon to him, with the casual words, *Paete non dole*, "It isn't painful."[1] I do not think, therefore, that Cleopatra need be blamed if she now hoped that Antony would make his exit from the stage of life.

Her fertile brain turned to the consideration of other

[1] Pliny, Epist. iii. 16.

means of holding her throne should Octavian's clemency
not be extended to her. Her dominant hope was now
the keeping of Egypt independent of Rome. The founding of an Egypto-Roman empire having been indefinitely
postponed by the defeat at Actium, her whole energies
would have to be given to the retention of some sort of
crown for her son. The dominions which Antony had
given her she could hardly expect to hold : but for Egypt,
her birthright, she must fight while breath remained in
her body. Under this inspiration her thoughts turned to
the Orient, to Media, Persia, Parthia, and India. Was
there not some means of forming an alliance with one or
all of these distant countries, thereby strengthening her
position ? Her son Alexander Helios was prospective
King of Media. Could not she find in Persia or India an
extension of the dominions which she could hand on to
Cæsarion ? And could not some great amalgamation of
these nations, which had never been conquered by Rome,
be effected ?

I imagine that her thoughts ran in these channels as
she sailed over the sea; but when she had dropped
Antony at Parætonium and was heading for Alexandria
the more immediate question of her entry into the capital
must have filled her mind. It was essential to prevent
the news of the defeat from being spread in the capital
until after she had once more obtained control of affairs.
She therefore seems to have arranged to sail into the
harbour some days before the arrival of the fleet, and
she caused her flagship to be decorated as though in
celebration of a victory. Her arrival took place at about
the end of September B.C. 31 ; and, with music playing,
sailors dancing, and pennants flying, the ship passed
under the shadow of the white Pharos and entered the

Great Harbour. Having moored the vessel at the steps of the Palace, Cleopatra was carried ashore in royal state, and was soon safely ensconced behind the walls of the Lochias. She brought, no doubt, written orders from Antony to the legions stationed in Alexandria; and, relying on the loyalty of these troops, she soon took the sternest measures to prevent any revolt or rioting in the city as the news of the disaster began to filter through. Several prominent citizens who attempted to stir up trouble were promptly arrested and put to death; and by the time that full confirmation of the news of the defeat had arrived, Cleopatra was in absolute control of the situation.

She now began to carry out her schemes in regard to the East, in pursuance of which her first step was, naturally, the confirmation of her treaty with the King of Media. It will be remembered that the elder son of Cleopatra and Antony, Alexander Helios, had been married to the King of Media's daughter, on the understanding, apparently, that he should be heir to the kingdoms of Media and Armenia. The little princess was now living at Alexandria; and it will be recalled that Artavasdes, the dethroned King of Armenia, the greater part of whose kingdom had been handed over to Media, remained a prisoner in the Egyptian capital, where he had been incarcerated since the Triumph in B.C. 34, three years previously. The defeat of Antony, however, would probably cause the reinstatement of the rulers deposed by him; and it seemed very probable that Octavian would restore Artavasdes to his lost kingdom, and that Media, on the other hand, by reason of its support of the Antonian party, would be stripped of as much territory as the Romans dared to seize. In order

CLEOPATRA.

to prevent this by removing the claimant to the Armenian throne, and perhaps owing to some attempt on the part of Artavasdes to escape or to communicate with Octavian, Cleopatra ordered him to be put to death ; and she thereupon sent an embassy to Media bearing his head to the King as a token of her good faith.[1]   I think it is probable that at the same time she sent the little Alexander and his child-wife Iotapa to the Median court in order that they might there live in safety; and there can be little doubt that she made various proposals to the King for joint action.

She then began an undertaking which Plutarch describes as " a most bold and wonderful enterprise." The northernmost inlet of the Red Sea, the modern Gulf of Suez, was separated from the waters of the Mediterranean by a belt of low-lying desert not more than thirty-five miles in breadth. Across the northern side of this isthmus the Pelusian branch of the Nile passed from the Delta down to the Mediterranean. Somewhat further south lay the Lakes of Balah and Timsah, and between these and the Gulf of Suez lay the so-called Bitter Lakes. These pieces of water had been linked together by a canal opened nearly five hundred years previously by the great Persian conqueror Darius I., who had thus sent his ships through from one sea to the other by a route not far divergent from that of the modern Suez Canal. King Ptolemy Philadelphus, three hundred years later, had reopened the waterway, and had built a great system of locks at its southern end, near the fortress

---

[1] In a very similar manner Herod, who had taken the part of Antony and who now feared that Octavian would dethrone him in favour of the earlier sovereign, Hyrcanus, put that claimant to death, so that Octavian, as Josephus indicates, should not find it easy to fill Herod's place.

Z

of Clysma;[1] but now a large part of the canal had
become blocked up once more by the encroaching sand,
and any vessel which had to be transported from the
Mediterranean to the Red Sea would have to be dragged
for several miles over the desert. In spite of the enormous labour involved, however, Cleopatra determined to
transfer immediately all her battleships which had survived Actium to the Red Sea, where they would be safe
from the clutches of Octavian, and would be in a position
to sail to India or to Southern Persia whenever she might
require them to do so. She also began with startling
energy to build other vessels at Suez, in the hope of
there fitting out an imposing fleet. Plutarch states
simply that her object was to go " with her soldiers and
her treasure to secure herself a home where she might
live in peace, far away from war and slavery"; but,
viewing the enterprise in connection with the embassy
to Media, it appears to me that she had determined to
put into partial execution the schemes of which she seems
to have talked with Julius Cæsar while he was staying
with her in Alexandria,[2] in regard to the conquest of the
East.

Media, Parthia, and India were all outside the influence
of Rome. Of these countries Media was now bound to
Egypt by the closest ties of blood, while India was
engaged in a thriving trade with Cleopatra's kingdom.
Parthia, now the enemy of Media, lay somewhere between
these vast lands; and if the Egyptian fleet could sail
round the coasts of Arabia and effect a junction with
the Median armies in the Persian Gulf, some sort of

---

[1] I found the remains of this fortress on an island behind the Governorat
at Suez.

[2] Page 116.

support might be given to the allies by the Indian
States, and Parthia could be conquered or frightened
into joining the confederacy. Syria and Armenia could
then be controlled, and once more the fight with the
West might be undertaken. In the meantime these far
countries offered a safe hiding-place for herself and her
family; and having, as I suppose, despatched her son
Alexander to his future kingdom of Media, she now
began to consider the sending of her beloved Cæsarion
to India,[1] there to prepare the way for the approach of
her fleet.

In these great schemes Antony played no part. During
their undertaking he was wandering about the desolate
shores of Parætonium, engrossed in his misfortunes and
bemoaning the ingratitude of his generals and friends
whom, in forgetfulness of his own behaviour at Actium,
he accused of deserting him. Cleopatra, as she toiled
at the organisation of her new projects, and struggled
by every means, fair or foul, to raise money for the
great task, must have heartily wished her husband out
of the way; and it must have been with very mixed
feelings that she presently received the news of his
approach. On his arrival, perhaps in November, he
was astonished at the Queen's activities; but, being
opposed to the idea of keeping up the struggle and of
setting out for the East, he tried to discourage her by
talking hopefully about the loyalty of the various garrisons of whose desertion he had not yet heard. He
seems also to have pointed out to her that some sort
of peace might be made with Octavian, which would
secure her throne to her family; and, in one way and

---

[1] Plutarch definitely states this, and I here use the fact as one of the main
arguments in my suppositions in regard to Cleopatra's plans.

another, he managed to dishearten her and to dull her
energies. He himself desired now to retire from public
life, and to take up his residence in some city, such as
Athens, where he might live in the obscurity of private
citizenship. He well knew the contempt in which Cleopatra held him, and at this time he thought it would be
best, in the long-run, if he left her to her fate. At all
events, he seems to have earnestly hoped that she would
not expect him to set out on any further adventures;
and in this his views must have met hers, for she could
have had no use for him. Her son Cæsarion was growing to manhood, and in the energy of his youth he would
be worth a hundred degenerate Antonys.

An unexpected check, however, was put to her schemes,
and once again misfortune seemed to dog her steps. The
Nabathæan Arabs from the neighbourhood of Petra, being
on bad terms with the Egyptians, raided the new docks
at Suez and, driving off the troops stationed there, burnt
the first galleys which had been dragged across from the
Mediterranean and those which were being built in the
docks. Cleopatra could not spare troops enough to
protect the work, and therefore the great enterprise had
to be abandoned.

Shortly after this Canidius himself arrived in Alexandria, apparently bringing the news that all Antony's
troops in all parts of the dominions had surrendered to
Octavian, and that nothing now remained to him save
Egypt and its forces. Thereupon, by the code of honour
then in recognition, Antony ought most certainly to have
killed himself; but a new idea had entered his head,
appealing to his sentimental and theatrical nature. He
decided that he would not die, but would live, like Timon
of Athens, the enemy of all men. He would build him-

self a little house, the walls buffeted by the rolling swell of the sea; and there in solitude he would count out the days of his life, his hand turned against all men.   There was a pier jutting out into the Great Harbour[1] just to the west of the Island of Antirrhodos, close to the Forum and the Temple of Neptune.   Though a powerful construction, some three hundred yards long, it does not appear to have been then in use; and Antony hit upon the idea of repairing it and building himself a little villa at its extreme end, wherein he might dwell in solitude. Cleopatra was far too much occupied with the business of life to care what her husband did; and she seems to have humoured him as she would a child, and to have caused a nice little house to be built for him on this site, which, in honour of the misanthrope whom Antony desired to emulate, she named the Timonium.   It appears that she was entirely estranged from him at this time, and he was, no doubt, glad enough to remove himself from the scorn of her eyes and tongue.   From his new dwelling he could look across the water to Cleopatra's palace; and at night the blaze of the Pharos beacon, and the many gleaming windows on the Lochias Promontory and around the harbour, all reflected with the stars in the dark water, must have formed a spectacle romantic enough for any dreamer.   In the daytime he could watch the vessels entering or leaving the port; and behind him the noise and bustle of Cleopatra's busy Alexandrians was wafted to his ears to serve as a correct subject for his Timonian curses.

The famous Timon, I need hardly say, was a citizen of

---

[1] I do not think it could have been begun to be built at this time, although Plutarch says so : it would have taken many months to complete.   It was more probably already in existence.

Athens, who lived during the days of the Peloponnesian war, and figures in the comedies of Aristophanes and Plato. He heartily detested his fellow-men, his only two associates being Alcibiades, whom he esteemed because he was likely to do so much mischief to Athens, and Apemantus, who also was a confirmed misanthrope. Once when Timon and Apemantus were celebrating a drinking festival alone together, the latter, wishing to show how much he appreciated the fact that no other of his hated fellow-men was present, remarked: "What a pleasant little party, Timon!" "Well, it would be," replied Timon, "if *you* were not here." Upon another occasion, during an assembly in the public meeting-place, Timon mounted into the speaker's place and addressed the crowd. "Men of Athens," he said, "I have a little plot of ground, and in it grows a fig-tree, from the branches of which many citizens have been pleased to hang themselves; and now, having resolved to build on that site, I wish to announce it publicly, that any of you who may so wish may go and hang yourselves there before I cut it down." Before his death he composed two epitaphs, one of which reads—

> "Timon, the misanthrope, am I below,
>   Go, and revile me, stranger—only *go!*"

The other, which was inscribed upon his tomb, reads—

> "Freed from a tedious life, I lie below.
>   Ask not my name, but take my curse and go."

Such was the man whom Antony now desired to imitate; and for the present the fallen Autocrator may be left seated in glum solitude, while Cleopatra's eager struggle for her throne occupies our attention. The

Queen's activities were now directed to urgent affairs
of State. She engaged herself in sending embassies to
the various neighbouring kingdoms in the attempt to
confirm her earlier friendships. Alexandria and Egypt
had to be governed with extreme firmness, in order to
prevent any insurrections or riots in these critical days;
and, at the same time, her subjects had to be heavily
taxed so that she might raise money for her projects.
The task of government must have been peculiarly
anxious, and the dread of the impending reckoning
with Octavian hung over her like a dark cloud. It
was quite certain that Octavian would presently invade
Egypt; but for the moment he was prevented from
doing so, mainly by financial embarrassments. After
his visit to Athens he had crossed into Asia Minor,
and now he was making arrangements for an advance
through Syria to Egypt, as soon as he should have
collected enough money for the expedition.

Towards the close of the year B.C. 31, the Jewish
King Herod seems to have come to Alexandria to discuss
the situation with Antony, his former friend and patron.
Herod's dislike of Cleopatra, and his desire to put her
to death when she was passing through his country,
will be recalled;[1] and now, after paying the necessary
compliments to the Queen, he appears to have engaged
himself in earnest conversation with Antony, perhaps
visiting him in his sea-girt hermitage. Josephus tells
us that he urged the fallen triumvir to arrange for the
assassination of Cleopatra, declaring that only by so
doing could he hope to have his life spared by Octavian.
Antony, however, would not entertain this proposal, for,
though anxious to escape his impending doom, he was

[1] Page 272.

not prepared to do so at the cost of his wife. Herod's object, of course, was to rid his horizon of the fascinating queen, who might very possibly play upon Octavian's sympathies and retain her Egyptian and Syrian dominions, thus remaining an objectionable and exacting neighbour to the kingdom of Judea. But failing to obtain Antony's co-operation in this plot, he returned to Jerusalem, and presently sailed for Rhodes to pay his respects to Octavian. Antony, hearing of his intention, sent after him a certain Alexis of Laodicea, to urge him not to abandon his cause. This Alexis had been instrumental in persuading Antony to divorce Octavia, and Cleopatra had often used him in persuading her husband to actions in regard to which he was undetermined; but he now showed the misapplication of the trust placed in him both by Antony and the Queen, for he did not return to Egypt from Herod's court, going on instead to place himself at the disposal of Octavian. His connection with Octavia's divorce, however, had not been forgotten by her revengeful brother, and his treachery was rewarded by a summary death. Herod, meanwhile, by boldly admitting that he had been Antony's friend, but was now prepared to change his allegiance, managed to win the favour of the conqueror, and his throne was not taken from him, although practically all the other kings and princes who had assisted Antony were dispossessed.

About the beginning of February B.C. 30, Octavian returned to Italy to quell certain disturbances arising from his inability to pay his disbanded troops, and there he stayed about a month, sailing once more for Asia Minor early in March. Dion tells us that the news of his voyage to Rome and that of his return to

Asia Minor were received simultaneously in Alexandria, probably late in April; but I think it very unlikely that the news of the first voyage was so long delayed, and, at any rate, some rumours of Octavian's retirement to Rome must have filtered through to Cleopatra during the month of March.

The news of this respite once more fired the Queen with hope, and she determined to make the best possible use of this precious gift of time. It will be remembered that her son Cæsarion, if I am not in error, was born at the beginning of July B.C. 47;[1] but a short time afterwards, some eighty days were added to the calendar in order to correct the existing inexactitude,[2] the real anniversary of the boy's birthday thereby being made to fall at about the middle of April.[3] The preparations for the celebration in this year B.C. 30, of his seventeenth birthday, were thus beginning to be put into motion at the time when Octavian was still thought to be struggling in Rome with his discontented troops. Cleopatra therefore determined to mark the festival by very great splendour, and to celebrate it more particularly by a public declaration of the fact that Cæsarion was now of age. I do not think it can be determined with certainty whether or not the seventeenth birthday was the customary age at which the state of manhood was sup-

---

[1] Page 130.   [2] Page 147.

[3] I do not think that the celebrations of this anniversary which now took place could possibly have occurred later than the middle of April, and therefore Cæsarion could not have been born later than the beginning of July, an argument which bears on the length of Julius Cæsar's stay in Egypt, discussed on page 128. It seems always to have been thought that the holding of the anniversary this year was anti-dated for political reasons, but it will be seen that the actual date was adhered to.

posed to be reached by an Egyptian sovereign, but it may certainly be said that the coming of age was, seldom, if ever, postponed to a later period. Cleopatra seems to have wished to make a very particular point of this fact of her son's majority, which would demonstrate to the Alexandrians, as Dion says, "that they now had a man as King." Let the public think, if they were so minded, that she herself was a defeated and condemned woman; but from this time onwards they had a grown man to lead them, a son of the divine Julius Cæsar, for whose rights she had fought while he was a boy, but who was henceforth capable of defending himself. Whatever her own fate might be, her son would, at any rate, have a better chance of retaining his throne by being firmly established upon it in the capacity of a grown man. In future she herself could work, as it were, behind the scenes, and her son could carry on the great task which she had so long striven to accomplish.

When the news of the coming celebrations was conveyed to Antony in his hermitage, he seems to have been much disturbed by it. Cæsarion and his rights had been to a large extent the cause of his ruin, and he must have been somewhat frightened at the audacity of the Queen in thus giving Octavian further cause for annoyance. Here was Alexandria preparing to celebrate in the most triumphant manner the coming of age of Octavian's rival, the claimant to Julius Cæsar's powers and estate. Was the move to be regarded as clever policy or as reckless effrontery? Leaving the passive solitude of his little Timonium, he seems to have entered once more into active discussions with Cleopatra; and as a result of these conversations, he

appears to have received the impression that his wife's
desire was now to resign her power to a large extent
into her son's hands, thus leaving to the energy of youth
the labours which middle age had failed to accomplish.
This aspect of the movement appealed to him, and he
determined in like manner to be represented in future
by a younger generation. His son by Fulvia, Antyllus,
who was a year or so younger than Cæsarion, was
living in the Alexandrian Palace; and Antony therefore
arranged with Cleopatra that the two youths should
together be declared of age (*ephebi*), Antyllus thenceforth being authorised to wear the legal dress of Roman
manhood. Cleopatra then appears to have persuaded
her husband to give up his ridiculous affectation of
misanthropy, and either to make himself useful in
organising her schemes of defence, or to leave Egypt
altogether.   Antony was by this time heartily tired
of his solitary life, and he was glad enough to abandon
his Timonian pose. He therefore took up his residence
once more in the Palace, and both he and Cleopatra
made some attempt to renew their old relationship.
Their paths had diverged, however, too far ever to
resume any sort of unity.   Antony had brooded in
solitude over his supposed wrongs, and he now regarded
his wife with a sort of suspicion; and she, on her part,
accepted him no longer as her equal, but as a creature
deserving her contempt, though arousing to some extent
her generous pity.

The birthday celebrations were conducted on the most
magnificent lines, and the whole city was given over to
feasting and revelling for many days.   The impending
storm was put away from the minds of all, and it would
have been indeed difficult for a visitor to Alexandria

during that time to believe that he had entered a city
whose rulers had recently been defeated by an enemy
already preparing to invade Egypt itself. Cleopatra, in
fact, could not be brought to admit that the game was
up; and in spite of the misery and anxiety weighing
upon her mind she kept a cheerful and hopeful demeanour
which ought to have won for her the admiration of all
historians. Antony, on the other hand, was completely
demoralised by the situation; and the birthday festivities
having whetted his appetite once more for the pleasures
of riotous living, he decided to bring his life to a close
in a round of mad dissipation. Calling together the
members of the order of Inimitable Livers, the banqueting club which he had founded some years before,[1] he
invited them to sign their names to the roll of member-
ship of a new society which he named the *Synapotha-
noumenoi* or the " Die-togethers." " Let us eat, drink,
and be merry, for to-morrow we die," must have been
his motto; and he seems to have thrown himself into
this new phase with as much shallow profundity as he
had displayed in his adoption of the Timonian pose.
Having no longer a world-wide audience before whom he
could play the jovial *rôle* of Bacchus or Hercules, he now
acted his dramatic parts before the eyes of an' inner
love of pretence; and with a kind of honest and boyish
charlatanism he paraded the halls of the Palace in the
grim but not original character of the reveller who
banqueted with his good friend Death. Antony actually
had no intention of dying: he hoped to be allowed to retire,
like his late colleague, Lepidus, the third triumvir, into
an unmolested private life; but the paradoxical situation
in which he now found himself, that of a state prisoner

[1] Page 246.

sent back, as it were, on bail to the luxuries of his home, could not fail to be turned to account by this "colossal child."

Cleopatra, on the other hand, was prepared for all eventualities; and, while she hoped somehow to be able to win her way out of her dilemma, she did not fail to make ready for the death which she might have to face. The news of Octavian's return to Asia Minor was presently received in Alexandria, and she must have felt that her chances of successfully circumventing her difficulties were remote. She therefore busied herself in making a collection of all manner of poisonous drugs, and she often went down to the dungeons to make eager experiments upon the persons of condemned criminals. Anxiously she watched the death-struggles of the prisoners to whom the different poisons had been administered, discarding those drugs which produced pain and convulsions, and continuing her tests and trials with those which appeared to offer an easy liberation from life. She also experimented with venomous snakes, subjecting animals and human beings to their poisonous bites; and Plutarch tells us that "she pretty well satisfied herself that nothing was comparable to the bite of the asp, which, without causing convulsion or groaning, brought on a heavy drowsiness and coma, with a gentle perspiration on the face, the senses being stupefied by degrees, and the victim being apparently sensible of no pain, but only annoyed when disturbed or awakened, like one who is in a profound natural sleep." [1] If the worst came to the worst, she decided that she would take her life in this manner; and this question being

[1] I fancy that the word asp is used in error, for I should think it much more probable that the deadly little horned viper was meant.

settled, she turned her undivided attention once more to the problems which beset her.

By May Octavian had marched into Syria, where all the garrisons surrendered to him.   He sent Cornelius Gallus to take command of the legions which had surrendered to him in North Africa, and this army had now taken possession of Parætonium, where Antony had stayed after his flight from Actium.   The news that this frontier fortress had passed into the hands of the enemy had not yet reached Alexandria, but that of Octavian's advance through Syria was already known in the city, and must have caused the greatest anxiety. Cleopatra thereupon decided upon a bold and dignified course of action.   Towards the end of May she sent her son Cæsarion, with his tutor Rhodon, up the Nile to Koptos,[1] and thence across the desert to the port of Berenice, where as many ships as she could collect were ordered to be in waiting for him.   The young Cæsar travelled, it would seem, in considerable state, and carried with him a huge sum of money.   He was expected to arrive at Berenice by about the end of June; and when, towards the middle of July,[2] the merchants journeying to India began to set out upon their long voyage, it was arranged that he should also set sail for those distant lands, there to make friends with the Kings of Hindustan, and perhaps to organise the great amalgamation of eastern nations of which Cleopatra had so often dreamed.   She herself decided to remain at Alexandria, first to negotiate with Octavian for the retention of her throne, and in the event of this proving

---

[1] In view of the activities of the Arabs of Petra, it is unlikely that she sent him by the sea route from Suez, which was little used by the merchants.

[2] Page 118.

unsuccessful, to fight him to the death.   No thought of
flight entered her mind;[1] and though, with a mother's
solicitous care, she made these adventurous arrangements for the safety of her beloved son, it does not
seem to have occurred to her to accompany him to the
East, where she might have expected at any rate to find
a temporary harbour of refuge.   Her parting with him
must have been one of the most unhappy events of her
unfortunate life.   For his safety and for his rights she
had struggled for seventeen years; and now it was
necessary to send him with the Indian merchants across
perilous seas to strange lands in order to save him from
the clutches of his successful rival Octavian, while she
herself remained to face their enemies and to fight for
their joint throne.   Her thoughts in these days of distress
were turning once more to the memory of the boy's
father, the great Julius Cæsar, for often, it would seem,
she gazed at his pictures or read over again the letters
which he had written to her; and now as she despatched
the young Cæsar upon his distant voyage to those lands
which had always so keenly interested his father, she
must have invoked the aid of that deified spirit which
all the Roman world worshipped as Divus Julius, and,
in an agony of supplication, must have implored him to
come to the assistance of his only earthly son and heir.

---

[1] When dying she is said to have regretted that she did not seek safety in
flight.

CHAPTER XIX.

OCTAVIAN'S INVASION OF EGYPT AND THE DEATH OF ANTONY.

THE historian must feel some reluctance in discrediting the romantic story of the attachment of Cleopatra and Antony at this period; but nevertheless the fact cannot be denied that they had now decided to live apart from one another, and there seems very little doubt that each regarded the other with distrust and suspicion. Antony had lived so long alone in his Timonium that he was altogether out of touch with his wife's projects; and she, on her part, had not, for many a month, admitted him fully into her confidence. Their relationship was marked, on his side, by mistrust, and on hers, by disdainful pity; and I can find no indication of that romantic passage, hand-in-hand to their doom, which has come to be regarded as the grand finale of their tragic tale. In its place, however, I would offer the spectacle of the lonely and courageous fight made by the little Queen against her fate, which must surely command the admiration of all men. Her husband having so signally failed her, the whole burden of the government of her country and of the organisation of her defence seems to have fallen upon her shoulders. Day and night she must have been harassed by fearful anxieties, and haunted by the thought of her probable doom; yet she conducted herself with undaunted courage, never deigning to consider the question of flight, and never once turning from the pathway of that personal and dynastic ambition which seems to me hardly able to be distinguished from her real duty to her country.

When Octavian was preparing in Syria, during the month of June B.C. 30, to invade Egypt, both Cleopatra and Antony attempted to open negotiations with him. They sent a certain Greek named Euphronius, who had been a tutor to one of the young princes, to the enemy bearing messages from them both. Cleopatra asked that, in return for her surrender, her son Cæsarion might be allowed to retain the throne of Egypt; but Antony prayed only that he might be allowed to live the life of a private man, either at Alexandria or else in Athens. With this embassy Cleopatra sent her crown, her sceptre, and her state-chariot, in the hope that Octavian would bestow them again upon her son, if not upon herself. The mission, however, was a partial failure. Octavian would not listen to any proposals in regard to Antony; but to Cleopatra he sent a secret message, conveyed by one of his freedmen, named Thyrsus, indicating that he was well-disposed towards her, and would be inclined to leave her in possession of Egypt, if only she would cause Antony to be put to death. Actually, Octavian had no intention of showing any particular mercy to Cleopatra, and his suggestions were intended to deceive her. He seems to have made up his mind how to act. Antony would have to be murdered or made to take his own life: it would be awkward to have to condemn him to death and formally to execute him. Cæsarion, his rival, would also have to meet with a violent end. Cleopatra ought to be captured alive so that he might display her in his Triumph, after which she would be sent into exile, while her country and its wealth would fall into his hands, the loot serving for the payment of his troops. In all his subsequent dealings with the Queen we shall observe his anxiety to take her alive, while towards Antony he will be seen to show a relentless hostility.

The freedman Thyrsus was a personage of tact and understanding, and with Cleopatra he was able to discuss the situation in all its aspects. The Queen was striving by every means to retain her throne, and she was quite capable of paying Octavian back in his own coin, deceiving him and leading him to suppose that she would trust herself to his mercy. She showed great attention to Thyrsus, giving him lengthy audiences, and treating him with considerable honour; and Antony, not being admitted to their secret discussions, grew daily more angry and suspicious. It is not likely that Cleopatra consented to the proposed assassination of her husband, but the situation was such that she could have had no great objection to the thought of his suicide, and I dare say she discussed quite frankly with Thyrsus the means of reminding him of his honourable obligations. It is said by Dion Cassius that Octavian actually conveyed messages of an amorous nature to Cleopatra, but this is probably incorrect, though Thyrsus may well have hinted that his master's heart had been touched by the brave manner in which she had faced her misfortunes, and that he was eager to win her regard. Possibly a rumour of the nature of their conferences reached Antony, or maybe his jealousy was aroused by the freedman's confidential attitude to the Queen; for he became even more suspicious than he had been before, and he appears to have conducted himself as though his mind were in a condition of extreme exasperation. Suddenly he caused Thyrsus to be seized by some of his men, and soundly thrashed, after which he sent him back to Octavian with a letter explaining his action. "The man's inquisitive, impertinent ways provoked me," he wrote, "and in my circumstances I cannot be expected to be very patient. But if it offend you, you have got my freedman, Hipparchus, with you : hang him up and whip him to make us even." Hipparchus had probably deserted from Antony to Octavian, and the whipping of Thyrsus and the suggested retaliation constituted a piece of grim humour which seems to have appealed at once to Cleopatra's instincts. The audacity of the action was of the kind which most delighted her; and she immediately began to pay more respect to her husband, who, she thus found, was still capable of asserting himself in a kingly manner. Plutarch tells us that to clear herself of his suspicions, which were quite unfounded, she now paid him more attention and humoured him in every way; and it seems that her change of attitude put new courage into his heart, substituting a brave bearing for that dejection of carriage which had lately been so noticeable. She seemed anxious to prove to him that she would not play him false, and to make her attitude clear to Octavian. When the anniversary of her birthday had occurred in the previous winter she had celebrated it very quietly; but Antony's birthday, which fell at about this time of year, she celebrated in the most elaborate manner, giving great presents to all those who had enjoyed her hospitality. It was as though she

desired all men to know that so long as Antony played
the man, and entered into this last fight with that spirit
of adventure which always marked her own actions, she
would stand by him to the last; but that if he lacked
the spirit to make a bid for success, then she could but
wish him well out of her way.   The thrashing of Thyrsus
proved to be the occasion of a temporary reconciliation
between the Queen and her husband,[1] and for a time
Antony acted with something of his old energy and
courage.

Hearing that the army under Cornelius Gallus was
marching through Cyrenaica, the modern Tripoli, towards
the western frontier of Egypt, he hastened with a few
ships to Paraetonium in order to secure the defence of
that place.   But on landing and approaching the walls
of the fortress and calling upon the commander to come
out to him, his voice was drowned by a blare of trumpets
from within.   A few minutes later the garrison made a
sortie, chased him and his men back to the harbour, set
fire to some of his ships, and drove him with considerable loss from their shores.   On returning to Alexandria
he heard that Octavian was approaching Pelusium, the
corresponding fortress on the eastern frontier of Egypt,
which was under the command of a certain officer named
Seleucus; and shortly after this, towards the middle of
July, the news arrived that that stronghold had surrendered.

Thereupon Antony, whose nerves were in a very highly-
strung condition, furiously accused Cleopatra of having
betrayed him by arranging secretly with Seleucus to
hand over the fortress to Octavian in the hope of
placating the approaching enemy.   Cleopatra denied

[1] This seems clearly indicated by Plutarch.

the accusation, and, to prove the truth of her words, she caused the wife and children of Seleucus to be arrested and handed over to her husband, that he might put them to death if it were shown that she had had any secret correspondence with the traitor,[1] a fact which seems to prove her innocence conclusively.

Antony's suspicions, however, unnerved him once more, and drove the flickering courage from his heart. Dispirited and agitated, he sent Euphronius to Octavian a second time, accompanied on this occasion by the young Antyllus, and provided with a large sum of money with which he hoped to placate his enemy. Octavian took the money but would not listen to the pleading of Antyllus on behalf of his father. The embassy must have been most distasteful to Cleopatra, who could not easily understand how a man could fall so low as to attempt to buy off his enemy with gold—and gold, let it be remembered, belonging to his wife. Her surprise and pain, however, must have been greatly increased when she discovered that Antony had next sent in chains to Octavian a certain ex-senator, named Turullius, who had been one of the murderers of Julius Cæsar, and was, in fact, the last survivor of all the assassins, each one of the others having met his death as though by the hand of a vengeful Providence. Turullius had now come into Antony's power, and, since Cleopatra's son was Julius Cæsar's heir, the man ought to have been handed over to the Queen for punishment. Instead, however, Antony had sent him on to his enemy in a manner which could only suggest that he admitted Octavian's right to act

---

[1] Dion Cassius suggests that Cleopatra did attempt to play into Octavian's hands, but the accusation is quite unfounded, and is an obvious one to make against the hated enemy.

as the Dictator's representative. Octavian at once put
Turullius to death, thereby performing the last necessary
act of vengeance in behalf of the murdered Cæsar; but
to Antony he did not so much as send an acknowledg-
ment of the prisoner's reception. Receiving no assurance
of mercy, Antony appears for a time to have thought of
flying to Spain or to some other country where he could
hide, or could carry on a guerilla warfare, until some
change in the politics of Rome should enable him to
reappear. His nobler nature, however, at length asserted
itself, owing to the example set by Cleopatra, who was
determined now to defend her capital; and once more
he pulled himself together, as though to stand by the
Queen's side until the end. Their position, though bad,
was not desperate. Alexandria was a strongly fortified
city. The four Roman legions which had been left in
Egypt during the war in Greece were still in the city;
the Macedonian household troops were also stationed
there; and no doubt a considerable body of Egyptian
soldiers were garrisoned within the walls; while in the
harbour lay the fleet which had retired from Actium,
together with numerous other ships of war. Thus a
formidable force was in readiness to defend the metropolis, and these men were so highly paid with the never-
ending wealth of the Egyptian treasury that they were
in much happier condition than were the legionaries of
Octavian, whose wages were months overdue.

Cleopatra, nevertheless, did not expect to come through
the ordeal alive; and although Octavian continued to
send her assurances of his goodwill, the price which he
asked for her safety was invariably the head of Antony,
and this she was not prepared to pay. I do not think that
the Queen's temptation in this regard has been properly

observed. Dion Cassius emphatically states that Octavian promised her that if she would kill Antony he would grant her both personal safety and the full maintenance of her undiminished authority; and Plutarch, with equal clearness, says that Octavian told her that there was no reasonable favour which she might not expect from him if only she would put Antony to death, or even expel him from his safe refuge in Egypt. Antony had proved himself a broken reed; he had acted in a most cowardly manner; he was generally drunk and always unreliable; and he appeared to be of no further use to her or to her cause. Yet, although his removal meant immunity to herself, she was too loyal, too proud, to sanction his assassination; and her action practically amounted to this, that she defied Octavian, telling him that if he wanted her drunken husband's useless head he must break down the walls of her city and hunt for it.

In accordance with the custom of the age the Queen had built herself, during recent years, a tomb and mortuary temple wherein her body should rest after death and her spirit should receive the usual sacrifices and priestly ministrations. This mausoleum, according to Plutarch, was surrounded by other buildings, apparently prepared for the royal family and for members of the court. They were not set up within the precincts of the Sema, or royal necropolis, which stood at the side of the Street of Canopus, but were erected beside the temple of Isis-Aphrodite, a building rising at the edge of the sea on the eastern side of the Lochias Promontory. I gather from the remarks of Plutarch that the Queen's tomb actually formed part of the temple buildings; and, if this be so, Cleopatra must have had it in

mind to be laid to rest within the precincts of the sanctuary of the goddess with whom she was identified.
Thus, after her death, the worshippers in the temple of
Isis would make their supplications, as it were, to her own
spirit, and her mortal remains would become holy relics
of their patron goddess.[1] The mausoleum was remarkable
for its height and for the beauty of its workmanship.
It was probably constructed of valuable marbles, and
appears to have consisted of several chambers. On the
ground floor I should imagine that a pillared hall, entered
through a double door of decorated cedar-wood, led to
an inner shrine wherein the sarcophagus stood ready
to receive the Queen's body; and that from this hall a
flight of stone stairs ascended to the upper chambers,
whose flooring was formed of the great blocks of granite
which constituted the roofing of the hall below. There
was, perhaps, a third storey, the chambers of which,
like those on the floor below, were intended to be used
by the mortuary priests for the preparation of the incense, the offerings, and the vestments employed in their
ceremonies. The large open casements in the walls of
these upper chambers must have overlooked the sea on
the one side and the courts of the Temple of Isis on
the other; but, as was usual in Egyptianised buildings,
there were no windows of any size in the lower hall
and sanctuary, the light being admitted through the
doorway and through small apertures close to the ceil-
ing. The heat of these July days did not penetrate to
any uncomfortable degree into this stone-built mausoleum, and the cool sea-wind must have blown continu-

---

[1] This fact, the significance of which has been overlooked, is an interesting
indication of Cleopatra's definite claim to be a manifestation of Venus-
Aphrodite-Isis. See pp. 121, 144, 228.

OCTAVIAN.

ously through the upper rooms, while the brilliant
sunlight outside was here subdued and softened in its
reflection upon the marble walls.   The rhythmic beat
of the breakers upon the stone embankment below the
eastern windows, and the shrill cries of the gulls, echoed
through the rooms; while from the western side the
chanting of the priests in the adjoining temple, and the
more distant hubbub of the town, intruded into the cool
recesses of these wind-swept chambers like the sounds
of a forsaken world.

Here Cleopatra decided to take up her residence so
soon as Octavian should lay successful siege to the walls
of the city.   She had determined that in the event of
defeat she would destroy herself; and, with this prospect
in view, she now caused her treasures of gold, silver,
ebony, ivory, and cinnamon, and her jewellery of pearls,
emeralds, and precious stones, to be carried into the
mausoleum, where they were laid upon a pyre of faggots
and tow erected on the stone floor of one of the upper
rooms.   If it should be necessary for her to put an end
to her miseries, she had decided to set the fangs of the
deadly asp into her flesh, and, with her last efforts, to fire
the tow, thus consuming her body and her wealth in a
single conflagration.   Meanwhile, however, she remained
in the Palace, and busied herself in the preparations of
the defence of the city.

In the last days of July Octavian's forces arrived before
the walls, and took up their quarters in and around the
Hippodromos, which stood upon rocky ground to the east
of the city.   Faced with the crisis, Antony once more
showed the flickering remnants of his former courage.
Gathering his troops together he made a bold sortie from
the city, and attacking Octavian's cavalry, routed them

with great slaughter and chased them back to their camp. He then returned to the Palace, where, meeting Cleopatra while still he was clad in his dusty and blood-stained armour, he threw his arms about her small form and kissed her in the sight of all men. He then commended to her especial favour one of his officers who had greatly distinguished himself in the fight; and the Queen at once presented the man with a magnificent helmet and breastplate of gold. That very night this officer donned his golden armour and fled to the camp of Octavian.

Upon the next morning Antony, with somewhat boyish effrontery, sent a messenger to Octavian challenging him to single combat, as he had done before the battle of Actium; but to this his enemy replied with the scathing remark that "he might find several other ways of ending his life." He thereupon decided to bring matters to a conclusion by a pitched battle on land and sea, rather than await the issue of a protracted siege; and, Cleopatra having agreed to this plan, orders were given for a general engagement upon August 1st. On the night before this date Antony, whose courage did not now fail him, bade the servants help him liberally at supper and not to be sparing with the wine, for that on the morrow they might be serving a new master, while he himself, the incarnation of Bacchus, the god of wine and festivity, lay dead upon the battlefield. At this his friends who were around him began to weep, but Antony hastily explained to them that he did not in the least expect to die, but hoped rather to lead them to glorious victory.

Late that night, when complete stillness had fallen upon the star-lit city, and the sea-wind had dropped, giving place to the hot silence of the summer darkness, on a sudden was heard the distant sound of pipes and

cymbals, and of voices singing a rollicking tune. Nearer
they came, and presently the pattering of dancing feet
could be heard, while the shouts and cries of a multitude
were blended with the wild music of a bacchanal song.
The tumultuous procession, as Plutarch described it,
seemed to take its course right through the middle of
the city towards the Gate of Canopus; and there the
commotion was most loudly heard. Then, suddenly,
the sounds passed out, and were heard no more. But
all those who had listened in the darkness to the wild
music were assured that they had heard the passage
of Bacchus as he and his ghostly attendants marched
away from the army of his fallen incarnation, and joined
that of the victorious Octavian.[1]

The next morning, as soon as it was light, Antony
marched his troops out of the eastern gates of the city,
and formed them up on rising ground between the walls
and the Hippodromos, a short distance back from the
sea. From this position he watched his fleet sail out
from the Great Harbour and make towards Octavian's
ships, which were arrayed near the shore, two or three
miles east of the city; but, to his dismay, the Alexandrian
vessels made no attempt to deliver an attack upon the
enemy as he had ordered them to do. Instead, they
saluted Octavian's fleet with their oars, and, on receiving
a similar salutation in response, joined up with the enemy,
all sailing thereupon towards the Great Harbour. Meanwhile, from his elevated position Antony saw the whole
of his cavalry suddenly gallop over to Octavian's lines,
and he thus found himself left only with his infantry,
who, of course, were no match for the enemy. It was

[1] The sounds perhaps came from Octavian's outposts, which were just outside
the Gate of Canopus.

useless to struggle further, and, giving up all hope, he fled back into the city, crying out that Cleopatra had betrayed him. As he rushed into the Palace, followed by his distracted officers, smiting his brow and calling down curses on the woman who, he declared, had delivered him into the hands of enemies made for her sake, the Queen fled before him from her apartments, as though she feared that in his fury and despair he might cut her down with his sword. Alone with her two waiting-women, Iras and Charmion, she ran as fast as she could through the empty halls and corridors of the Palace, and at length, crossing the deserted courtyard, she reached the mausoleum adjoining the temple of Isis. The officials, servants, and guards, it would seem, had all fled at the moment when the cry had arisen that the fleet and the cavalry had deserted; and there were probably but a few scared priests in the vicinity of the temple, who could hardly have recognised the Queen as she panted to the open door of the tomb, deserted by the usual custodians. The three women rushed into the dimly-lighted hall, bolting and barring the door behind them, and no doubt barricading it with benches, offering-tables, and other pieces of sacerdotal furniture. They then made their way to the habitable rooms on the upper floor, where they must have flung themselves down upon the rich couches in a sort of delirium of horror and excitement, Cleopatra herself preparing for immediate suicide. From the window they must have seen some of Antony's staff hastening towards them, for presently they were able to send a message to tell him that the Queen was on the point of killing herself. After a short time, however, when the tumult in her brain had somewhat subsided, Cleopatra made up her mind to wait awhile before taking the final step, so that she might ascertain Octavian's attitude towards her; and, having determined upon this course of action, she seems to have composed herself as best she could, while through the eastern windows, her eyes staring over the summer sea, she watched the Egyptian ships and those of the enemy rowing side by side into the Great Harbour.

There is no reason to suppose that Cleopatra had betrayed her husband, or that she was in any way a party to the desertions which had just taken place. The sudden collapse of their resistance, while yet it was but mid-morning, must have come to her as a staggering shock; and Antony's accusations were doubtless felt to be only in keeping with the erratic behaviour which had characterised his last years. On the previous day Antony had offered a large sum of money to every one of Octavian's legionaries who should desert; and it is more than likely that Octavian had made a similar offer to the Egyptian sailors and soldiers. Only a year previously these sailors had fraternised with the Romans of the Antonian party in the Gulf of Ambracia, and the latter, having deserted to Octavian after the battle of Actium, were now present in large numbers amongst the opposing fleet. The Egyptians were thus called upon to fight with their friends whose hospitality they had often accepted, and whose fighting qualities, now that they were combined with Octavian's victorious forces, they had every reason to appreciate. Their desertion, therefore, needed no suggestion on the part of Cleopatra: it was almost inevitable.

Antony, however, was far too distracted and over-wrought to guard his tongue, and he seems to have paced his apartments in the Palace in a condition bordering upon madness, cursing Cleopatra and her country, and calling down imprecations upon all who had deserted him. Presently those of his staff who had followed the Queen to her mausoleum brought him the news that she had killed herself, for so they had interpreted her message; and instantly Antony's fury seems to have left him, the shock having caused a collapse of his energy. At first he was probably dazed by the tidings; but when their full significance had penetrated to his bewildered brain there was no place left for anger or suspicion. "Now Antony," he cried, "why delay longer? Fate has taken away the only thing for which you could say you still wanted to live." And with these words he rushed into his bedchamber, eagerly tearing off his armour, and calling upon his slave Eros to assist him. Then, as he bared the upper part of his body, he was heard to talk aloud to the Queen, whom he believed to be dead. "Cleopatra," he said, "I am not sad to be parted from you now, for I shall soon be with you; but it troubles me that so great a general should have been found to have slower courage than a woman." Not long previously he had made Eros solemnly promise to kill him when he should order him to do so; and now, turning to him, he gave him that order, reminding him of his oath. Eros drew his sword, as though he intended to do as he was bid, but suddenly turning round, he drove the blade into his own breast, and fell dying upon the floor. Thereupon Antony bent down over him and cried to him as he lost consciousness, "Well done, Eros! Well done!" Then, picking up the sword, he added, "You have shown your master how to do what you had not the heart to do yourself;" and so saying, he drove the sword upwards into his breast from below the ribs, and fell back upon his bed.

The wound, however, was not immediately mortal, and presently, the flow of blood having ceased, he recovered consciousness. Some of the Egyptian servants had gathered around him, and now he implored them to put him out of his pain. But when they realised that he was not dead they rushed from the room, leaving him groaning and writhing where he lay. Some of them must have carried the news to the Queen as she sat at the window of the mausoleum, for, a few moments later, a certain Diomedes, one of her secretaries, came to Antony telling him that she had not yet killed herself, and that she desired his body to be brought to her. Thereupon Antony eagerly gave orders to the servants to carry him to her, and they, lifting him in their arms, placed him upon an improvised stretcher and hurried with him to the mausoleum. A crowd seems now to have collected around the door of the building, and when the Queen saw the group of men bringing her husband to her, she must have feared lest some of them, seeking a reward, would seize her as soon as they had entered her stronghold and carry her alive to Octavian. Perhaps, also, it was a difficult matter to shoot back the bolts of the door which in her excitement she had managed to drive deep into their sockets. She, therefore, was unable to admit Antony into the mausoleum; and there he lay below her window, groaning and entreating her to let him die in her arms. In the words of Plutarch, Cleopatra thereupon "let down ropes and cords to which Antony was fastened; and she and her two women, the only persons she had allowed to enter the mausoleum, drew him up. Those who were present say that nothing was ever more sad than this spectacle, to see Antony, covered all over with blood and just expiring, thus drawn up, still holding up his hands to her, and raising up his body with the little force he had left. And, indeed, it was no easy task for the women; for Cleopatra, with all her strength clinging to the rope and straining at it with her head bent towards the ground, with difficulty pulled him up, while those below encouraged her with their cries and joined in all her efforts and anxiety." The window must have been a considerable distance from the ground, and I do not think that the three women could ever have succeeded in raising Antony's great weight so far had not those below fetched ladders, I suppose, and helped to lift him up to her, thereafter, no doubt, watching the terrible scene from the head of these ladders outside the window.

Dragging him through the window the women carried him to the bed, upon which he probably swooned away after the agonies of the ascent. Cleopatra was distracted by the pitiful sight, and fell into uncontrolled weeping. Beating her breast and tearing her clothes, she made some attempts, at the same time, to stanch the scarlet stream which flowed from his wound; and soon her face and neck were smeared with his blood. Flinging herself down by his side she called him her lord, her husband, and her emperor. All her pity and much of her old love for him was aroused by his terrible sufferings, and so intent was she upon his pain that her own desperate situation was entirely forgotten. At last Antony came to his senses, and called for wine to drink; after which, having revived somewhat, he attempted to soothe the Queen's wild lamentations, telling her to make her terms with Octavian, so far as might honourably be done, and advising her to trust only a certain Proculeius amongst all the friends of the conqueror. With his last breath, he begged her, says Plutarch, "not to pity him in this last turn of fate, but rather to rejoice for him in remembrance of his past happiness, who had been of all men the most illustrious and powerful, and in the end had fallen not ignobly, a Roman by a Roman vanquished." With these words he lay back upon the bed, and soon had breathed his last in the arms of the woman whose interests he had so poorly served, and whom now he left to face alone the last great struggle for her throne and for the welfare of her son.

CHAPTER XX.

THE DEATH OF CLEOPATRA AND THE
TRIUMPH OF OCTAVIAN.

CLEOPATRA'S situation was at this moment terrible in
the extreme. The blood-stained body of her husband lay
stretched upon the bed, covered by her torn garments
which she had thrown over it. Charmion and Iras, her
two waiting-women, were probably huddled in the corner
of the room, beating their breasts and wailing as was the
Greek habit at such a time. Below the open window a
few Romans and Egyptians appear to have gathered in
the sun-baked courtyard; and, I think, the ladders still
rested against the wall where they had been placed by
those who had helped to raise Antony up to the Queen.
It must now have been early afternoon, and the sunlight
of the August day, no doubt, beat into the room, light-
ing the disarranged furniture and revealing the wet
blood-stains upon the tumbled carpets over which the
dying man's heavy body had been dragged. From the
one side the surge of the sea penetrated into the
chamber; from the other the shouts of Octavian's
soldiers and the clattering of their arms came to
Cleopatra's ears, telling her of the enemy's arrival in
the Palace. She might expect at any moment to be
asked to surrender, and more than probably an attempt
would be made to capture her by means of an entry

through the window. She had determined, however, never to be made prisoner in this manner, and she had, no doubt, given it to be clearly understood that any effort to seize her would be her signal for firing the funeral pyre which had been erected in the adjoining room and destroying herself upon it. To be made a captive probably meant her degradation at Octavian's Triumph and the loss of her throne; but to surrender by mutual arrangement might assure her personal safety and the continuity of her dynasty. With this in view, it seems likely that she now armed her two women to resist any assault upon the windows, and told them to warn all who attempted to climb the ladders that she, with her priceless jewellery and treasures, would be engulfed in the flames before ever they had reached to the level of her place of refuge.

Antony had been dead but a few minutes when Proculeius, of whom he had spoken to Cleopatra just before he expired, arrived upon the scene, demanding, in the name of Octavian, an audience with the Queen. He knocked upon the barred door of the main entrance to the mausoleum, calling upon Cleopatra to admit him, and the sound must have echoed through the hall below and come to her ears, where she listened at the top of the stairs, like some ominous summons from the powers of the Underworld; but, fearing that she might be taken prisoner, she did not dare open to him, even if she could have shot back the heavy bolts, and she must have paced to and fro beside her husband's corpse in an agony of indecision. At last, however, she ran down the marble staircase to the dimly-lighted hall below, and, standing beside the barricade which she had constructed against the inner side of the door, called out to Proculeius by name. He answered her from the outside, and in this manner they held a short parley with one another, she offering to surrender if she could receive Octavian's word that her Kingdom of Egypt would be given to her son Cæsarion, and Proculeius replying only with the assurance that Octavian was to be trusted to act with clemency towards her. This was not satisfactory to her, and presently the Roman officer returned to his master, leaving Cleopatra undisturbed until late in the afternoon. He described the Queen's situation to Octavian, and pointed out to him that it would probably not be difficult to effect an entrance to the mausoleum by means of the ladders, and that, with speed and a little manœuvring, Cleopatra could be seized before she had time to fire the pyre. Thereupon Octavian sent him with Cornelius Gallus,[1] who had now reached Alexandria, to attempt her capture, and the latter went straight to the door of the mausoleum, knocking upon it to summon the Queen. Cleopatra at once went down the stairs and entered into conversation with Cornelius Gallus through the closed door; and it would seem that her two women, perhaps eager to hear what was said, left their post at the window of the upper room and stood upon the steps behind her. As soon as the Queen was heard to be talking and reiterating her conditions of surrender, Proculeius ran round to the other side of the building, and, adjusting the ladders, climbed rapidly up to the window, followed by two other Roman officers. Entering the disordered room, he ran past the dead body of Antony and hurried down the stairs, at the bottom of which he encountered Charmion and Iras, while beyond them in the dim light of the hall he saw Cleopatra

[1] Page 366.

standing at the shut door, her back turned to him. One of the women uttered a cry, when she saw Proculeius, and called out to her mistress: "Unhappy Cleopatra, you are taken prisoner!" At this the Queen sprang round, and, seeing the Roman officer, snatched a dagger from its sheath at her waist and raised it for the stroke which should terminate the horror of her life. Proculeius, however, was too quick for her. He sprang at her with a force which must have hurled her back against the door, and, seizing her wrist, shook the dagger from her small hand. Then, holding her two arms at her side, he caused his men to shake her dress and to search her for hidden weapons or poison. "For shame, Cleopatra," he said to her, scolding her for attempting to take her life; "you wrong yourself and Octavian very much in trying to rob him of so good an opportunity of showing his clemency, and you would make the world believe that the most humane of generals was a faithless and implacable enemy." He then seems to have ordered his officers to remove the barriers and to open the door of the mausoleum, whereupon Cornelius Gallus and his men were able to assist him to guard the Queen and her two women. Shortly after this, Octavian's freedman, Epaphroditus, arrived with orders to treat Cleopatra with all possible gentleness and civility, but to take the strictest precautions to prevent her injuring herself; and, acting on these instructions, the Roman officers seem to have lodged the Queen under guard in one of the upper rooms of the mausoleum, after having made a thorough search for hidden weapons or poisons.

Just before sunset Octavian made his formal entry into Alexandria. He wished to impress the people of the city with the fact of his benevolent and peace-loving nature, and therefore he made a certain Alexandrian philosopher named Areius, for whom he had a liking, ride with him in his chariot.   As the triumphal procession passed along the beautiful Street of Canopus, Octavian was seen by the agitated citizens to be holding the philosopher's hand and talking to him in the most gentle manner.   Stories soon went the rounds that when the conqueror had received the news of Antony's death he had shed tears of sorrow, and had read over to his staff some of his enemy's furious letters to him and his own moderate replies, thus showing how the quarrel had been forced upon him.   Orders now seem to have been issued forbidding all outrage or looting; and presently the frightened Alexandrians ventured from their hiding-places, most of the local magnates being ordered to gather themselves together in the Gymnasium.   Here, in the twilight, Octavian rose to address them; and as he did so, they all prostrated themselves upon the ground before him in abject humiliation.   Commanding them to rise, he told them that he freely acquitted them of all blame: firstly, in memory of the great Alexander who had founded their city; secondly, for the sake of the city itself which was so large and beautiful; thirdly, in honour of their god Serapis;[1] and lastly, to gratify his dear friend Areius, at whose request he was about to spare many lives.

Having thus calmed the citizens, who now must have hailed him as a kind of deliverer and saviour, he retired to his quarters, whence, in his sardonic manner, he appears to have issued orders for the immediate slaughter

[1] Plutarch does not give Serapis as one of the reasons of Octavian's clemency, but Dion says this was so.

of those members of the court of Cleopatra and Antony for whom Areius had not any particular liking. The unfortunate Antyllus, Antony's son, having been betrayed to Octavian by his faithless tutor Theodorus, was at once put to death in the temple erected by Cleopatra to Julius Cæsar, whither he had fled. As the executioner cut off the boy's head, Theodorus contrived to steal a valuable jewel which hung round his neck; but the theft was discovered, and he was carried before Octavian, who ordered him to be crucified forthwith. A strict guard was set over the two children of Cleopatra, Ptolemy and Cleopatra Selene,[1] who were still in Alexandria; and Octavian seems to have given Cleopatra to understand that if she attempted to kill herself he would put these two children to death. Thus he was able to assure himself that she would refrain from taking her life, for, as Plutarch says, "before such engines her purpose (to destroy herself) shook and gave way."

Antony's body was now, I suppose, prepared for burial. Though mummification was still often practised in Alexandria by Greeks and Egyptians, I do not think that any elaborate attempt was made to embalm the corpse, and it was probably ready for the funeral rites within a few days. Out of respect to the dead general a number of Roman officers and foreign potentates who were with Octavian's army begged to be allowed to perform these rites at their own expense; but in deference to Cleopatra's wishes the body was left in the Queen's hands, and instructions were issued that her orders were to be obeyed in regard to the funeral. Thus Antony was buried, with every mark of royal splendour and pomp,

[1] Page 355.

in a tomb which had probably long been prepared for him, not far from his wife's mausoleum. Cleopatra followed him to his grave, a tragic, piteous little figure, surrounded by a group of her lamenting ladies; and, while the priests burnt their incense and uttered their droning chants, the Queen's fragile hands ruthlessly beat her breasts as she called upon the dead man by his name. In these last terrible hours only the happier character of her relationship with Antony was remembered, and the recollection of her many disagreements with him were banished from her mind by the piteous scenes of his death, and by the thought of his last tender words to her as he lay groaning upon her bed. In her extreme loneliness she must have now desired his buoyant company of earlier years with an intensity which she could hardly have felt during his lifetime; and it must have been difficult indeed for her to refrain from putting an end to her miserable life upon the grave of her dead lover. Yet Octavian's threat in regard to her children held her hand; and, moreover, even in her utter distress, she had not yet abandoned her hope of saving Egypt from the clutch of Rome. Her own dominion, she knew, was over, and the best fate which she herself could hope for was that of an unmolested exile; yet Octavian's attitude to her indicated in every way that he would be willing to leave the throne to her descendants. She did not know how falsely he was acting towards her, how he was making every effort to encourage hope in her heart in order that he might bring her alive to Rome to be exhibited in chains to the jeering populace. She did not understand that his messages of encouragement, and even of affection, to her were written with sardonic cunning, that his cheerful assurances in regard to her children were made at a time when he was probably actually sending messages post-haste to Berenice to attempt to recall Cæsarion in order to put him to death. She did not understand Octavian's character: perhaps she had never even seen him; and she hoped somehow to make a last appeal to him. She had played her wonderful game for the amalgamation of Egypt and Rome into one vast kingdom, ruled by her descendants and those of the great Julius Cæsar, and she had lost. But there was yet hope that out of the general wreck she might save the one asset with which she had started her operations —the independent throne of Egypt; and to accomplish this she must live on for a while longer, and must face with bravery the nightmare of her existence.

Coming back, after the funeral, to her rooms in the mausoleum, wherein she had now decided to take up her residence, she fell into a high fever; and there upon her bed she lay in delirium for several days. She suffered, moreover, very considerable pain, due to the inflammation and ulceration caused by the blows which she had rained upon her delicate body in the abandonment of her despair. Over and over again she was heard to utter in her delirium the desolate cry, " I *will not* be exhibited in his Triumph," and in her distress she begged repeatedly to be allowed to die. At one time she refused all food, and begged her doctor, a certain Olympus, to help her to pass quietly out of the world.[1] Octavian, however, hearing of her increasing weakness, warned her once more that unless she made an effort to live he would not be lenient to her children; whereupon, as though galvanised into life by this pressure upon

---

[1] Plutarch tells us that this doctor wrote a full account of these last scenes, from which he evidently quotes.

her maternal instincts, she made the necessary struggle to recover, obediently swallowing the medicine and stimulants which were given to her.

Thus the hot August days passed by, and at length the Queen, now fragile and haggard, was able to move about once more. Her age at this time was thirty-eight years, and she must have lost that freshness of youth which had been her notable quality; but her brilliant eyes had now perhaps gained in wonder by the pallor of her face, and the careless arrangement of her dark hair must have enhanced her tragic beauty. The seductive tones of her voice could not have been diminished, and that peculiar quality of elusiveness may well have been accentuated by her illness and by the nervous strain through which she had passed. Indeed, her personal charm was still so great that a certain Cornelius Dolabella, one of the Roman officers whose duty it was to keep watch over her, speedily became her devoted servant, and was induced to promise that he would report to her any plans in regard to her welfare which Octavian should disclose.

On August 28th, as she lay upon a small pallet-bed in the upper room, gazing in utter desolation, as I imagine, over the blue waters of the Mediterranean, her women ran in to her to tell her that Octavian had come to pay his respects to her. He had not yet visited her, for he had very correctly avoided her previous to and during Antony's funeral; and since that time she had been too ill to receive him. Now, however, she was convalescent, and the conqueror had arrived unexpectedly to congratulate her, as etiquette demanded, upon her recovery. He walked into the room before the Queen had time to prepare herself; and Plutarch describes how, "on his entering, she sprang from her bed, having nothing on but the one garment next her body, and flung herself at his feet, her hair and face looking wild and disfigured, her voice trembling, and her eyes sunken and dark. The marks of the blows which she had rained upon herself were visible about her breast, and altogether her whole person seemed to be no less afflicted than was her spirit. But for all this, her old charm and the boldness of her youthful beauty had not wholly left her, and, in spite of her present condition, still shone out from within and allowed itself to appear in all the expressions of her face."

The picture of the distraught little Queen, her dark hair tumbled over her face, her loose garment slipping from her white shoulders, as she crouches at the feet of this cold, unhealthy-looking man, who stands somewhat awkwardly before her, is one which must distress the mind of the historian who has watched the course of Cleopatra's warfare against the representative of Rome. Yet in this scene we are able to discern her but stripped of the regal and formal accessories which have often caused her to appear more imposing and awe-inspiring than actually her character justified. She was essentially a woman, and now, in her condition of physical weakness, she acted precisely as any other overwrought member of her sex might have behaved under similar circumstances. Her wonderful pluck had almost deserted her, and her persistence of purpose was lost in the wreck of all her hopes. We have often heard her described as a calculating woman, who lived her life in studied and callous voluptuousness, and who died in unbending dignity; but, as I have tried to indicate in this volume, the Queen's nature was essentially feminine—highly-strung, and liable to rapid changes from joy to despair. Keen, independent, and fearless though she was, she was never a completely self-reliant woman, and in circumstances such as those which are now being recorded we obtain a view of her character, which shows her to have been capable of needing desperately the help and sympathy of others.

Octavian raised her to her feet, and, assisting her once more on to her bed, sat himself down beside her. At first she talked to him in a rambling manner, justifying her past movements, and attributing certain actions, such, I suppose, as her hiding in the mausoleum, to her fear of Antony; but when Octavian pointed out to her the discrepancies in her statements she made no longer any attempt to excuse her conduct, begging him only not to take her throne from her son, and telling him that she was willing enough to live if only he would insure the safety of her country and dynasty, and would be merciful to her children. Then, rising from the bed, she brought to Octavian a number of letters written to her by Julius Cæsar, and also one or two portraits of him painted for her during his lifetime. "You know," she said,[1] "how much I was with your father,[2] and you are aware that it was he who placed the crown of Egypt upon my head; but, so that you may know something of our private affairs, please read these letters. They are all written to me with his own hand."

Octavian must have turned the letters over with some curiosity, but he does not seem to have shown a desire to read them; and, seeing this, Cleopatra cried: "Of what use are all these letters to me? Yet I seem to see

---

[1] Dion Cassius.

[2] Octavian now always spoke of the Dictator as his father, and he called himself "Cæsar."

him living again in them." The thought of her old lover and friend, and the memories recalled by the letters and portraits before her seem to have unnerved her; and, being in so overwrought and weak a condition, she now broke down completely. Between her sobs she was heard to exclaim, "Oh, I wish to God you were still alive," as though referring to Julius Cæsar.

Octavian appears to have consoled her as best he could; and at length she seems to have agreed that, in return for his clemency, she would place herself entirely in his hands, and would hand over to him without reserve all her property. One of her stewards, named Seleucus, happened to be awaiting her orders in the mausoleum at the time, and, sending for him, she told him to hand over to Octavian the list which they together had lately made of her jewellery and valuables, and which now lay with her other papers in the room. Seleucus seems to have read the document to Octavian; but, wishing to ingratiate himself with his new master, and thinking that loyalty to Cleopatra no longer paid, he volunteered the information that various articles were omitted from the list, and that the Queen was purposely secreting these for her own advantage. At this Cleopatra sprang from her bed, and, dashing at the astonished steward, seized him by the hair, shook him to and fro, and furiously slapped his face. So outraged and overwrought was she that she might well have done the man some serious injury had not Octavian, who could not refrain from laughing, withheld her and led her back to her seat. "Really it is very hard," she exclaimed to her visitor, "when you do me the honour to come to see me in this condition I am in, that I should be accused by one of my own servants of setting aside some women's trinkets—

not so as to adorn my unhappy self, you may be sure, but so that I might have some little presents by me to give to your sister Octavia and your wife Livia, that by their intercession I might hope to find you to some extent disposed to mercy."

Cæsar was delighted to hear her talk in this manner, for it seemed to indicate that she was desirous of continuing to live; and he was most anxious that she should do so, partly, as I have said, that he might have the satisfaction of parading her in chains through the streets of Rome, and partly, perhaps, in order to show, thereafter, his clemency and his respect to the late Dictator's memory by refraining from putting her to death. He therefore told her that she might dispose of these articles of jewellery as she liked; and, promising that his usage of her would be merciful beyond her expectation, he brought his visit to a close, well satisfied that he had won her confidence, and that he had entirely deceived her. In this, however, he was mistaken, and he was himself deceived by her.

Cleopatra had observed from his words and manner that he wished to exhibit her in Rome, and that he had little intention of allowing her son Cæsarion to reign in her place, but purposed to seize Egypt on behalf of Rome. Far from reassuring her, the interview had left her with the certainty that the doom of the dynasty was sealed; and already she saw clearly that there was nothing left for which to live. Presently a messenger from Cornelius Dolabella came to her, and broke the secret news to her that Octavian, finding her now recovered from her illness, had decided to ship her off to Rome with her two children in three days' time or less. It is possible, also, that Dolabella was already able to tell her that there was no hope for her son Cæsarion, for that Octavian had decided to kill him so soon as he could lay hands on him, realising, at the instance of his Alexandrian friend Areius, that it was unwise to leave at large one who claimed to be the rightful successsor of the great Dictator.

On hearing this news the Queen determined to kill herself at once, for her despair was such that the fact of existence had become intolerable to her. In her mind she must have pictured Octavian's Triumph in Rome, in which she and her children would figure as the chief exhibits. She would be led in chains up to the Capitol, even as she had watched her sister Arsinoe paraded in the Triumph of Julius Cæsar; and she could hear in imagination the jeers and groans of the townspeople, who would not fail to remind her of her former boast that she would one day sit in royal judgment where then she would be standing in abject humiliation. The thought, which of itself was more than she could bear, was coupled with the certainty that, were she to prolong her life, she would have to suffer also the shock of her beloved son's cruel murder, for already his death seemed inevitable.

Having therefore made up her mind, she sent a message to Octavian asking his permission for her to visit Antony's tomb, in order to make the usual oblations to his spirit. This was granted to her, and upon the next morning, August 29th, she was carried in her litter to the grave, accompanied by her women. Arriving at the spot she threw herself upon the gravestone, embracing it in a very passion of woe. "Oh, dearest Antony," she cried, the tears streaming down her face, "it is not long since with these hands I buried you. Then they were free;

now I am a captive; and I pay these last duties to you
with a guard upon me, for fear that my natural griefs and
sorrows should impair my servile body and make it less
fit to be exhibited in their Triumph over you. Expect no
further offerings or libations from me, Antony; these are
the last honours that Cleopatra will be able to pay to
your memory, for she is to be hurried far away from you.
Nothing could part us while we lived, but death seems to
threaten to divide us. You, a Roman born, have found a
grave in Egypt. I, an Egyptian, am to seek that favour,
and none but that, in your country. But if the gods
below, with whom you now are dwelling, can or will do
anything for me, since those above have betrayed us, do
not allow your living wife to be abandoned, let me not be
led in Triumph to your shame; but hide me, hide me:
bury me here with you. For amongst all my bitter misfortunes nothing has been so terrible as this brief time
that I have lived away from you." [1]

For some moments she lay upon the tombstone passionately kissing it, her past quarrels with the dead man
all forgotten in her desire for his companionship now in
her loneliness, and only her earlier love for him being
remembered in the tumult of her mind. Then, rising
and placing some wreaths of flowers upon the grave,
she entered her litter and was carried back to the
mausoleum.

As soon as she had arrived she ordered her bath to
be prepared, and having been washed and scented, her
hair being carefully plaited around her head, she lay
down upon a couch and partook of a sumptous meal.

---

[1] Plutarch. It is very probable that Cleopatra's doctor, Olympus, was by
her side, and afterwards wrote these words down in the diary which we know
Plutarch used.

THE NILE.

AN EXAMPLE OF ALEXANDRIAN ART.

After this she wrote a short letter to Octavian, asking that she might be buried in the same tomb with Antony; and, this being despatched, she ordered everybody to leave the mausoleum with the exception of Charmion and Iras, as though she did not wish to be disturbed in her afternoon's siesta. The doors were then closed, and the sentries mounted guard on the outside in the usual manner.

When Octavian read the letter which Cleopatra's messenger had brought him, he realised at once what had happened, and hastened to the mausoleum. Changing his mind, however, he sent some of his officers in his place, who, on their arrival, found the sentries apprehensive of nothing. Bursting open the door they ran up the stairs to the upper chamber, and immediately their worst fears were realised. Cleopatra, already dead, lay stretched upon her bed of gold, arrayed in her Grecian robes of state, and decked with all her regal jewels, the royal diadem of the Ptolemies encircling her brow. Upon the floor at her feet Iris was just breathing her last; and Charmion, scarce able to stand, was tottering at the bedside, trying to adjust the Queen's crown.

One of the Roman officers exclaimed angrily: "Charmion, was this well done of your lady?" Charmion, supporting herself beside the royal couch, turned her ashen face towards the speaker. "Very well done," she gasped, "and as befitted the descendant of so many Kings"; and with these words she fell dead beside the Queen.

The Roman officers, having despatched messengers to inform Octavian of the tragedy, seem to have instituted an immediate inquiry as to the means by which the

2 C

deaths had taken place.[1]   At first the sentries could
offer no information, but at length the fact was elicited
that a peasant carrying a basket of figs had been allowed
to enter the mausoleum, as it was understood that the
fruit was for the Queen's meal.   The soldiers declared
that they had lifted the leaves with which the fruit was
covered and had remarked on the fineness of the figs,
whereupon the peasant had laughed and had invited
them to take some, which they had refused to do.   It
was perhaps known that Cleopatra had expressed a
preference for death by the bite of an asp,[2] and it was
therefore thought that perhaps one of these small snakes
had been brought to her concealed under the figs.
A search was made for the snake, and one of the
soldiers stated that he thought he saw a snake-track
leading from the mausoleum over the sand towards the
sea.   An attendant who had admitted the peasant seems
now to have reported that when Cleopatra saw the figs
she exclaimed, " So here it is ! " a piece of evidence which
gave some colour to the theory.   Others suggested that
the asp had been kept at hand for some days in a vase,
and that the Queen had, at the end, teased it until she
had made it strike at her.   An examination of the body
showed nothing except two very slight marks upon the
arm, which might possibly have been caused by the bite
of a snake.   On the other hand, it was suggested that
the Queen might have carried some form of poison in
a hollow hair-comb or other similar article ; and this
theory must have received some support from the fact
that there were the three deaths to account for.

[1] The following evidence as to the manner of the Queen's death is given by
Plutarch, and it is clear that it was the result of an investigation such as I have
described.

[2] Page 365.

Presently Octavian seems to have arrived, and he at once sent for snake-doctors, *Psylli*, to suck the poison from the wound; but they came too late to save her. Though Octavian expressed his great disappointment at her death, he could not refrain from showing his admiration for the manner in which it had occurred. Personally, he appears to have favoured the theory that her end was caused by the bite of the asp, and afterwards in his Triumph he caused a figure of Cleopatra to be exhibited with a snake about her arm. Though it is thus quite impossible to state with certainty how it occurred, there is no reason to contradict the now generally accepted story of the introduction of the asp in the basket of figs. I have no doubt that the Queen had other poisons in her possession, which were perhaps used by her two faithful women; and it is to be understood that the strategy of the figs, if employed at all, was resorted to only in order that she herself might die by the means which her earlier experiments had commended to her.

Octavian now gave orders that the Queen should be buried with full honours beside Antony, where she had wished to lie. He had sent messengers, it would seem, to Berenice to attempt to stop the departure of Cæsarion for India, having heard, no doubt, that the young man had decided to remain in that town until the last possible moment. His tutor, Rhodon, counselled him to trust himself to Octavian; and, acting upon this advice, they returned to Alexandria, where they seem to have arrived very shortly after Cleopatra's death. Octavian immediately ordered Cæsarion to be executed, his excuse being that it was dangerous for *two Cæsars* to be in the world together; and thus died the last of the Ptolemaic

Pharaohs of Egypt, the son and only real heir of the great Julius Cæsar. The two other children who remained in the Palace, Ptolemy and Cleopatra Selene, were shipped off to Rome as soon as possible, and messengers seem to have been despatched to Media to take possession of Alexander Helios who had probably been sent thither, as we have already seen.

In my opinion, Octavian now decided to take over Egypt as a kind of personal possession. He did not wish to cause a revolution in the country by proclaiming it a Roman province; and he seems to have appreciated the ceaseless efforts of Cleopatra and her subjects to prevent the absorption of the kingdom in this manner. He therefore decided upon a novel course of action. While not allowing himself to be crowned as actual King of Egypt, he assumed that office by tacit agreement with the Egyptian priesthood. He seems to have claimed, in fact, to be heir to the throne of the Ptolemies. Julius Cæsar had been recognised as Cleopatra's husband in Egypt, and he, Octavian, was Cæsar's adopted son and heir. After the elimination of Cleopatra's three surviving children he was, therefore, the rightful claimant to the Egyptian throne. The Egyptians at once accepted him as their sovereign, and upon the walls of their temples we constantly find his name inscribed in hieroglyphics as " King of Upper and Lower Egypt, Son of the Sun, Cæsar, living for ever, beloved of Ptah and Isis." He is also called by the title Autocrator, which he took over from Antony, and which, in the Egyptian inscriptions, was recognised as a kind of hereditary royal name, being written within the Pharaonic cartouche.[1] His descendants,

---

[1] In hieroglyphs this reads *Aut'k'r'd'r K's'r's.*

the Emperors of Rome, were thus successively Kings of Egypt, as though heads of the reigning dynasty; and each Emperor as he ascended the Roman throne was hailed as Monarch of Egypt, and was called in all Egyptian inscriptions " Pharaoh " and " Son of the Sun." The Egyptians, therefore, with the acquiescence of Octavian, came to regard themselves not as vassals of Rome, but as subjects of their own King, who happened at the same time to be Emperor of Rome; and thus the great Egypto-Roman Empire for which Cleopatra had struggled actually came into existence.   All Emperors of Rome came to be recognised in Egypt not as sovereigns of a foreign empire of which Egypt was a part, but as *actual Pharaohs of Egyptian dominions of which Rome was a part.*

The ancient dynasties had passed away, the Amenophis and Thutmosis family, the house of Rameses, the line of Psammetichus, and many another had disappeared. And now, in like manner, the house of the Ptolemies had fallen, and the throne of Egypt was occupied by the dynasty of the Cæsars.   This dynasty, as it were, supplied Rome with her monarchs; and the fact that Octavian was hailed by Egyptians as King of Egypt long before he was recognised by Romans as Emperor of Rome, gave the latter throne a kind of Pharaonic origin in the eyes of the vain Egyptians.   It has usually been supposed that Egypt became a Roman province; but it was never declared to be such.   Octavian arranged that it should be governed by a *praefectus*, who was to act in the manner of a viceroy,[1] and he retained the greater part of the Ptolemaic revenues as his personal property.

[1] Strabo, xvii. i. 14; Tacitus, Hist. i. 11.

While later in Rome he pretended that Cleopatra's
kingdom had been annexed, in Egypt it was distinctly
understood that the country was still a monarchy.

He treated the Queen's memory with respect, since he
was carrying on her line; and he would not allow her
statues to be overthrown.[1] All her splendid treasures,
however, and the gold and silver plate and ornaments
were melted down and converted into money with which
to pay the Roman soldiers. The royal lands were seized,
the palaces largely stripped of their wealth; and when at
last Octavian returned to Rome in the spring of B.C. 29,
he had become a fabulously rich man.

On August 13th, 14th, and 15th of the same year three
great Triumphs were celebrated, the first day being devoted to the European conquests, the second to Actium,
and the third to the Egyptian victory. A statue of
Cleopatra, the asp clinging to her arm, was dragged
through the streets of the capital, and the Queen's twin
children, Alexander Helios and Cleopatra Selene, were
made to walk in captivity in the procession. Images
representing Nilus and Egypt were carried along, and an
enormous quantity of interesting loot was heaped up on
the triumphal cars. The poet Propertius tells us how in
fancy he saw " the necks of kings bound with golden
chains, and the fleet of Actium sailing up the Via Sacra."
All men became unbalanced by enthusiasm, and stories
derogatory to Cleopatra were spread on all sides.
Horace, in a wonderful ode, expressed the public sentiments, and denounced the unfortunate Queen as an
enemy of Rome. Honours were heaped upon Octavian;

---

[1] This was said to have been due to a bribe received from one of Cleopatra's
friends, but it was more probably political.

and soon afterwards he was given the title of Augustus, and was named *Divi filius*, as being heir of *Divus Julius*. He took great delight in lauding the memory of the great Dictator, who was now accepted as one of the gods of the Roman world; and it is a significant fact that he revived and reorganised the Lupercalia, as though he were in some manner honouring Cæsar thereby.[1]

Meanwhile the three children of Cleopatra and Antony found a generous refuge in the house of Octavia, Antony's discarded wife. With admirable tact Octavian seems to have insisted upon this solution of the difficulty as to what to do with them. Their execution would have been deeply resented by the Egyptians, and, since Octavian was now posing as the legal heir to the throne of Egypt, the dynastic successor of Cleopatra, and not a foreign usurper, it was well that his own sister should look after these members of the royal family. Octavia, always meek and dutiful, accepted the arrangement nobly, and was probably unvaryingly kind to these children of her faithless husband, whom she brought up with her two daughters, Antonia Major and Minor, and Julius Antonius, the second son of Antony and Fulvia, and brother of the murdered Antyllus. When the little Cleopatra Selene grew up she was married to Juba, the King of Numidia, a learned and scholarly monarch, who was later made King of Mauretania. The son of this marriage was named Ptolemy, and succeeded his father about A.D. 19. He was murdered by Caligula, who, by the strange workings of Fate, was also a descendant of Antony. We do not know what became of Alexander Helios and his brother Ptolemy. Tacitus tells us[2] that

---

[1] Page 174.   [2] Tacitus, Hist., v. 9.

Antonius Felix, Procurator of Judæa under the Emperor Nero, married (as his second wife) Drusilla, a granddaughter of Cleopatra and Antony, who was probably another of the Mauretanian family. Octavia died in B.C. 11. Antony's son, Julius Antonius, in B.C. 2, was put to death for his immoral relations with Octavian's own daughter Julia, she herself being banished to the barren island of Pandateria. Octavian himself, covered with honours and full of years, died in A.D. 14, being succeeded upon the thrones of Egypt and of Rome by Tiberius, his son.

During the latter part of the reign of Octavian, or Augustus, as one must call him, the influence of Alexandria upon the life of Rome began to be felt in an astonishing degree; and so greatly did Egyptian thought alter the conditions in the capital that it might well be fancied that the spirit of the dead Cleopatra was presiding over that throne which she had striven to ascend. Ferrero goes so far as to suggest that the main ideas of splendid monarchic government and sumptuous Oriental refinement which now developed in Rome were due to the direct influence of Alexandria, and perhaps to the fact that the new emperors were primarily Kings of Egypt. Alexandrian artists and artisans swarmed over the sea to Italy, and the hundreds of Romans who had snatched estates for themselves in Egypt travelled frequently to that country on business, and unconsciously familiarised themselves with its arts and crafts. Alexandrian sculpture and painting was seen in every villa, and the poetry and literature of the Alexandrian school were read by all fashionable persons. Every Roman wanted to employ Alexandrians to decorate his house, everybody studied the manners and refinements of the Græco - Egyptians. The old austerity went to pieces before the buoyancy of Cleopatra's subjects, just as the aloofness of London has disappeared under the Continental invasion of the last few years.

Thus it may be said that the Egypto-Roman Empire of Cleopatra's dreams came to be founded in actual fact, with this difference, that its monarchs were sprung from the line of Octavian, Cæsar's nephew, and not from that of Cæsarion, Cæsar's son. But while Egypt and Alexandria thus played such an important part in the creation of the Roman monarchy, the memory of Cleopatra, from whose brain and whose influence the new life had proceeded, was yearly more painfully vilified. She came to be the enemy of this Orientalised Rome, which still thought itself Occidental; and her struggle with Octavian was remembered as the evil crisis through which the party of the Cæsars had passed. Abuse was heaped upon her, and stories were invented in regard to her licentious habits. It is upon this insecure basis that the world's estimate of the character of Cleopatra is founded; and it is necessary for every student of these times at the outset of his studies to rid his mind of the impression which he will have obtained from these polluted sources. Having shut out from his memory the stinging words of Propertius and the fierce lines of Horace, written in the excess of his joy at the close of the period of warfare which had endangered his little country estate, the reader will be in a position to judge whether the interpretation of Cleopatra's character and actions, which I have laid before him, is to be considered as unduly lenient, and whether I have made unfair use of the merciful prerogative of the historian, in behalf of an often lonely and sorely tried woman, who fought all her life for the fulfilment of a patriotic and splendid ambition, and who died in a manner "befitting the descendant of so many kings."

THE END.